Day-by-Day Math Mats

by Mary Rosenberg

SCHOLASTIC
PROFESSIONAL BOOKS

New York ★ Toronto ★ London ★ Auckland ★ Sydney ★ Mexico City ★ New Delhi ★ Hong Kong ★ Buenos Aires

Dedication
With special thanks to Barbara and Mario Baca for their friendship, support, and encouragement.

Cover design by Pamela Simmons

Cover artwork by Tammie Lyon

Interior artwork by Maxie Chambliss

Interior design by Ellen Matlach Hassell
for Boultinghouse & Boultinghouse, Inc.

ISBN: 0-439-21569-2

Printed in the U.S.A.

★ 1 2 3 4 5 6 7 8 9 ★ 1 2 3 4 5 6 7 8 9 ★ 1 2 3 4 5 6 7 8 9 ★

Contents

★ 1 2 3 4 5 6 7 8 9 ★ 1 2 3 4 5 6 7 8 9 ★ 1 2 3 4 5 6 7 8 9 ★

Map Skills and Location

Measurement: U.S. Standard

Measurement: Metric System

Money

Early Multiplication and Division

★ 1 2 3 4 5 6 7 8 9 ★ 1 2 3 4 5 6 7 8 9 ★ 1 2 3 4 5 6 7 8 9 ★

Number Patterns

Numerals and Number Words

Patterns, Shapes, and Fractions

Place Value

Time

★ 1 2 3 4 5 6 7 8 9 ★ 1 2 3 4 5 6 7 8 9 ★ 1 2 3 4 5 6 7 8 9 ★

Introduction

Welcome to *Day-by-Day Math Mats*! These 180 fun and interactive math activities are designed to capture your students' interest and build essential math skills every day of the school year. The activity pages in *Day-by-Day Math Mats* have been created with teachers of grades 1 and 2 in mind, helping you teach students the skills they need to know.

Each reproducible math activity page complements your curriculum and serves as a handy springboard for teaching specific skills. The activities help students learn the important math skills addressed in the National Council of Teachers of Mathematics (NCTM) standards for first and second grade. Math topics within those content and process standards include addition, subtraction, patterns, money, measurement, place value, time, and graphing. Within each topic, math mats address similar skills and concepts using a variety of approaches, providing students with opportunities to learn according to their individual learning styles. What's more, your students will love them!

How to Use Math Mats

Day-by-Day Math Mats is designed so that it can be used in a variety of settings and situations. Simply photocopy the math mats you want to cover with the students, and you're ready to go! The only other materials needed for the activities are crayons, glue, scissors, paper clips, and occasionally dominoes and string.

Each math mat presents a basic skill in the main area of the page and extra follow-up activities or "cut-and-paste" items on the right side of the page.

Consider using the math mats in any or all of the following ways:

- **Preview and review:** Math mats are wonderful to use to introduce new concepts or skills to students and to review concepts already covered in class.
- **Learning center activities:** You can photocopy and assemble math mats into individual learning packets. For example, all of the pages on the topic "time" can be assembled to supplement a unit on time while students are doing individual activities in a learning center.
- **Paired or group activities:** Many of the math mats work well as group assignments. The math mats that are games, such as "Partner Bingo," require students to play with a partner. Those that require the use of a spinner, such as "Which Spinner Is the Fair One?," or the development of graphs, such as "A Roll of the Die!" or "Penny Toss," allow students to work together in pairs and learn from each other. The logic puzzles are also a natural activity for pairs or groups because the questions prompt discussion of possibilities.
- **Quick checks:** Math mats can be used as ready-to-use diagnostic tools. They're a terrific, fun way to see if a student already knows a concept before you begin teaching it or is grasping the concept while you are teaching your unit. Students aren't likely to feel that they are being "tested" because the activities are engaging and enjoyable.
- **Homework:** Parents and students will find that math mats are easy to use and enhance learning. The skill highlighted at the top of each math mat helps parents see the math topics their children are studying, and each page gives kids lots of opportunities to show their parents what they are learning, what they've mastered, and where they might need some extra guidance.

Helpful Hints

The following are some suggestions to make using math mats enjoyable for both you and your students:

- The first few times that students use the math mats, show them how the page is set up.

There are often pictures to cut out on the right side of the pages. Help students to understand that they should have a pencil, a pair of scissors, crayons, and glue handy when they work with a math mat. At times they may need paper clips, dominoes, or string. If you are using the math mats in a learning center, keep those materials easily accessible.

- Consider photocopying some of the mats onto heavy card stock, especially the mats that have parts that need to be shuffled, such as those in "Playing Card Addition."
- In math mats with find-the-word puzzles, show students how words can appear either horizontally or vertically.
- In math mats with number boxes, show students beforehand how addition and subtraction can work within these boxes.
- The first time your students encounter math mats with graphic organizers, show them how to place Xs in boxes as they narrow choices. For example, in "Sports Tally," help students see that once they learn that Kate plays football, Xs need to be written in the "football" column for both Angela and Mark.
- Encourage your students to color the mats after they've completed the activities on the page. Provide students with color pencils, markers, and crayons.
- Have your students develop stories that show how numbers can be used in real-life or imaginative settings. For example, with "Counting Cats," have them develop a story about Paula's trip to the park or why the cats have come to the park to play and sleep. The more students use words to help them understand numbers, the more fluent they will be in both expressive language and mathematics.
- Once your students are comfortable with the format of math mats, have them develop their own. Make copies for their classmates and have a Homemade Math Mats Party to celebrate their accomplishments in mathematics over the course of the year.

Connections With the NCTM Standards

The activity pages in *Day-by-Day Math Mats* are linked with the NCTM's content and process standards on the first and second grade levels. As the NCTM suggests, math mats teach these skills in a real-world context. Important math skills and concepts are not taught as abstractions, but as situations that children encounter and problem solve in their daily lives. For easy reference as you plan your daily lessons, at the top of each math mat page you'll find the primary skill (within the NCTM's standards) on which the math mat focuses. As you'll note, most pages include several activities and address more than one of the NCTM standards, providing your students with opportunities to practice other skills as well as the skill you are currently teaching.

The activity pages in this book cover many of the NCTM standards for content and processes: number and operation; patterns, functions, and algebra; geometry and spatial sense; measurement; data analysis, statistics, and probability; problem solving; reasoning and proof; communication; connections; and representation. Your students will build on what they have learned previously by using, for example, their experience in counting by 5s and establishing patterns in the early math mats to understand the reasoning required for the later math mats that focus on finding mystery numbers.

Enjoy using *Day-by-Day Math Mats* and seeing how much your students look forward to learning mathematics in this fun and interactive format!

Connections With the NCTM Standards

	Number and Operation	Patterns, Functions, and Algebra	Geometry and Spatial Sense	Measurement	Data Analysis, Statistics, and Probability	Problem Solving	Reasoning and Proof	Communication	Connections	Representation
	Content Standards					Process Standards				
Mat Addition and Subtraction										
1 Adding 1 to 5	◆									
2 Ways to Make 5	◆									
3 Counting Cats	◆							◆		◆
4 Gathering Acorns	◆					◆				
5 Dog Bone Directions	◆					◆				
6 Brown Bear's Berries: Song	◆					◆				
7 Stars on Flags	◆									
8 Bird Nests	◆					◆		◆		◆
9 Many Mice	◆					◆		◆		◆
10 Frogs in a Bucket	◆					◆		◆		◆
11 Apple Picking	◆									
12 Butterfly Wing Addition	◆									
13 Sort the Fish!	◆				◆					
14 Cat and Dog Pogs	◆									
15 Domino Sort and Tally	◆				◆					
16 Birthday Candles	◆					◆				◆
17 Party Balloons	◆					◆				◆
18 Playing Card Addition	◆									
19 Four in a Row	◆									
20 Scarecrow Subtraction	◆					◆				
21 Finding the Difference	◆									
22 Count and Subtract	◆									
23 Dominoes Subtraction	◆									
24 How Many Are Left?	◆					◆				
25 At the Fruit Stand	◆					◆				
26 Rupert's Cheese	◆					◆				◆
27 On the Ranch	◆					◆				
28 Apples in a Row	◆									
29 1, 2, 3, Go!	◆					◆				
30 Number Sentences	◆									
31 Spin the Spinners	◆									
32 Apple Number Line	◆									
33 Find the Missing Number	◆									
34 Ready, Set, Start!	◆									
35 Arabic and Roman Numerals	◆									
36 Subtraction Crossword Puzzle	◆									
Venn Diagrams										
37 Apples and Cores	◆				◆	◆				
38 Stinky Skunks!	◆				◆	◆				
39 Animal Sorting	◆				◆	◆				
40 Chocolate Desserts	◆				◆	◆				
41 Ladybugs and Butterflies	◆				◆	◆				
Problem Solving										
42 Find Me!					◆	◆				
43 Woodland Animal Clues					◆	◆				
44 My Favorite Hat					◆	◆				
45 Albert Goes to School					◆	◆				
46 Sports Tally					◆	◆				

	Number and Operation	Patterns, Functions, and Algebra	Geometry and Spatial Sense	Measurement	Data Analysis, Statistics, and Probability	Problem Solving	Reasoning and Proof	Communication	Connections	Representation
	Content Standards					Process Standards				
47 Favorite Fruits					◆	◆				
48 At the Toy Store					◆	◆				
49 Who Lives Where?	◆				◆	◆				
50 Animal Order	◆				◆	◆				
51 Mix and Match Caps		◆				◆				◆
Charts and Graphs										
52 A Fall Day	◆				◆	◆				
53 Favorite Ways to Eat an Apple	◆				◆	◆				
54 A Roll of the Die!	◆				◆					
55 Jason's Classmates	◆				◆	◆				
56 Cowboys and Cowgirls	◆				◆	◆				
57 Maria's Gardening Equipment	◆				◆	◆				
58 Favorite Hearts	◆				◆					
59 Letters and Names	◆				◆	◆		◆		
60 Voting for Presidents	◆				◆					
61 Penny Toss	◆				◆	◆		◆		
62 A Trip to the Orchard	◆				◆	◆				
63 Flower Picking	◆				◆	◆				
64 Fair and Square					◆			◆		
65 Circles and Squares					◆			◆		
Map Skills and Location										
66 Bear Buddies	◆		◆			◆				
67 Animal Addresses	◆		◆							
68 Creepy Crawlies	◆		◆			◆				
69 The Playground			◆			◆				
70 Tiny Town			◆			◆				
71 A Trip to the Zoo			◆			◆				
72 Our Classroom			◆			◆		◆		
73 Design a Bedroom			◆					◆		
74 Tasty Treat	◆		◆							
75 Furry Friend	◆		◆							
76 Me and My Big Trunk!	◆		◆							
Measurement: U.S. Standard										
77 Pencil Lengths	◆			◆						
78 Ribbon Lengths	◆			◆						
79 Shape Sizes	◆			◆						
80 Estimating Weights				◆	◆	◆				
81 What's the Temperature?	◆			◆						
82 More or Less Water				◆						
83 About a Cup				◆	◆					
84 Ways to Measure Volume	◆			◆		◆				
85 More Ways to Measure Volume	◆			◆						
86 Animal Pens	◆			◆						
87 Measuring Me	◆			◆						
88 Our Classroom	◆			◆						
89 Campground Map	◆			◆				◆		
Measurement: Metric System										
90 Camping Out	◆			◆						
91 Find the Area	◆			◆						

	Content Standards					Process Standards				
	Number and Operation	Patterns, Functions, and Algebra	Geometry and Spatial Sense	Measurement	Data Analysis, Statistics, and Probability	Problem Solving	Reasoning and Proof	Communication	Connections	Representation
92 About Meters	◆			◆						
93 Kilometers	◆			◆		◆				
94 Grams and Kilograms	◆			◆						
95 Liters	◆			◆						
96 °Celsius	◆			◆	◆					
Money										
97 Coin Values	◆									
98 Making Cents	◆									
99 Change for a Nickel	◆									
100 Change for a Dime	◆									
101 School Store	◆					◆				
102 Counting With Nickels	◆									
103 Counting With Dimes	◆									
104 Counting With Quarters	◆									
105 Counting Loose Change	◆									
106 Sweet Shop	◆									
107 Pennies and Dimes	◆									
108 Frisbee Dog	◆					◆				
109 Dollars and Cents	◆									
110 Bait and Tackle Shop	◆					◆				
111 Matching Money	◆									
112 Money Review	◆							◆		
Early Multiplication and Division										
113 Plenty of Penguins	◆									◆
114 Fabulous Fish	◆									◆
115 Busy Bees	◆									◆
116 Fresh Fruit	◆									
117 Multiplication Chart	◆					◆				
118 Apple Division	◆									◆
119 In the Woods	◆					◆				
120 Pizza Parlor	◆									
121 Division Review	◆									
Number Patterns										
122 Pencil Pairs	◆									
123 Odd or Even?	◆				◆					
124 Lost Mittens	◆				◆	◆				
125 What's the Pattern?	◆	◆						◆		
126 What's the Pattern?	◆	◆						◆		
127 What's the Pattern?	◆	◆						◆		
Numerals and Number Words										
128 Planes and Trains	◆									
129 Counting Apples	◆									
130 Snack Food	◆									
131 How Many Shoes?	◆									
132 School Supplies	◆									
133 Counting Books	◆									
134 Mice Count	◆									
135 Seeing Stars	◆	◆				◆				
136 Pennies	◆					◆				

	Content Standards					Process Standards				
	Number and Operation	Patterns, Functions, and Algebra	Geometry and Spatial Sense	Measurement	Data Analysis, Statistics, and Probability	Problem Solving	Reasoning and Proof	Communication	Connections	Representation
137 Pet Math	◆									
138 Missing Numbers	◆	◆								
139 Teddy-ominoes	◆									
140 Partners Bingo	◆									
Patterns, Shapes, and Fractions										
141 Naming Shapes			◆					◆		
142 What Comes Next?		◆	◆							
143 Button Patterns		◆	◆							
144 Seeing Patterns		◆	◆							
145 Shapes, Sides, and Corners			◆			◆				
146 Seeing Shapes			◆		◆			◆		
147 Sorting Shapes			◆		◆					
148 Shape Symmetry	◆		◆							
149 Dividing Shapes	◆		◆							
150 Fraction Fun	◆		◆							
Place Value										
151 How Many Tens and Ones?	◆									
152 Apples	◆									◆
153 Who Is My Neighbor?	◆					◆				
154 Find the Mystery Number!	◆							◆		
155 How Many Miles?	◆				◆					
156 The Garden Shop's Inventory	◆				◆	◆				
157 Hundreds Puzzle	◆	◆								
158 Grape Going!	◆					◆				◆
159 Making Numbers	◆					◆				
160 Number Hunt	◆					◆				
161 Using Symbols	◆									
162 Making Numbers	◆					◆				
163 Magic Number	◆					◆				
164 Adding Large Numbers	◆	◆								
165 What's the Secret Number?	◆					◆				
166 Subtracting Large Numbers	◆									
Time										
167 The Hands of a Clock	◆									◆
168 Telling Time	◆									
169 What Time Is It?	◆									
170 Reading Clocks	◆					◆				
171 Half Past or Thirty Minutes	◆					◆				
172 A Quarter of an Hour	◆					◆				
173 A.M. or P.M.	◆				◆	◆				
174 The Weather Calendar	◆				◆	◆				
175 Happy New Year!	◆				◆	◆				
176 Roberto's Busy Month	◆				◆	◆				
177 Latisha's Plans	◆				◆	◆				
178 A Caterpillar's Life	◆					◆	◆			
179 Holidays	◆					◆	◆			
180 Birthdays	◆					◆	◆			

Math Mat 1 Name ____________

ADDING HORIZONTAL ARRAYS

Adding 1 to 5

Solve each problem.

1

3 + 2 = ____

2

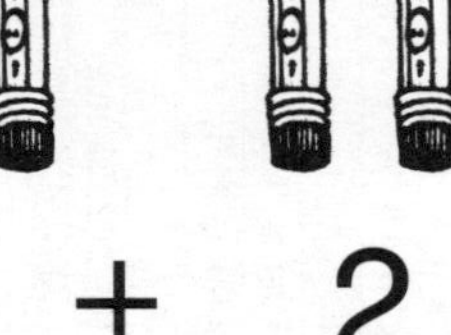

4 + 0 = ____

3

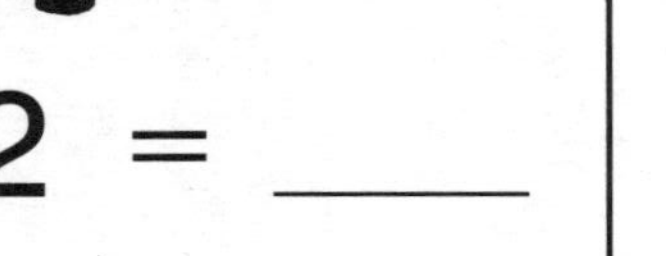

1 + 4 = ____

4

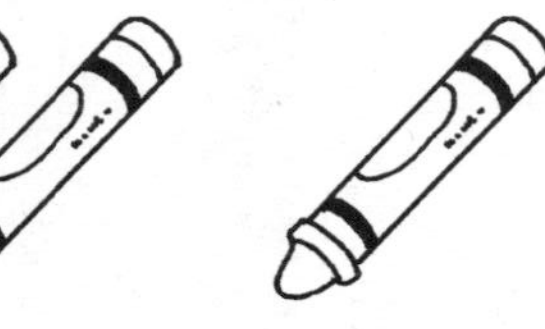

2 + 1 = ____

5

1 + 3 = ____

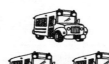

6

5 + 0 = ____

7 Circle each pair of numbers that equals 5.

3	2	4	1
5	0	1	3
0	5	2	4

8 Circle apples to show how many sets of 5 can you make.

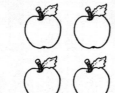

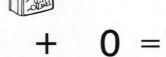

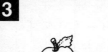

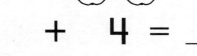

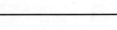

I made ____ sets of 5.

9 How many apples are left?

____

Name ____________________

FORMING ADDITION SENTENCES

Ways to Make 5

Cut out the pictures and arrange them to show the different ways of making 5.
Glue the pictures down and write the addition sentences. Example:

1.  +  1 + 4 = 5
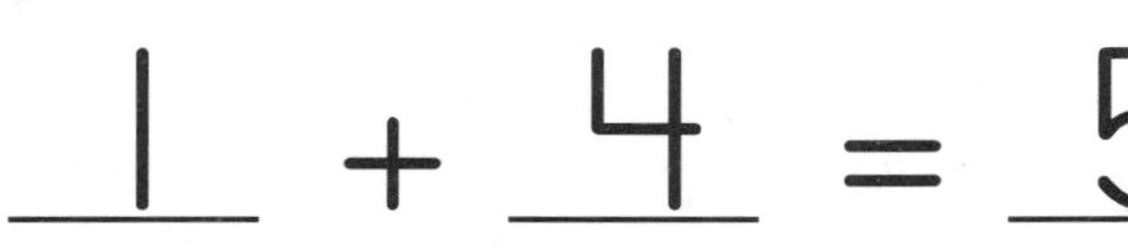

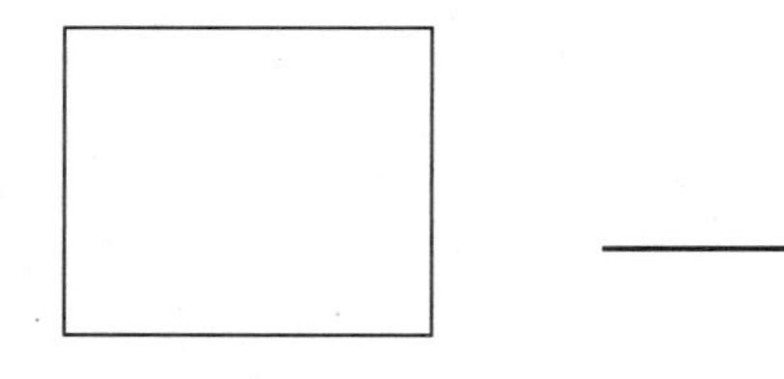
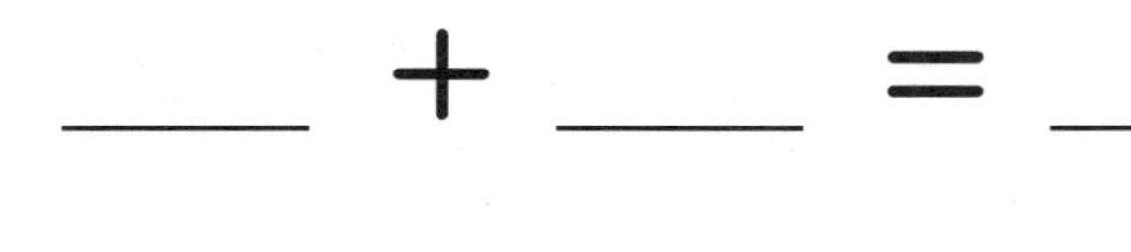
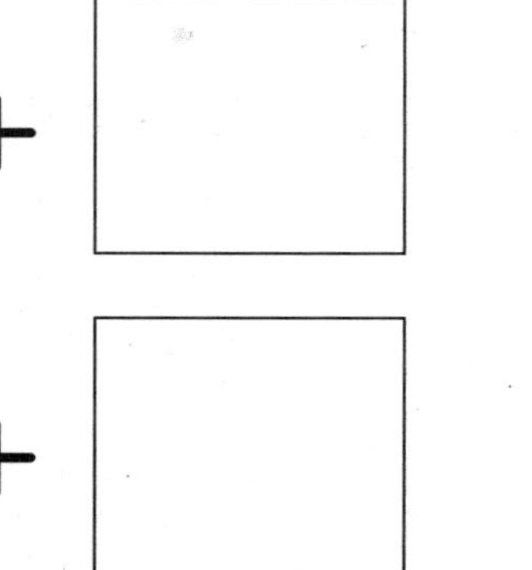

2. ☐ + ☐ ___ + ___ = ___

3. ☐ + ☐ ___ + ___ = ___

4. ☐ + ☐ ___ + ___ = ___

5. ☐ + ☐ ___ + ___ = ___

Count the fingers.

6.  ___

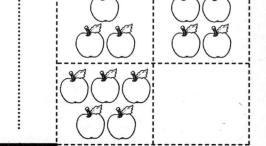

7.  ___

8.   ___

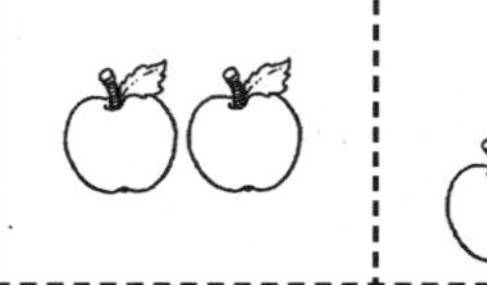

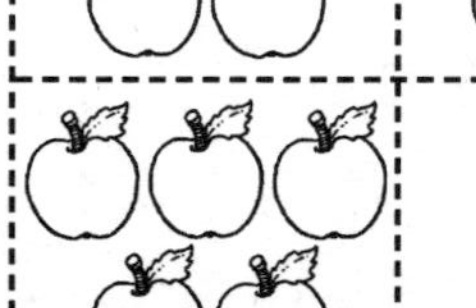

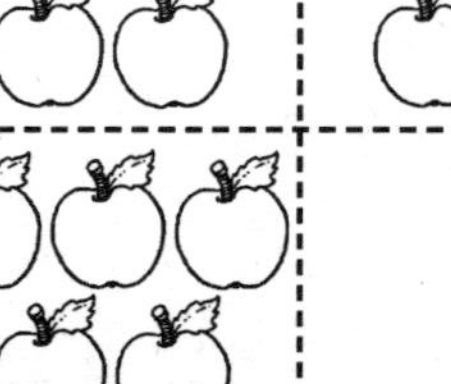

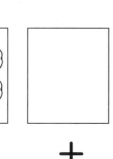

Math Mat 3 Name ______________________

SOLVING WORD PROBLEMS

Counting Cats

Paula went for a walk in the park. She saw 4 cats playing in the grass and 1 cat sleeping in the tree. Cut out the cats and glue them into the correct place on the picture. How many cats did Paula see in the park?

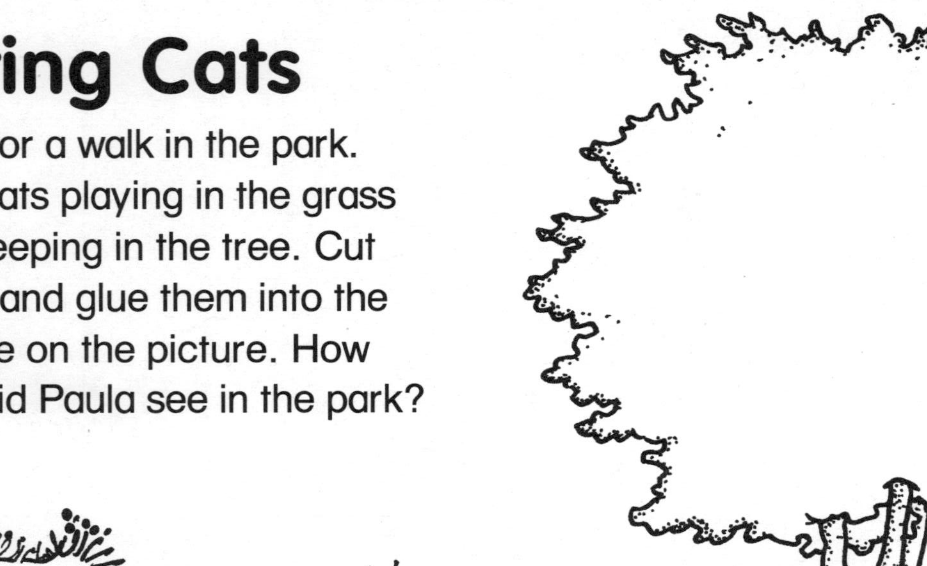

1 Write the math problem and a sentence telling about the answer.

____

____

About Cats

2 How many cat pictures are left?

____

3 How many ears are there in all?

____

4 How many legs are there in all?

____

Name ______________________

ADDING HORIZONTAL ARRAYS

Gathering Acorns

Samantha Squirrel was busy gathering and storing acorns. She gathered 6 acorns in the morning and 4 acorns in the afternoon. Cut out the acorns and glue them to show how many acorns Samantha gathered in the morning and afternoon. How many acorns did Samantha gather in all?

Morning	+	**Afternoon**

_____ + _____ = _____

Samantha gathered _____ acorns.

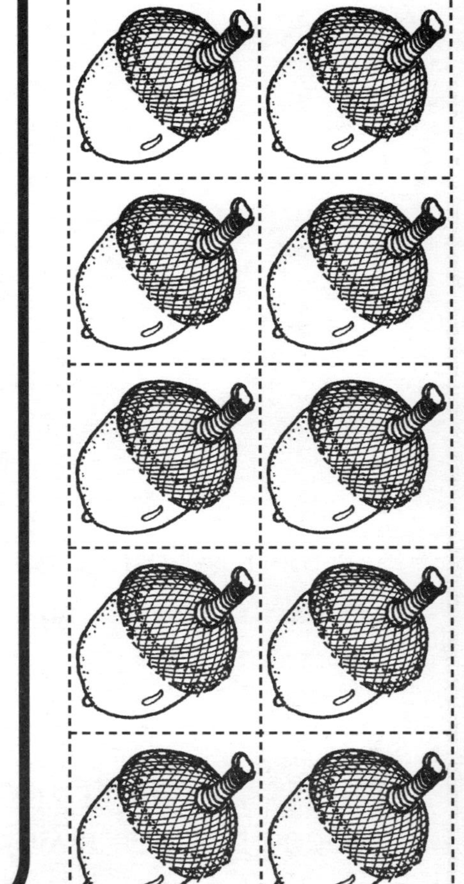

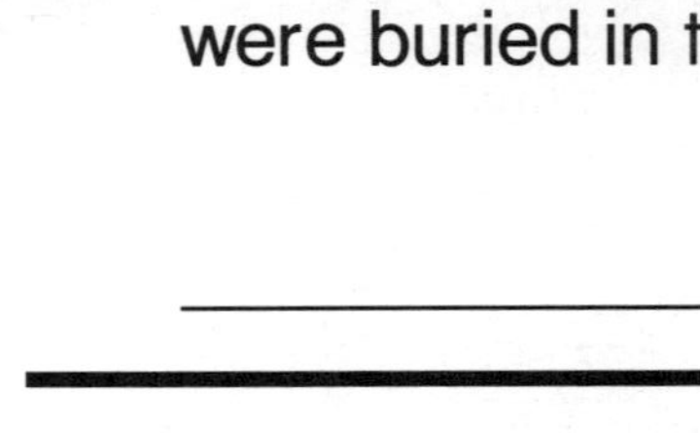

Math Mat 5

Name ______________________

USING DEDUCTIVE REASONING

Dog Bone Directions

Cut out the dog bones and follow the directions.

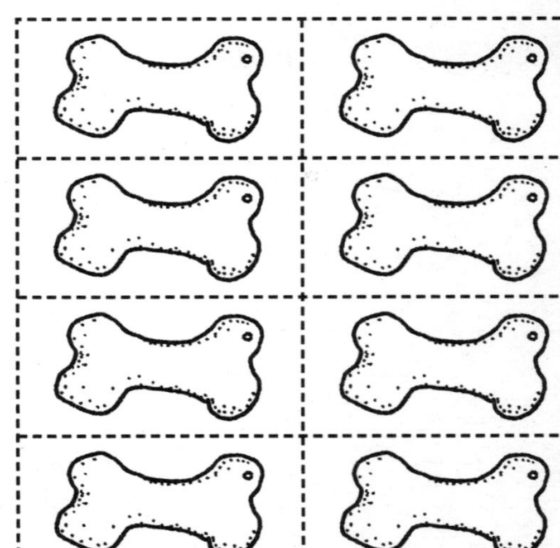

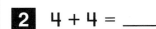

Directions

1. Put a bone next to the bowl of food.
2. Put a bone in the wheelbarrow.
3. Put a bone in the grass below the tree.
4. Put a bone under the front tire on the wheelbarrow.
5. Put a bone in front of the fence on the grass.

1 How many dog bones were buried in the yard?

____

Solve each problem.

2 $4 + 4 =$ ______

3 $5 + 3 =$ ______

4 $8 - 0 =$ ______

5 $10 - 2 =$ ______

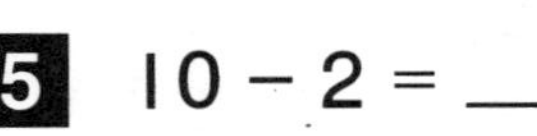

Name ______________________

REPRESENTING ADDITION SENTENCES

Brown Bear's Berries: Song

Sing the song. Use the berries to illustrate the math problem presented in the song. Cut out and color the berries according to the song. Color the extra berries orange.

Brown Bear, Brown Bear
(Sung to "Twinkle, Twinkle Little Star")

Brown Bear, Brown Bear in the tree,
How many berries do you need?
 1 red berry
 2 blue ones
 3 raspberries
 Growing in the sun.
Brown Bear, Brown Bear in the tree,
How many berries do you need?

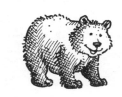

1 How many berries does Brown Bear need?

____

2 How many extra berries does Brown Bear have?

____

3 Write the math sentence telling about the answer.

____

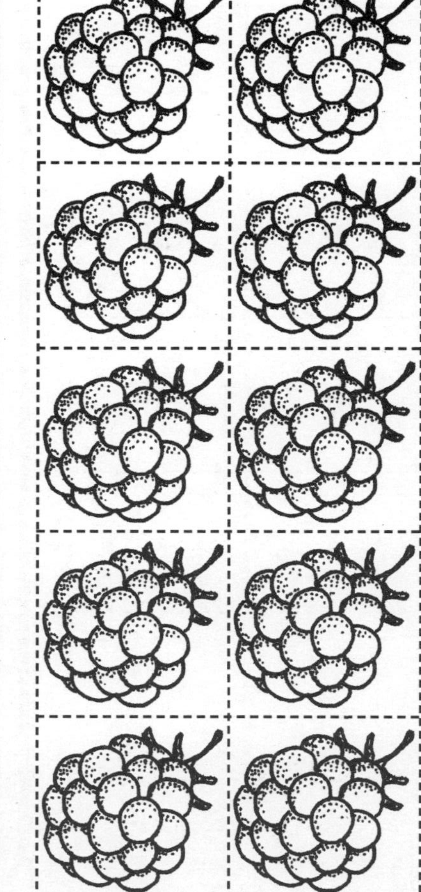

Math Mat 7

Name ________________

REPRESENTING ADDITION SENTENCES

Stars on Flags

Arrange the stars on the flags so that there are 5 stars in each box.
Write the addition sentence for each set of flags and stars.

1

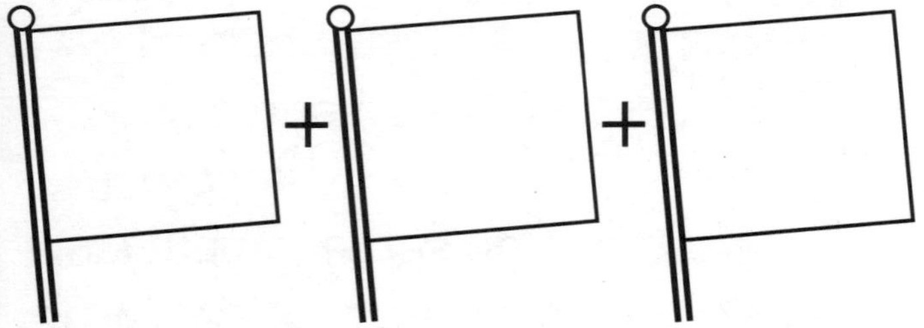

____ + ____ + ____ = 5

2

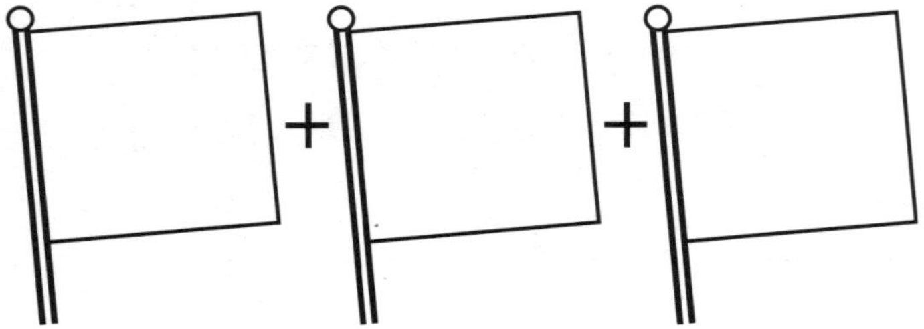

____ + ____ + ____ = 5

3

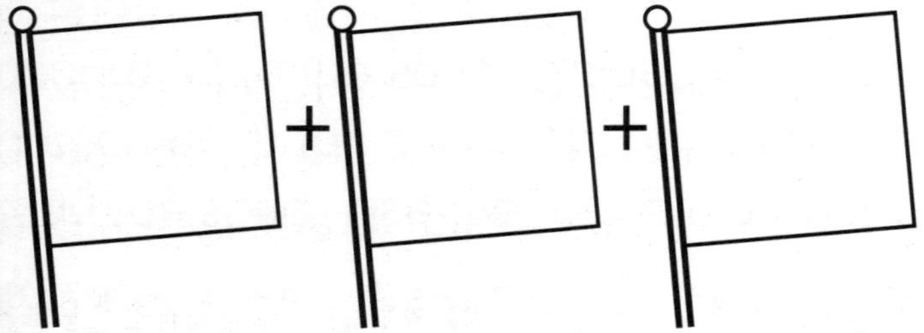

____ + ____ + ____ = 5

4

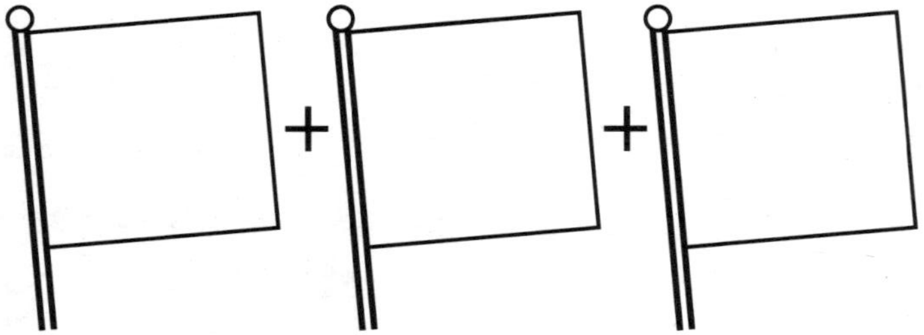

____ + ____ + ____ = 5

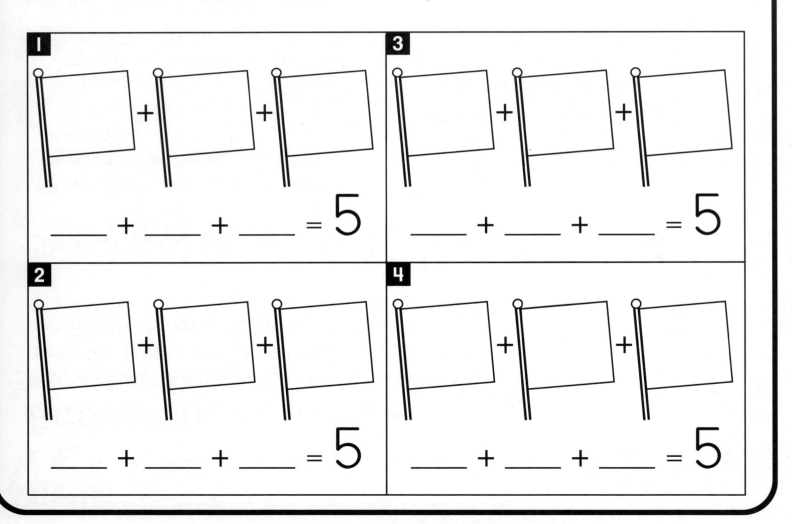

Name ____________________

REPRESENTING ADDITION SENTENCES

Bird Nests

Betsy Bird needs to build nests for her 5 babies. Only 3 baby birds can fit in one nest. How many nests does Betsy Bird need to build? Draw the number of nests Betsy Bird needs. Glue the correct number of babies in each nest.

1 Write the math problem and a sentence telling about the answer.

____

____

2 What do all the birds have in common?

____

____

____

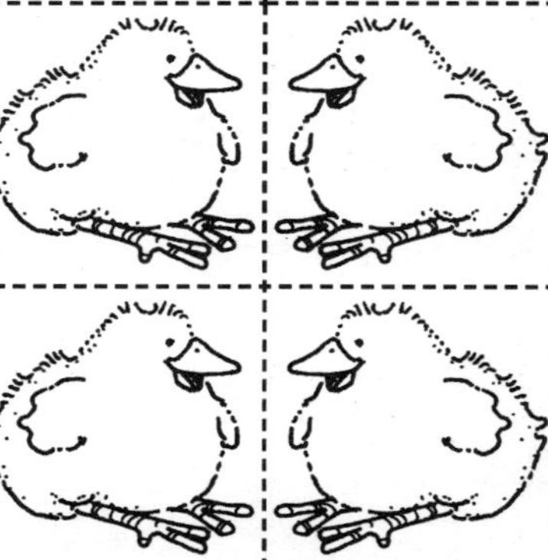

Name ______________________

REPRESENTING ADDITION SENTENCES

Many Mice

One afternoon, Chester the cat went into the kitchen to look for something to eat. Chester saw 3 mice running into the cupboard and 4 mice running into a hole in the wall. How many mice did Chester see in all? Draw a picture of the cupboard and the hole in the wall. Glue the correct number of mice in the picture.

Write the math problem and a sentence telling about the answer.

____

____

Name ______________

SOLVING WORD PROBLEMS

Frogs in a Bucket

Sam caught 9 frogs and put them in his bucket. 6 of the frogs jumped out of the bucket and ran away. How many frogs were left? Cut out the frogs and glue them to the picture to illustrate the story.

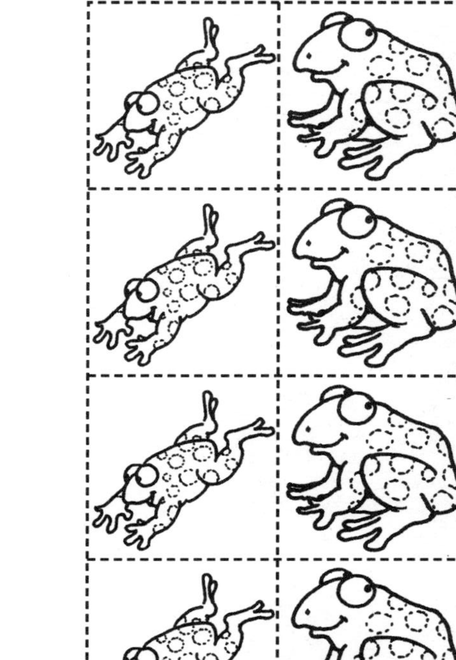

1 Write the math problem and a sentence telling about the answer.

____

____

2 If Sam sells the frogs left in his bucket for 5¢ each, how much money will he earn?

____

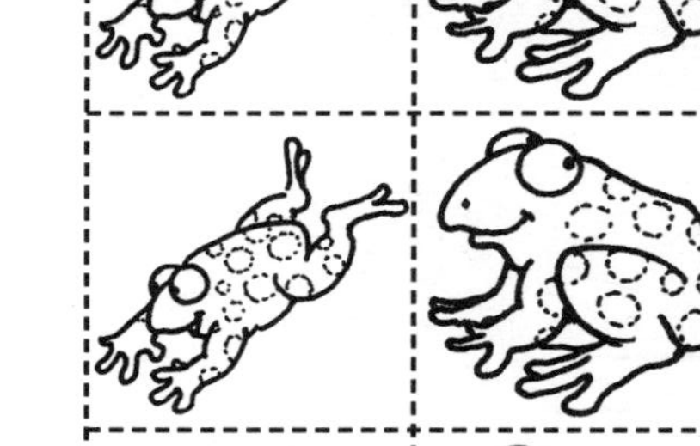

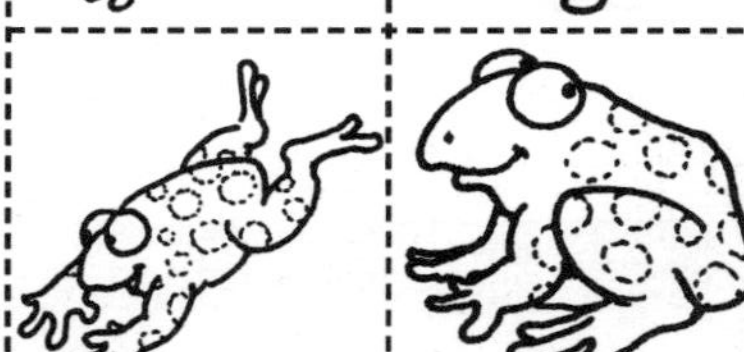

Name ____________

Apple Picking

Roll two dice and add the numbers together. Write the addition problem on the line. Color the apple that shows the answer.

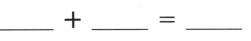

____ + ____ = ____　　　　____ + ____ = ____

____ + ____ = ____　　　　____ + ____ = ____

____ + ____ = ____　　　　____ + ____ = ____

____ + ____ = ____　　　　____ + ____ = ____

How many apples are on this page? ________

Name ______

Butterfly Wing Addition

Roll two dice and record the numbers rolled on each butterfly wing. Add the numbers and write the total on the butterfly's body.

Extension: Play with a partner. Taking turns, roll the dice and record the numbers on the butterfly. The player with the larger (or smaller) answer wins and can color in his or her butterfly.

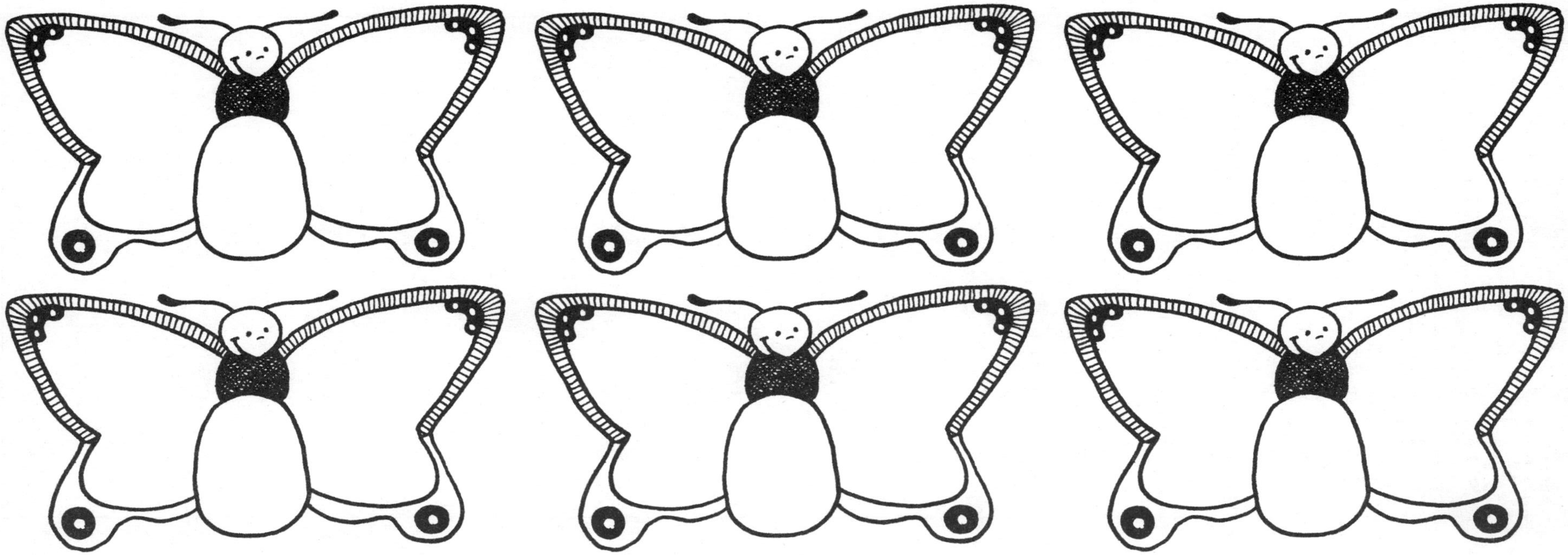

1 Write the math problem with the largest answer. ______

2 Write the math problem with the smallest answer. ______

Math Mat 13 Name ____________________ SORTING ANSWERS

Sort the Fish!

Cut out the fish. Sort and glue each fish by its answer.

10	11	12

12 − 0

3 + 9

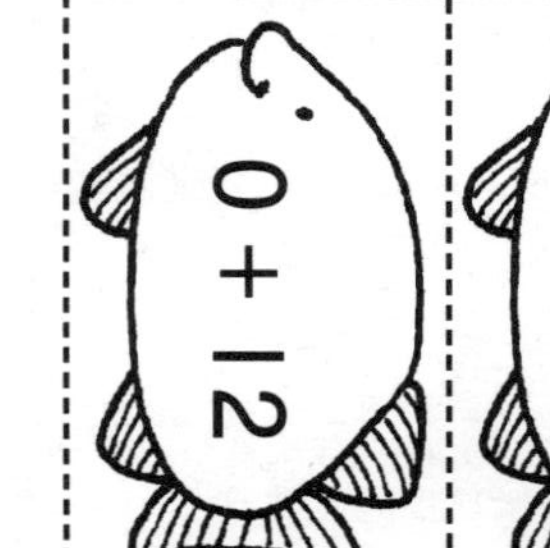

0 + 12

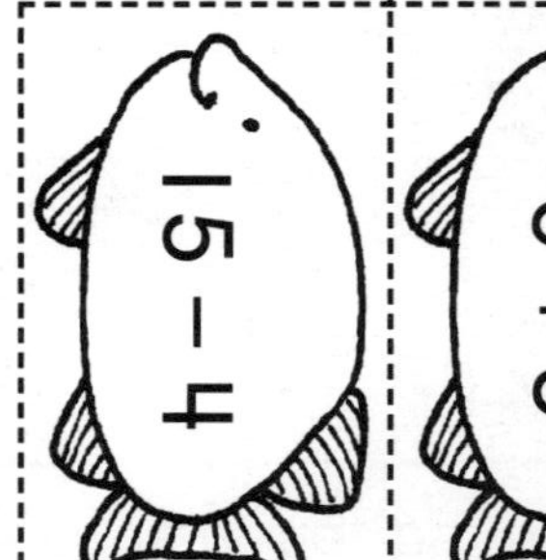

15 − 4

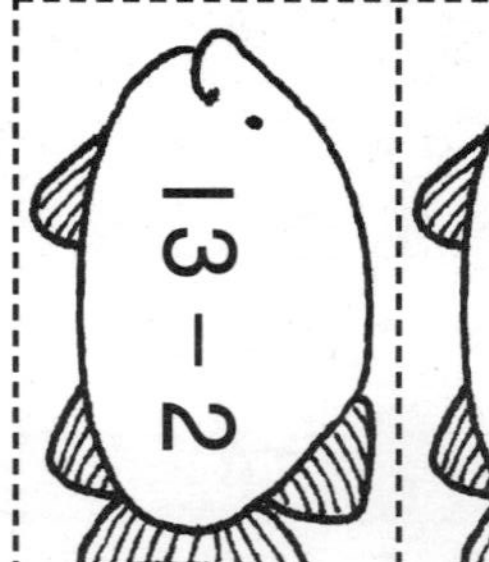

13 − 2

Name ____________________

WRITING NUMBER SENTENCES

Cat and Dog Pogs

1. Cut out the pictures and glue them back to back to make "pogs."
2. Place the pogs in a paper bag. Then shake the bag and pour the pogs onto the desk.
3. Write the two addition problems and two subtraction problems that you can make.

Example:

3 cats and 5 dogs

Addition problems:

$3 + 5 = 8$ $5 + 3 = 8$

Subtraction problems:

$8 - 3 = 5$ $8 - 5 = 3$

Shake 1	Shake 2	Shake 3
___ + ___ = ___	___ + ___ = ___	___ + ___ = ___
___ + ___ = ___	___ + ___ = ___	___ + ___ = ___
___ − ___ = ___	___ − ___ = ___	___ − ___ = ___
___ − ___ = ___	___ − ___ = ___	___ − ___ = ___

Name ______________________

USING TALLY MARKS

Domino Sort and Tally

Pick up a domino and count the number of pips. Write a tally mark in the correct column. Repeat 10 times.

Example:
8 pips
Make a tally mark under **Less than 10**.

Less than 10	Exactly 10	More than 10
Write the number. ______	Write the number. ______	Write the number. ______

Write the number.

1 |||| ______

2 ~~||||~~ |||| ______

3 ~~||||~~ ~~||||~~ |||| ______

On the back of this page, play tic-tac-toe with a classmate. Use tally marks to keep track of who wins each game.

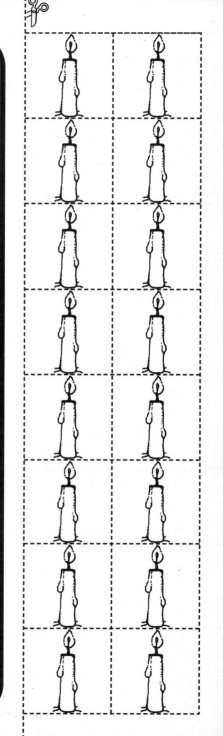

Name ____________________

CREATING SETS

Birthday Candles

Jenny put some candles on the birthday cake. She made 2 rows of candles with 3 candles in each row. How many candles did Jenny put on the birthday cake? Cut out the candles and glue them to the cake to illustrate the story.

Write the math problem and finish the sentence telling about the answer.

____

Jenny put ________ candles on the birthday cake.

Math Mat 17 Name ____________________

SOLVING WORD PROBLEMS

Party Balloons

Della blew up 16 balloons for the party. 5 of the balloons were red.
3 of the balloons were orange. 4 of the balloons were yellow.
The rest of the balloons were green. How many balloons were green?
Cut out the balloons and glue them in the boxes to illustrate the story.

Red Balloons	Orange Balloons
Yellow Balloons	**Green Balloons**

Finish the sentence.

There were ______ green balloons.

Name ____________________

WRITING ADDITION SENTENCES

Playing Card Addition

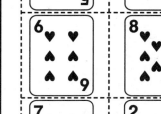

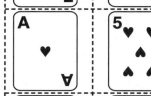

Make addition problems using the cards. Cut out the cards, shuffle them, and place them in a stack facedown. Turn over the top two cards and glue them in the spaces below. Write the answer to the addition problem in the box. (Hint: An ace equals 1.)

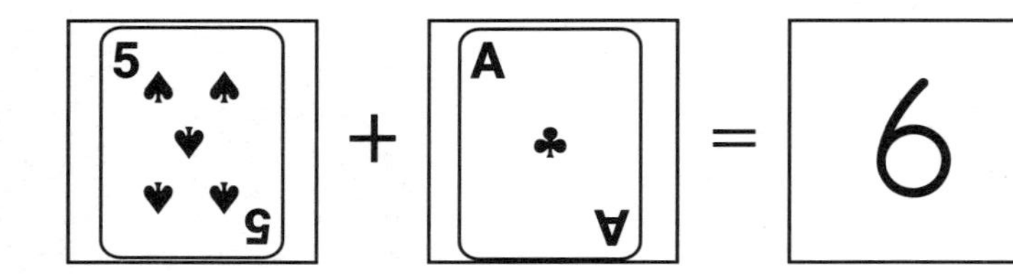

+ =

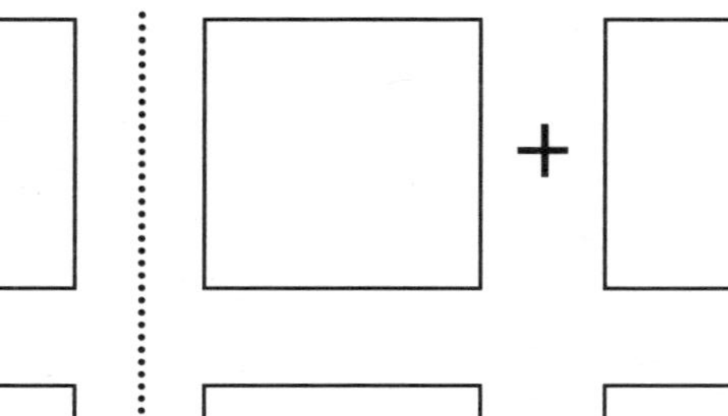

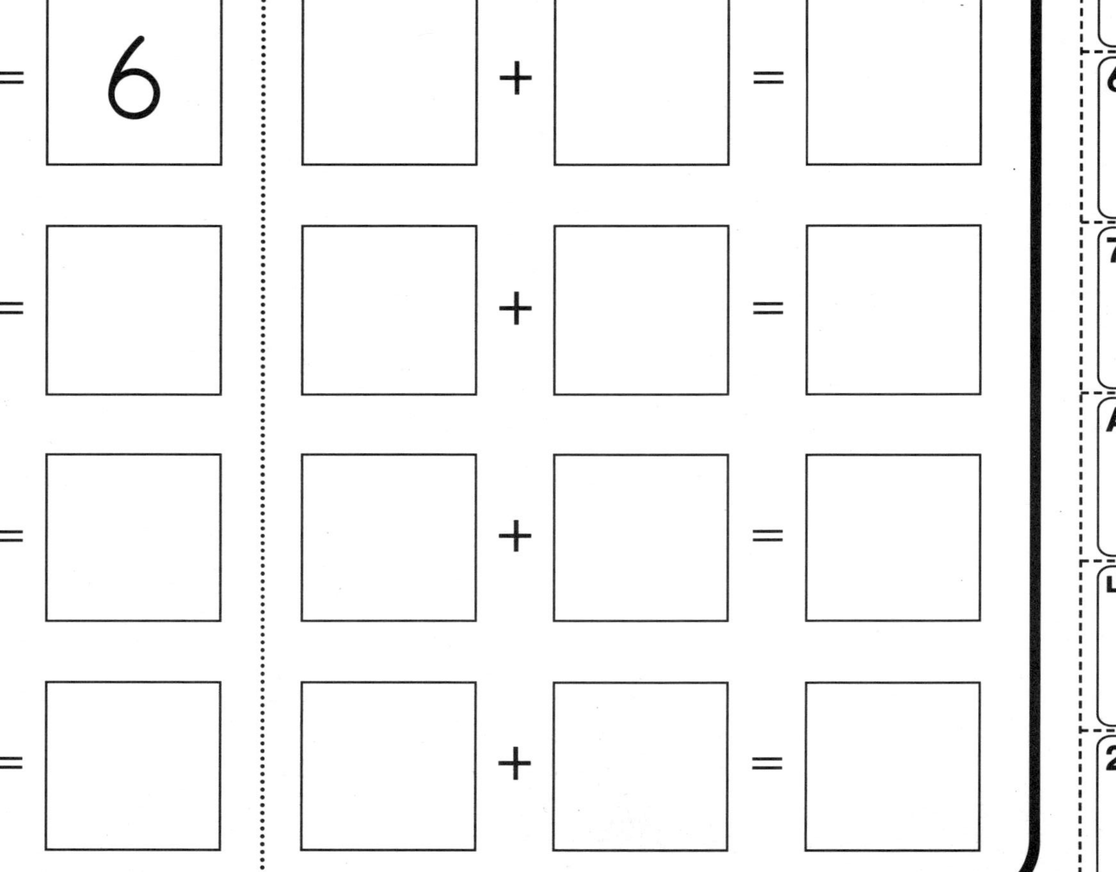

☐ + ☐ = ☐ ☐ + ☐ = ☐

☐ + ☐ = ☐ ☐ + ☐ = ☐

☐ + ☐ = ☐ ☐ + ☐ = ☐

☐ + ☐ = ☐ ☐ + ☐ = ☐

A 8 3 4 5 6 6 8 7 2 A 5 4 8 2 3

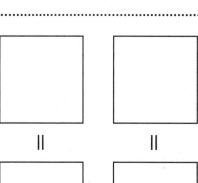

Name ______________________

SOLVING SUBTRACTION PROBLEMS

Four in a Row

Cut out the flash cards, shuffle them, and place them in a stack facedown. Turn over the top card and solve the subtraction problem. Color a box with the correct answer on the playing board. When you have four in row, you win!

1	0	2	0
0	3	2	1
1	3	1	2
2	0	3	1

$3 - 2$	$3 - 3$	$2 - 1$
$4 - 4$	$4 - 3$	$5 - 4$
$2 - 2$	$2 - 0$	$3 - 1$
$5 - 2$	$4 - 2$	$5 - 3$
$5 - 5$	$1 - 1$	$3 - 0$
$1 - 0$	$4 - 1$	$5 - 2$

Name ________________

SOLVING SUBTRACTION SENTENCES

Scarecrow Subtraction

Cross out the pictures to solve each problem.

1

6 − 4 = ____

2

5 − 3 = ____

3

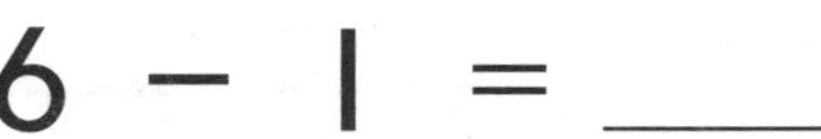

6 − 1 = ____

Solve each word problem.

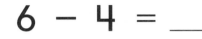

4 4 crows are in the field. The scarecrow scares 3 of the crows away. How many crows are left?

4 − 3 = ____

5 Jasper made 6 scarecrows. He sold 3 of them to Farmer Brown. How many scarecrows does Jasper have left?

6 − 3 = ____

Name ______________________

Finding the Difference

Count the legs.

1 _____ legs

2 _____ legs

3 _____ legs

4 _____ legs

5 _____ legs

6 _____ legs

Count the legs on each animal. Use the information to solve the math problems below. The first problem is done for you.

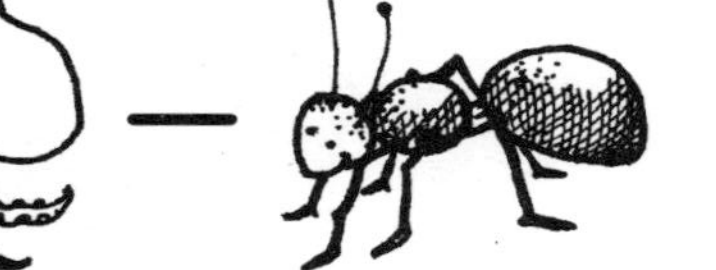

7 8 (legs) – 6 (legs) = 2 (legs)

10 _____ – _____ = _____

8 _____ – _____ = _____

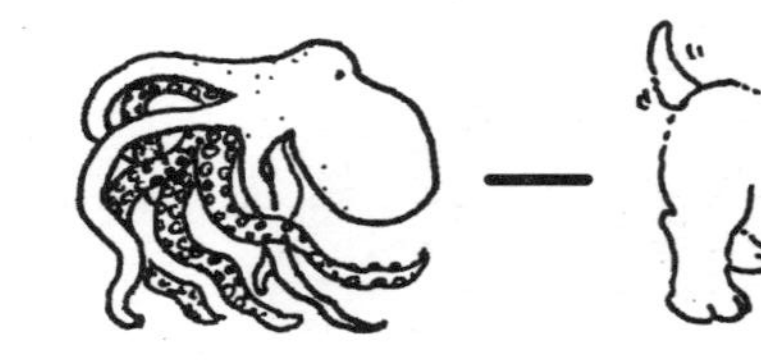

11 _____ – _____ = _____

9 _____ – _____ = _____

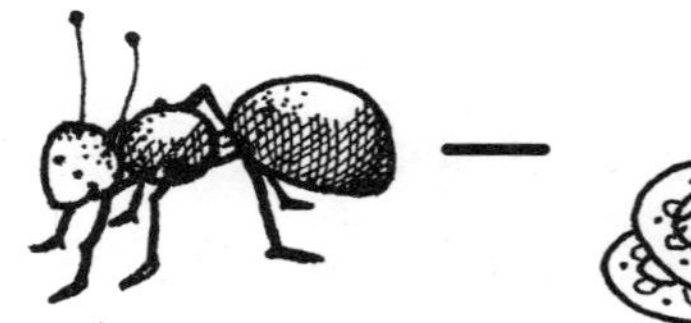

12 _____ – _____ = _____

Name ____________________

SUBTRACTING FROM ARRAYS

Count and Subtract

Cross out 3 items from each set. Complete the subtraction sentence.

1

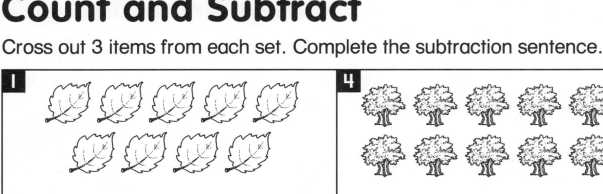

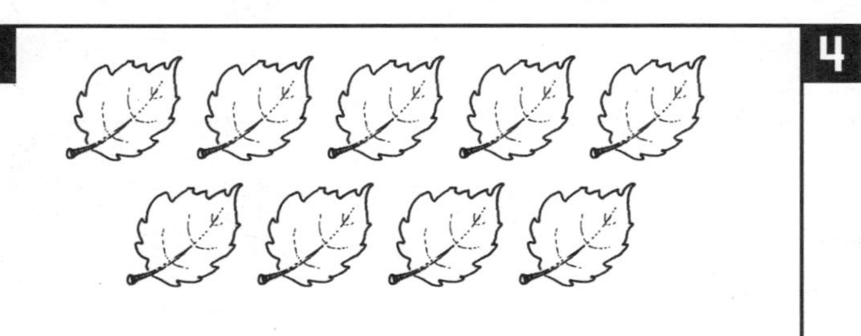

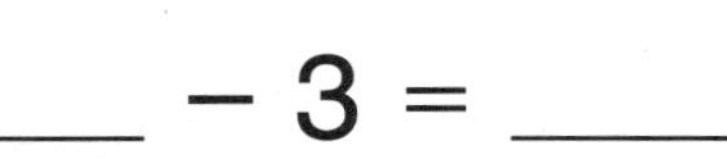

____ − 3 = ____

2

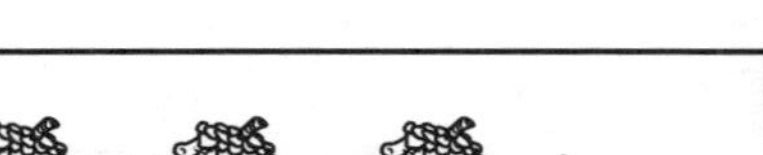

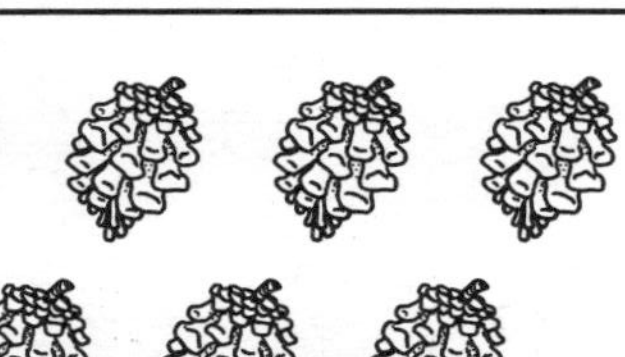

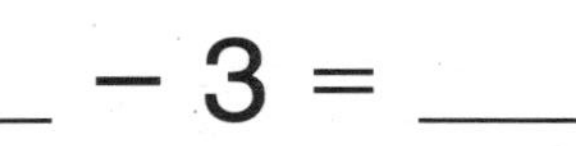

____ − 3 = ____

3

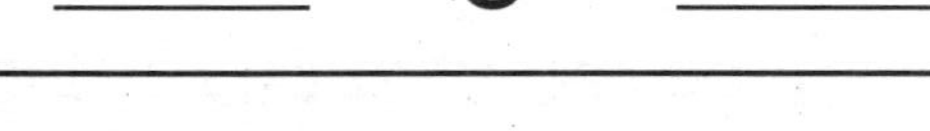

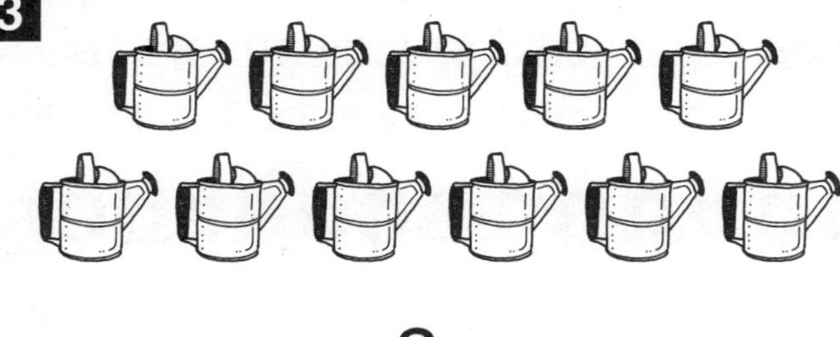

____ − 3 = ____

4

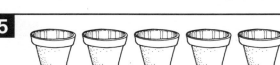

____ − 3 = ____

5

____ − 3 = ____

6

____ − 3 = ____

Complete the subtraction squares. Subtract going across and down.

7

9	8	
5	4	
		■

8

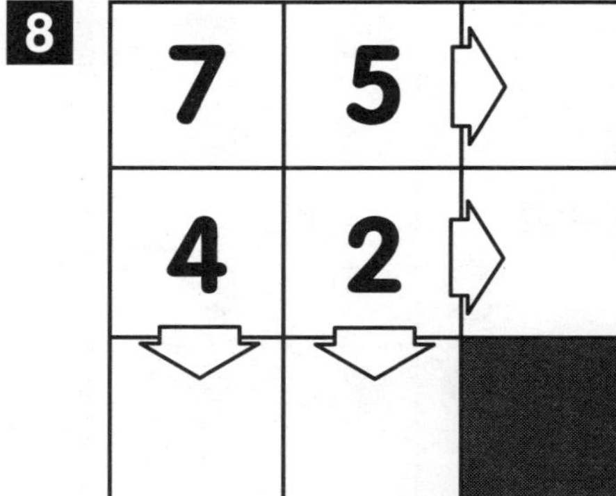

7	5	
4	2	
		■

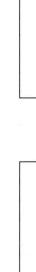

Math Mat 23

Name ______________________

WRITING SUBTRACTION SENTENCES

Dominoes Subtraction

Cut out the dominoes. Glue each domino in one of the boxes. Circle the smaller number of pips on the domino. Subtract the smaller number from the larger number. Write the math problem.

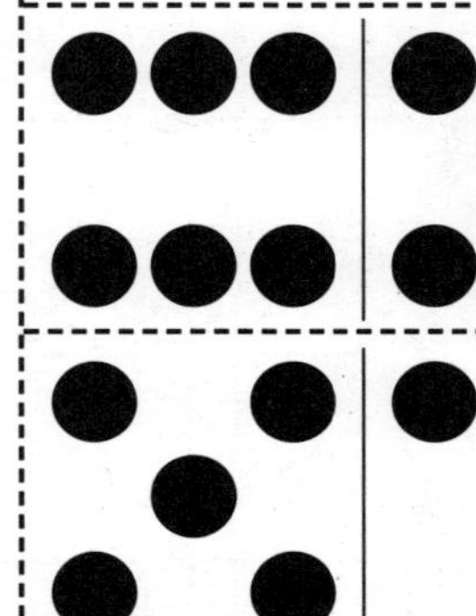
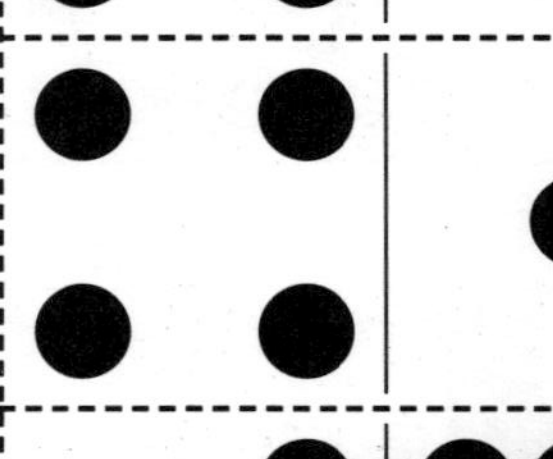

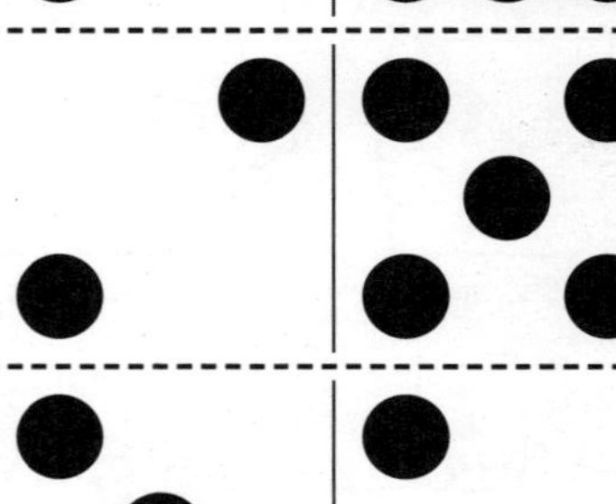
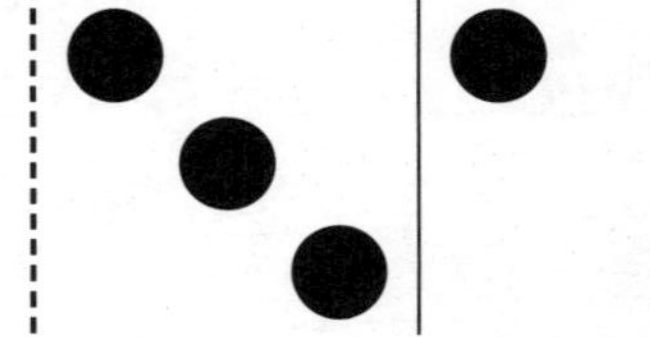

____ – ____ = ____   ____ – ____ = ____   ____ – ____ = ____

____ – ____ = ____   ____ – ____ = ____   ____ – ____ = ____

Name ______________________

WRITING SUBTRACTION SENTENCES

How Many Are Left?

Read and solve each word problem. Then write the math sentence.

1 Jason had 8 balloons. 4 balloons were red and the rest were blue. How many balloons were blue?

_____ – _____ = _____

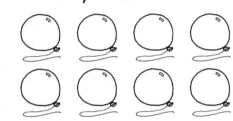

2 Abner had 9 pencils. He gave 7 pencils to a friend. How many pencils does Abner have left?

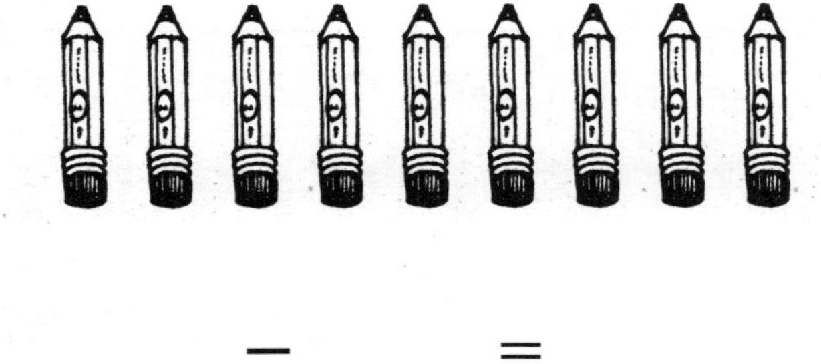

_____ – _____ = _____

3 Dana had 10 boxes of crayons. She gave 7 boxes away. How many boxes does Dana have left?

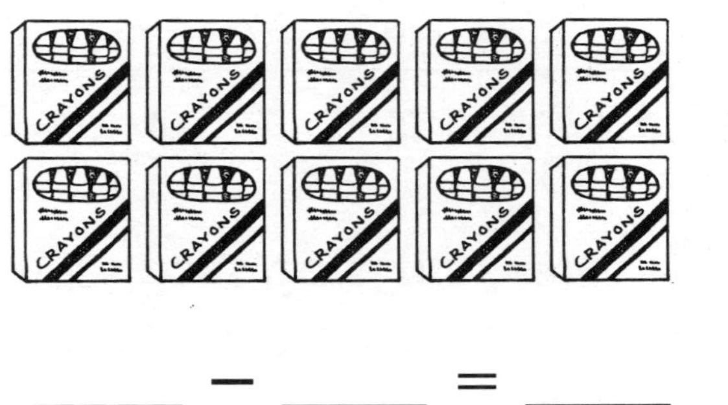

_____ – _____ = _____

4 Liz had 10 hats. She sold 1 of the hats. How many hats does Liz have left?

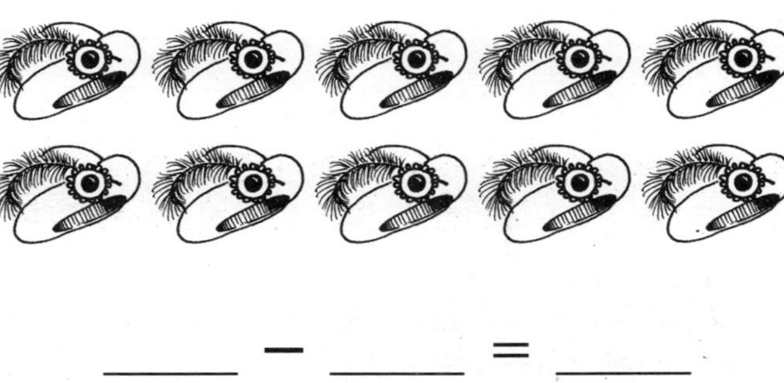

_____ – _____ = _____

What is $\frac{1}{2}$ of each group?

Example:

$\frac{1}{2}$ of 6 hats =

3 hats

5 $\frac{1}{2}$ of 4 crayons =

_____ crayon(s)

6 $\frac{1}{2}$ of 2 balloons =

_____ balloon(s)

7 $\frac{1}{2}$ of 10 crayons =

_____ crayon(s)

Name ______________________

SOLVING SUBTRACTION WORD PROBLEMS

At the Fruit Stand

Read and solve each word problem.

1

Amy had 10 apples. She used 5 to make a pie. How many apples does Amy have left?

Amy has ______ apples left.

2

Jerry had 9 bananas. He gave 6 to his sister. How many bananas does Jerry have left?

Jerry has ______ bananas left.

3

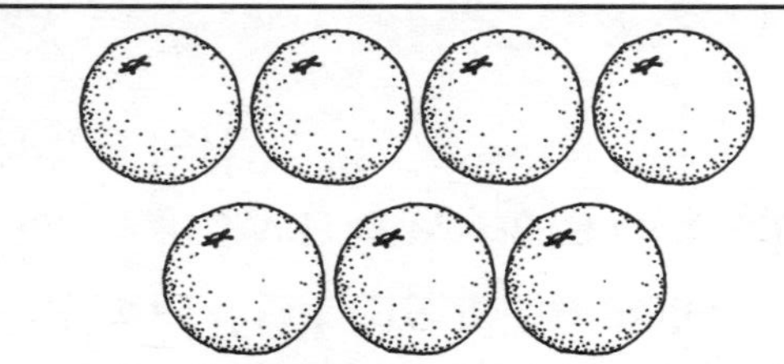

Carol picked 7 oranges. She used 4 to make juice. How many oranges does Carol have left?

Carol has ______ oranges left.

4

Peter gathered 8 strawberries. He ate 2 of them. How many strawberries does Peter have left?

Peter has ______ strawberries.

Crossword Puzzle

zero	one	two	three
four	five	six	seven
eight	nine	ten	

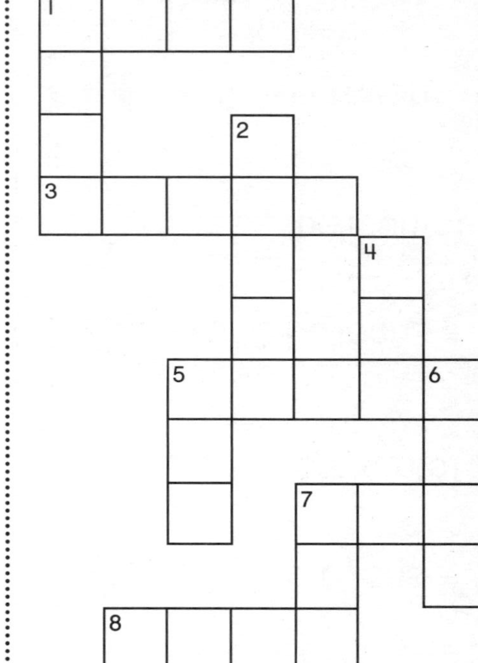

Across	Down
1. 3 + 1	1. 2 + 3
3. 9 − 1	2. 0 + 3
5. 10 − 3	4. 4 − 3
7. 8 + 2	5. 3 + 3
8. 6 − 6	6. 5 + 4
	7. 2 + 0

Name ____________________

SOLVING SUBTRACTION WORD PROBLEMS

Rupert's Cheese

Rupert the mouse had 9 pieces of cheese. He ate 3 pieces of cheese for lunch. How many pieces of cheese does Rupert have left? (Hint: Cross out the pieces of cheese Rupert ate for lunch.)

Finish the sentence.

1 Rupert has ______ pieces of cheese left.

Cross out the cheese to solve each problem.

2 9 – 2 = ______

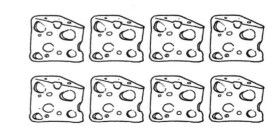

3 10 – 5 = ______

4 8 – 3 = ______

Math Mat 27 Name ____________________

SOLVING SUBTRACTION WORD PROBLEMS

On the Ranch

Read and solve each word problem.

1

Missy had 10 cows. She put 4 cows in the field. How many cows does Missy have left?

Missy has ______ cows left.

2

Sybil had 7 horses in the pasture. She put 7 in the barn. How many horses does Sybil have left in the pasture?

Sybil has ______ horses left.

3

Rusty had 8 sheep. He sheared 5 of them. How many sheep does Rusty still have left to shear?

Rusty still has to shear ______ sheep.

4

Cam had 9 chickens. He fed 7 chickens. How many chickens does Cam still have to feed?

Cam has to feed ______ chickens.

Count the animals.
Circle the answer.

5 15 hens 5 hens

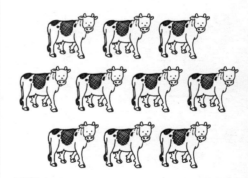

6 10 cows 20 cows

7 12 pigs 2 pigs

Math Mat 28 Name ______________________ **ADDING VERTICAL NUMERALS**

Apples in a Row

Use the apple number line to solve each problem.

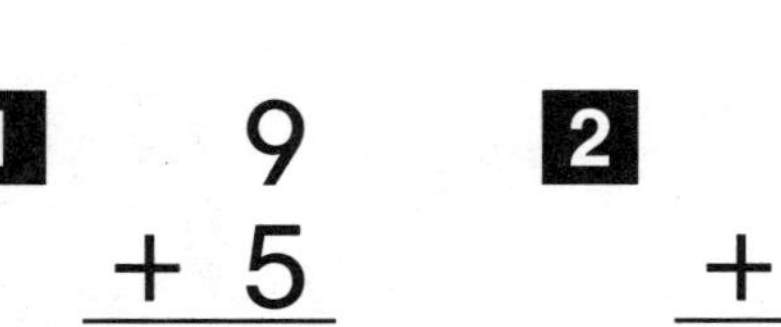

1 $\begin{array}{r} 9 \\ +\ 5 \\ \hline \end{array}$

2 $\begin{array}{r} 6 \\ +\ 5 \\ \hline \end{array}$

3 $\begin{array}{r} 7 \\ +\ 2 \\ \hline \end{array}$

4 $\begin{array}{r} 8 \\ +\ 2 \\ \hline \end{array}$

5 $\begin{array}{r} 6 \\ +\ 2 \\ \hline \end{array}$

6 $\begin{array}{r} 5 \\ +\ 4 \\ \hline \end{array}$

7 $\begin{array}{r} 7 \\ +\ 5 \\ \hline \end{array}$

8 $\begin{array}{r} 9 \\ +\ 3 \\ \hline \end{array}$

9 $\begin{array}{r} 9 \\ +\ 9 \\ \hline \end{array}$

10 $\begin{array}{r} 9 \\ +\ 0 \\ \hline \end{array}$

Cut out the numbers. Use the numbers to complete the addition square.

6		3	→ 10
			→ 10
1		5	→ 10
↓ 10	↓ 10	↓ 10	

Check your work. Then glue the numbers in place.

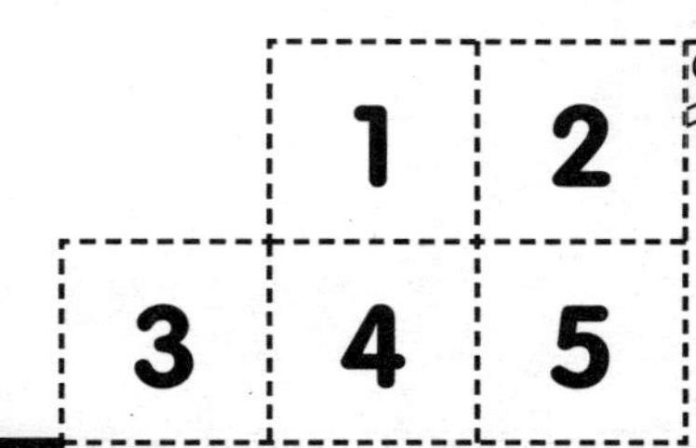

Math Mat 29 Name ____________

ADDING THREE VERTICAL NUMERALS

1, 2, 3, Go!

Follow the arrows to solve each addition problem.

1. 3 + 6 + 2 → 9 → 11

$$\begin{array}{r} 3 \\ 6 \\ +\ 2 \\ \hline 11 \end{array}$$

2. $$\begin{array}{r} 2 \\ 4 \\ +\ 8 \\ \hline \end{array}$$

3. $$\begin{array}{r} 1 \\ 0 \\ +\ 9 \\ \hline \end{array}$$

4. 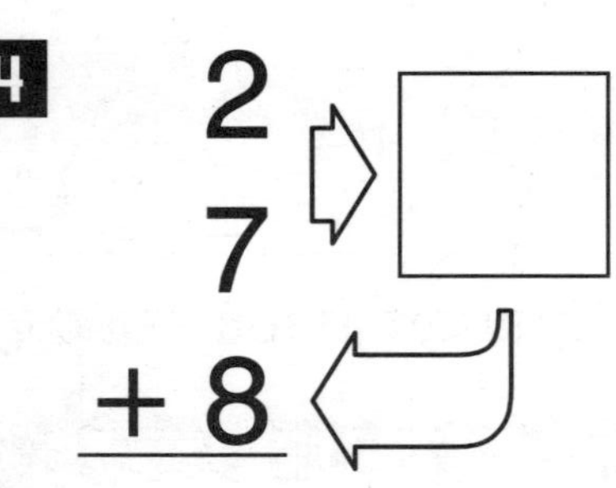

$$\begin{array}{r} 2 \\ 7 \\ +\ 8 \\ \hline \end{array}$$

5. 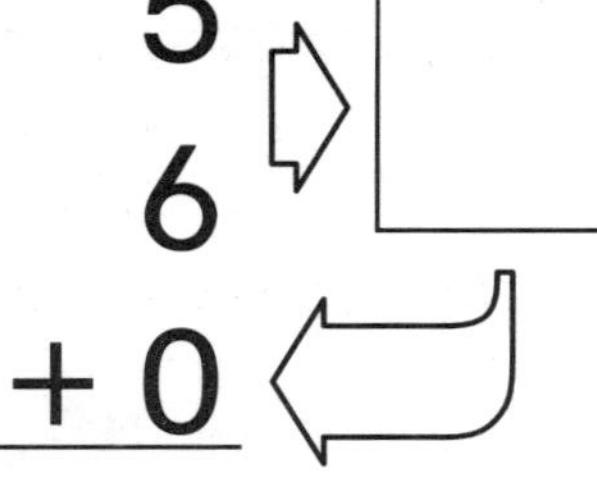

$$\begin{array}{r} 5 \\ 6 \\ +\ 0 \\ \hline \end{array}$$

6. $$\begin{array}{r} 4 \\ 4 \\ +\ 4 \\ \hline \end{array}$$

Math Riddles

Circle the answer.

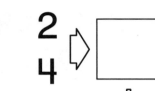

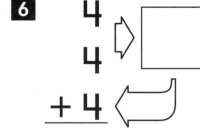

7. I have three digits in my number. All three numbers are the same. Which number am I?

444 **542**

8. I have three digits in my number. I have an 8 in the ones place and a 7 in the tens place. Which number am I?

178 **187**

9. I have three digits in my number. I have a 5 in the tens place and a 6 in the ones place. Which number am I?

865 **856**

Name ____________________

MATCHING SUMS AND SENTENCES

Number Sentences

Draw a line matching each math problem to its answer.

8 + 9	13	6 + 9
6 + 8	14	4 + 9
9 + 7	15	8 + 6
9 + 6	16	10 + 8
9 + 4	17	9 + 8
8 + 10	18	7 + 9

Circle all of the ways to make 15.

9 8 7 6 5 7 8
8 7 6 5 9 6 9
7 6 5 9 8 7 5
6 5 9 8 7 9 6
8 7 5 6 9 7 8
9 6 9 6 5 8 7
6 7 8 9 5 7 6

Write the math sentences.

___ + ___ = 15

___ + ___ = 15

___ + ___ = 15

___ + ___ = 15

Name ______________________

Spin the Spinners!

Spin one spinner. Write the subtraction sentence and the answer. Repeat these steps with the other spinner.

9 – ______ = ______

9 – ______ = ______

9 – ______ = ______

9 – ______ = ______

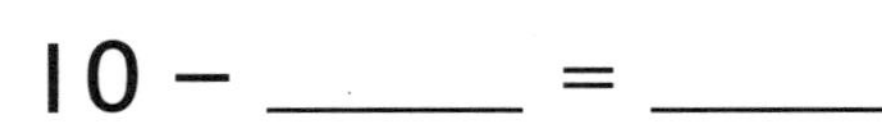

10 – ______ = ______

10 – ______ = ______

10 – ______ = ______

10 – ______ = ______

Make the spinner using a paper clip and a pencil.

Use the >, <, and = signs to compare the answers to the following math problems.

1 3 + 2 ☐ 4 – 1

2 5 – 5 ☐ 6 + 3

3 10 – 2 ☐ 2 + 7

4 6 – 0 ☐ 1 + 5

Name ______________ USING NUMBER LINES

Apple Number Line

Use the number line to solve each problem.

1 Start on 8.
Add 7 more.

8 + 7 = ______

2 Start on 18.
Add 0 more.

18 + 0 = ______

3 Start on 20.
Subtract 9.

20 − 9 = ______

4 Start on 16.
Add 4 more.

16 + 4 = ______

5 Start on 11.
Add 8 more.

11 + 8 = ______

6 Start on 19.
Subtract 5.

19 − 5 = ______

7 Start on 10.
Add 5 more.

10 + 5 = ______

8 Start on 15.
Add 2 more.

15 + 2 = ______

9 Start on 17.
Subtract 7.

17 − 7 = ______

Write the missing + or − sign to solve each problem.

10 12 ☐ 2 = 10

11 14 ☐ 1 = 15

12 13 ☐ 10 = 3

13 18 ☐ 18 = 0

14 20 ☐ 11 = 9

15 10 ☐ 3 = 13

Math Mat 33

Name ______________________

FINDING MISSING ADDENDS

Find the Missing Number

Cut out the numbers. Use each number to solve the addition or subtraction sentence.

1. $\square + 3 = 6$
2. $10 - \square = 3$
3. $9 - 4 = \square$
4. $\square - 6 = 2$
5. $7 - 6 = \square$
6. $\square + 0 = 6$
7. $5 - \square = 1$
8. $6 + \square = 8$

Unscramble each number word.

9. eroz ______________
10. nnie ______________
11. gheti ______________
12. rethe ______________
13. net ______________

1	2
3	4
5	6
7	8

Name ____________________

FINDING MISSING ADDENDS

Ready, Set, Start!

Cut out the numbers and use them to solve each math problem. Each number can be used only once.

1 ☐ − 8 = 5

2 19 − 8 = ☐

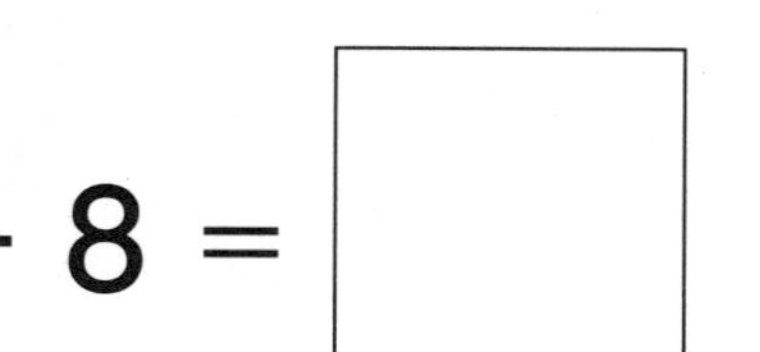

3 14 − 2 = ☐

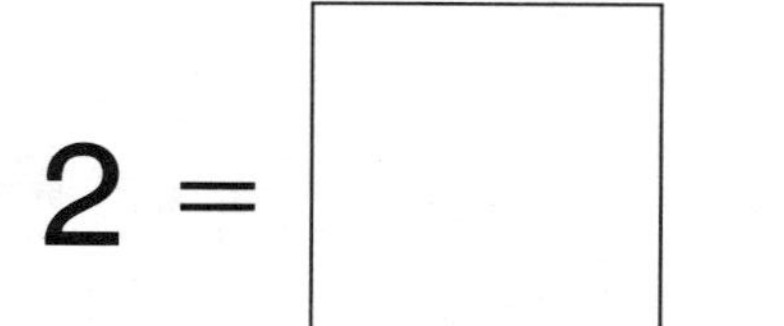

4 ☐ − 6 = 9

5 11 − ☐ = 3

6 ☐ − 8 = 6

7 18 − 9 = ☐

8 20 − ☐ = 10

Math Riddle

Sam had 12 apples in his left pocket. He put 5 of those apples in his right pocket and 2 apples in his back pocket. How many apples does Sam now have in his left pocket?

____

8	9
10	11
12	13
14	15

Math Mat 35 Name ______________

CONVERTING ROMAN AND ARABIC NUMERALS

Arabic and Roman Numerals

Rewrite each math problem with Arabic numerals and solve.

1 XII – IX =

12 – 9 = 3

2 XVII – I =

____

3 XV – VI =

____

4 X – V =

____

5 XIX – VII =

____

6 XIV – II =

____

Rewrite the Arabic numerals with Roman numerals.

7 25 ______________

8 30 ______________

Arabic Numerals	Roman Numerals
1	I
2	II
3	III
4	IV
5	V
6	VI
7	VII
8	VIII
9	IX
10	X
11	XI
12	XII
13	XIII
14	XIV
15	XV
16	XVI
17	XVII
18	XVIII
19	XIX
20	XX

Name ____________________

WRITING NUMBER WORDS

Subtraction Crossword Puzzle

Write the answer to each math problem in the crossword puzzle.

Across

1. 19 − 1 = ____

3. 20 − 0 = ____

5. 15 − 13 = ____

7. 17 − 10 = ____

8. 15 − 11 = ____

9. 12 − 12 = ____

10. 15 − 6 = ____

Down

2. 18 − 8 = ____

3. 19 − 7 = ____

4. 20 − 9 = ____

5. 10 − 7 = ____

6. 14 − 13 = ____

8. 14 − 9 = ____

Number Word Bank

zero
one
two
three
four
five
six
seven
eight
nine
ten
eleven
twelve
thirteen
fourteen
fifteen
sixteen
seventeen
eighteen
nineteen
twenty

Name ______________________

GATHERING INFORMATION

Apples and Cores

Use the information shown below to answer the questions.

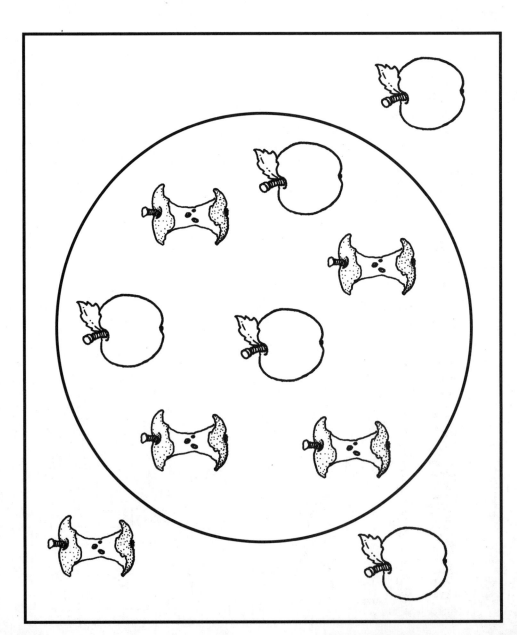

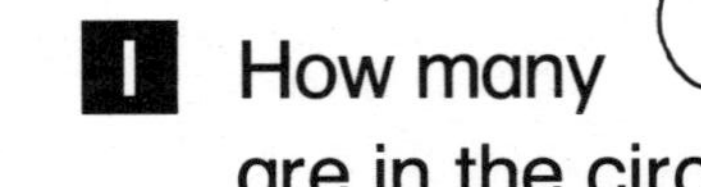
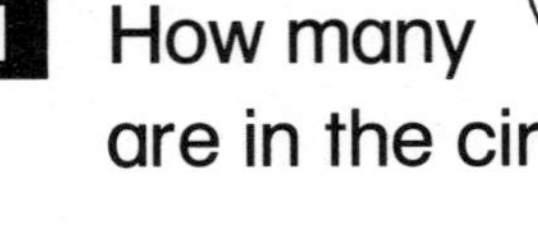

1 How many 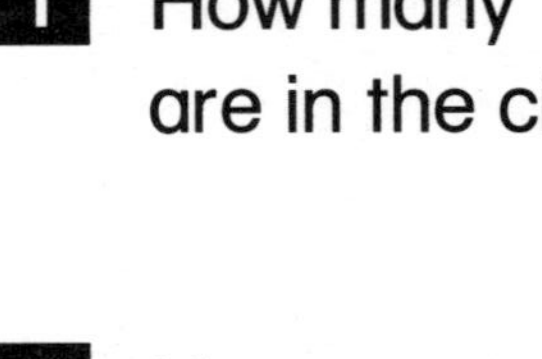 are in the circle? ______

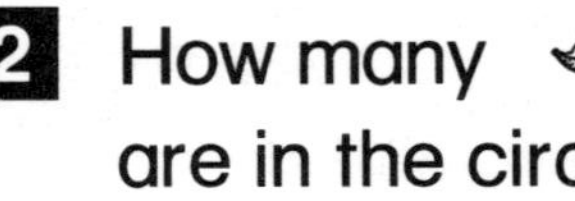

2 How many  are in the circle? ______

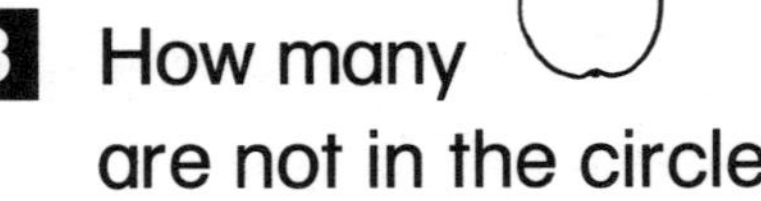

3 How many 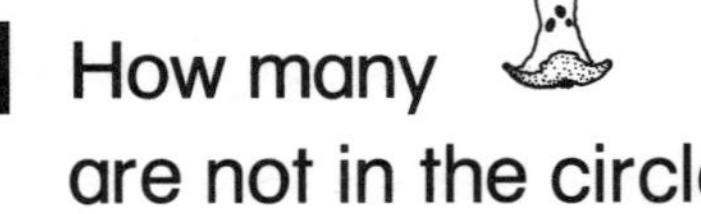 are not in the circle? ______

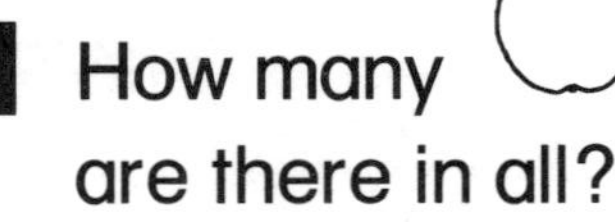

4 How many  are not in the circle? ______

5 How many  are there in all? ______

6 How many  are there in all? ______

Name ____________________

GATHERING INFORMATION

Stinky Skunks!

Answer the questions about the diagram.

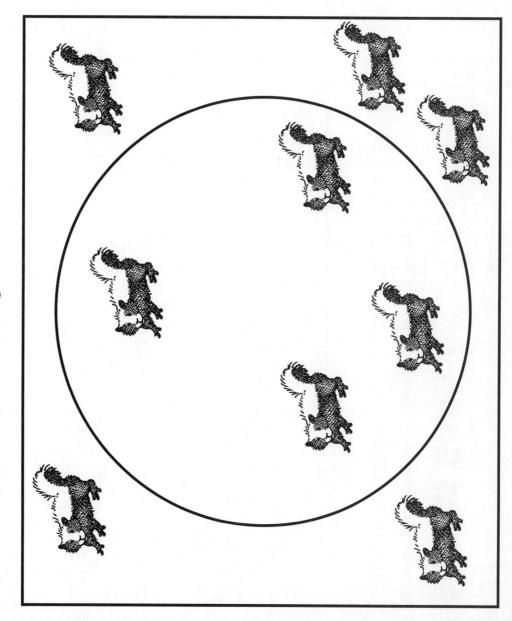

1 How many skunks are in the circle? ______

2 How many skunks are not in the circle? ______

3 How many skunks are there in all? ______

Complete each pattern.

2, 4, ______, 8, ______

5, ______, 9, 11, ______

28, 30, ______, ______

What's the rule?

____

Name ____________________

Animal Sorting

Answer the questions using the information shown on the diagram.

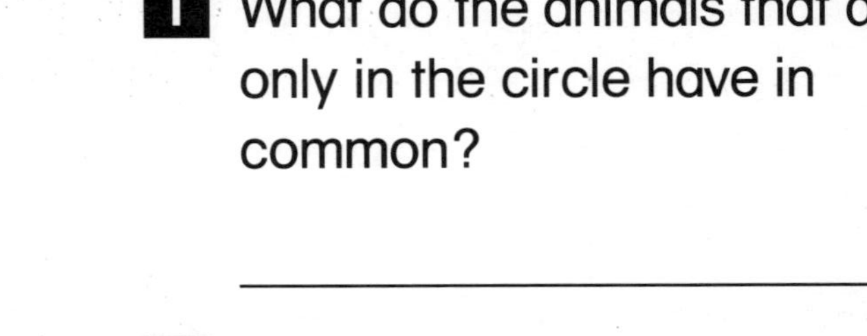

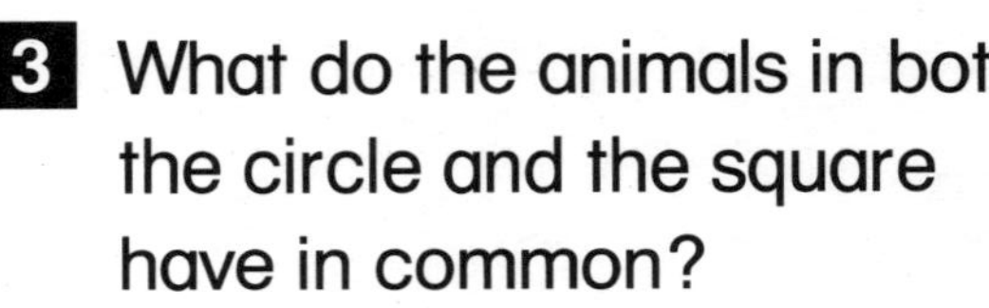

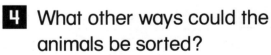

1 What do the animals that are only in the circle have in common?

____

2 What do the animals that are only in the square have in common?

____

3 What do the animals in both the circle and the square have in common?

____

4 What other ways could the animals be sorted?

____

____

____

Name ______________________

USING A VENN DIAGRAM

Chocolate Desserts

Cut out the pictures. Read the statements and glue the chocolate dessert pictures in the correct spaces.

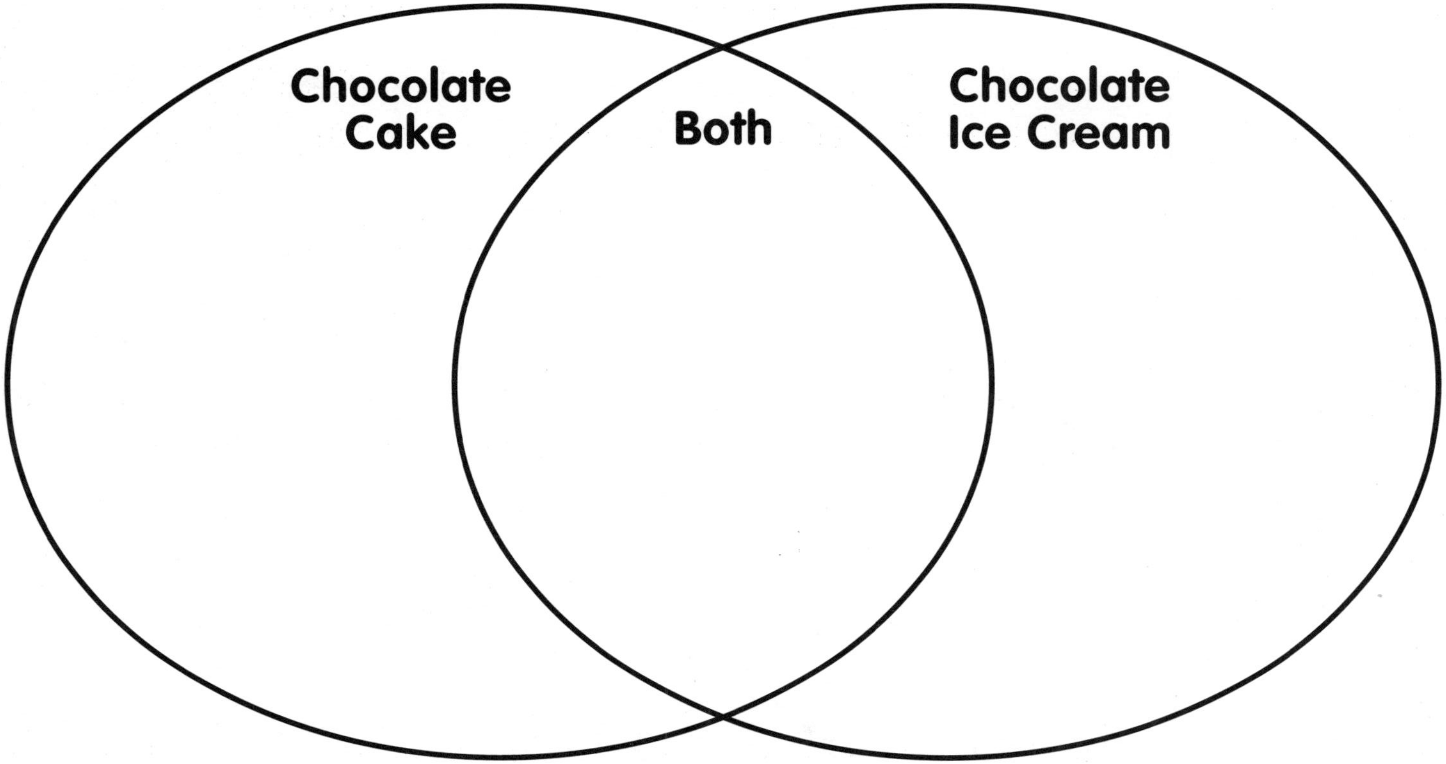

Chocolate Cake

Both

Chocolate Ice Cream

1. 2 people liked only chocolate cake.
2. 3 people liked chocolate ice cream.
3. 1 person liked both chocolate cake and chocolate ice cream.

How many people voted? ________

Name ____________

Ladybugs and Butterflies

Cut out the pictures.
Then follow the directions.

1. Glue 3 ladybugs in the circle but not in the square.
2. Glue 2 butterflies in both the circle and the square.
3. Glue 1 butterfly in the circle but not in the square.
4. Glue 2 ladybugs in the square but not in the circle.
5. Glue 1 ladybug in both the circle and the square.

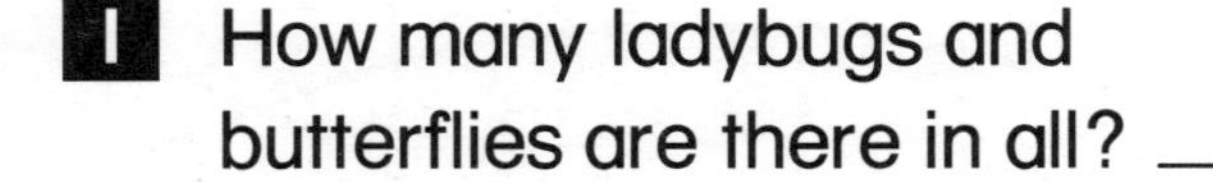

1 How many ladybugs and butterflies are there in all? ________

2 Which insect is in the circle, in the square, and in both the circle and the square? ________

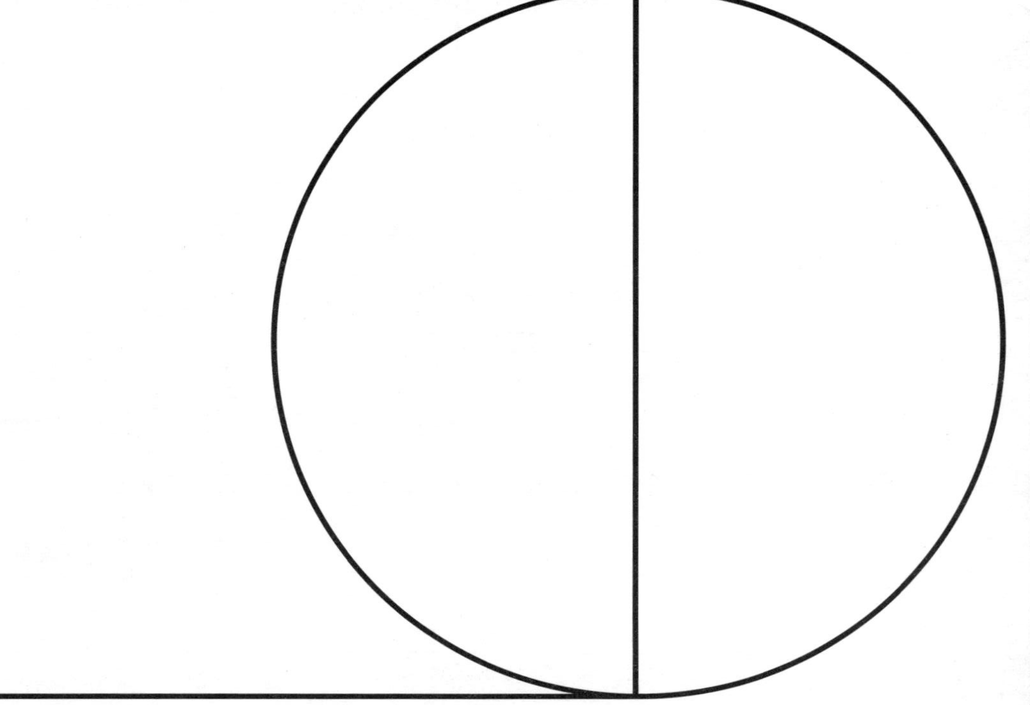

Name ____________________

USING DEDUCTIVE REASONING

Find Me!

Read the clues. If a picture does not fit the clue, make an X on that animal.

1. I have 4 legs.
2. I do not carry my home on my back.
3. I can hop.

1 Which animal am I?

____

Write a clue that would fit the animal.

____

____

Look at each set of animals. What do they all have in common?

2 They all ____________________.

3 They all ____________________.

4 They all ____________________.

Name ____________________

FOLLOWING DIRECTIONS

Woodland Animal Clues

Follow the directions.

1. Draw an X on the animals that do not have legs.
2. Draw an X on the animals that have big ears.
3. Draw an X on the animals that have stripes.
4. Draw an X on the animals that do not have wings.

1 Which animal is left?

____

Read each question and circle the answer.

2 Which animal can fly?

3 Which animal can hang by its tail?

4 Which animal can make a bad smell?

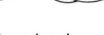

5 Which animal has no legs?

Name ______________________

USING DEDUCTIVE REASONING

My Favorite Hat

Read the clues to find my favorite hat. If a hat does not fit the clue, make an X on that hat.

1. My hat does not have horns or a tail.
2. My hat is not a helmet.
3. My hat does not have any feathers or bows.
4. My hat does not have any jewels.
5. My hat covers my head.
6. My hat has lots of decorations on it.
7. I wear my hat on Cinco de Mayo.

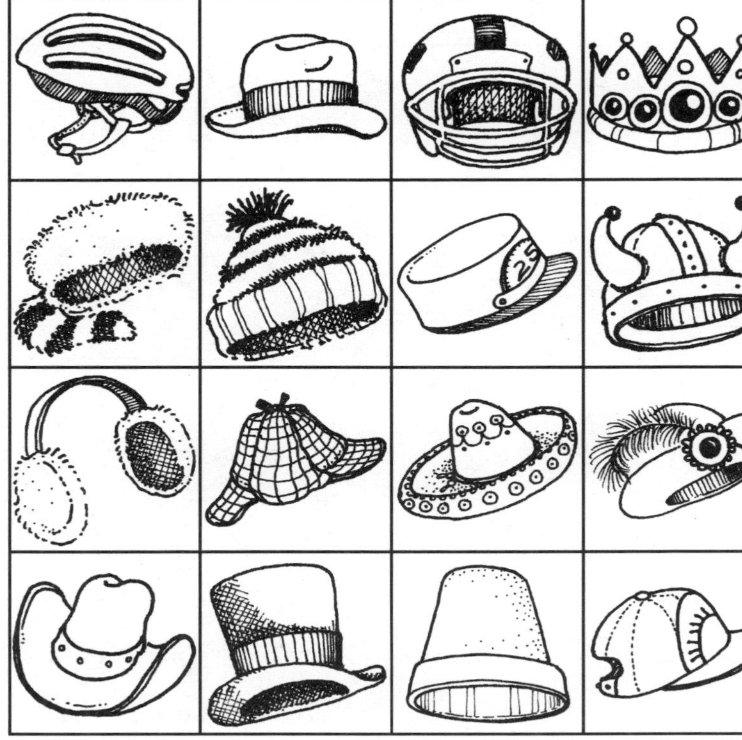

Which hat am I?

____

Cut out the hats. Sort them two different ways on the back of the paper. Write a sentence describing one of the ways.

Name ____________

USING DEDUCTIVE REASONING

Albert Goes to School

Read the clues and cross out the pictures that do not fit the clues to find the way Albert gets to school.

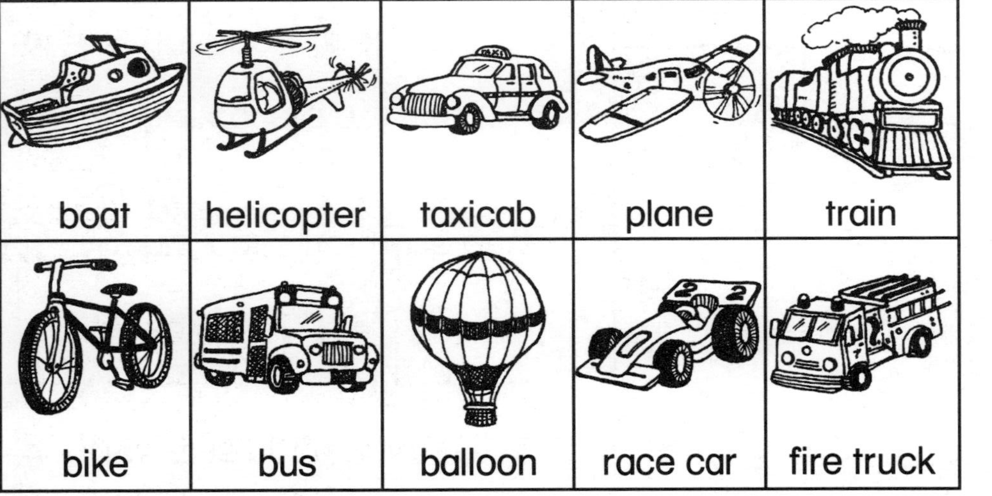

1. It has wheels.
2. It can carry more than one person at a time.
3. It can go on a road.
4. It does not charge a fare for each ride.
5. It does not go to fires.
6. It carries many students together to school each day.

How does Albert get to school each day? ____________

Draw a picture showing your favorite way to get to school.

Write a clue describing your favorite way of getting to school.

____

____

____

____

Name ____________________

USING GRAPHIC ORGANIZERS

Sports Tally

Read each clue.If the answer is **no**, make an **X** in the square. If the answer is **yes**, make an **O** in the square.

Clues

1. Angela does not play Frisbee or football.
2. Kate plays only football.
3. Mark does not play football or basketball.

	football	Frisbee	basketball
Angela			
Kate			
Mark			

Which sport does each person play?

Angela ____________________

Kate ____________________

Mark ____________________

Ask ten classmates which sport they like best. Use tally marks to record each vote.

football ____________

Frisbee ____________

basketball ____________

baseball ____________

hockey ____________

cycling ____________

skating ____________

soccer ____________

swimming ____________

Name ______________________

Favorite Fruits

Read each clue.
If the answer is **no**, make an **X** in the box.
If the answer is **yes**, make an **O** in the box.

Clues

1. Leo eats only pears.
2. Henry does not like grapes, pears, and strawberries.
3. Sonja eats nothing but strawberries.
4. Rebecca likes fruit that comes in bunches.

Draw lines matching each person to his or her favorite fruit.

On the back of the page, write a clue about your favorite fruit. Share the clue with a classmate. Can the classmate guess what your favorite fruit is?

Name ____________________

At the Toy Store

Read each clue.
If the answer in **no**, make an **X** in the square.
If the answer is **yes**, make an **O** in the square.

Clues

1. Lisa did not buy a bear, dog, or turtle.
2. Daniel bought a dog.
3. Maria does not like cats, dogs, or bears.
4. Bill bought a bear.

What did each person buy?

Daniel bought a ____________________.

Lisa bought a ____________________.

Maria bought a ____________________.

Bill bought a ____________________.

Name ______________________

USING GRAPHIC ORGANIZERS

Who Lives Where?

Cut out the pictures. Read the clues to discover where each person lives. Glue each picture on the correct floor.

Clues

1. Chris lives on the 3rd floor.
2. Sarah lives 2 floors above Chris.
3. Kevin lives 3 floors below Sarah.
4. Sam does not live on the 1st floor or the 6th floor.
5. Steve does not live on the 6th floor.
6. Alanna lives on the highest numbered floor.

Write the floor number next to each person.

Sam ________ Sarah ________

Alanna ________ Chris ________

Steve ________ Kevin ________

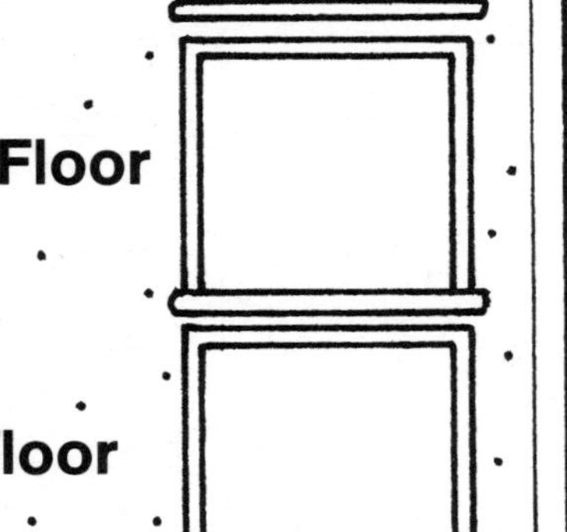

Find and color each word.

first	second	third
fourth	fifth	sixth

```
F O T H E A S J P H
N K A S C F I F T H
T J S E C O N D U O
H J Y Q E J N T Y P
A I H Q D T H I R D
W W P S D S H Q F B
F I R S T L O F C Z
E M J F O U R T H P
V D H U S I X T H T
```

Name ____________

USING ORDINAL NUMBERS

Animal Order

Cut out the animal pictures. Read the clues and place the animals in the correct order.

first	second	third	fourth
1st	2nd	3rd	4th

Logic Clues 1

- The cat is first.
- The dog is last.
- The chick is third.

Where is the lamb? ____________

Logic Clues 2

- The lamb is first.
- The dog is third.
- The cat is after the dog.

Where is the chick? ____________

Logic Clues 3

- The chick is second.
- The lamb is third.
- The cat is not last.

Where is the dog? ____________

Logic Clues 4

- The dog is fourth.
- The lamb is second.
- The chick is not first.

Where is the cat? ____________

5 Circle the 4th cat.

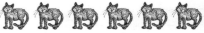

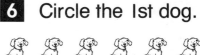

6 Circle the 1st dog.

7 Circle the 6th chick.

8 Circle the 3rd lamb.

Name ____________________ **PROBLEM SOLVING**

Mix and Match Caps

How many ways can you hang the caps? Cut out and arrange the caps on the hooks. Record the order of each arrangement.

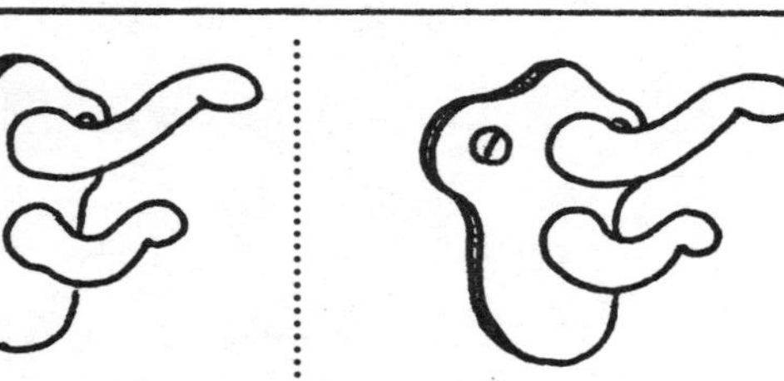

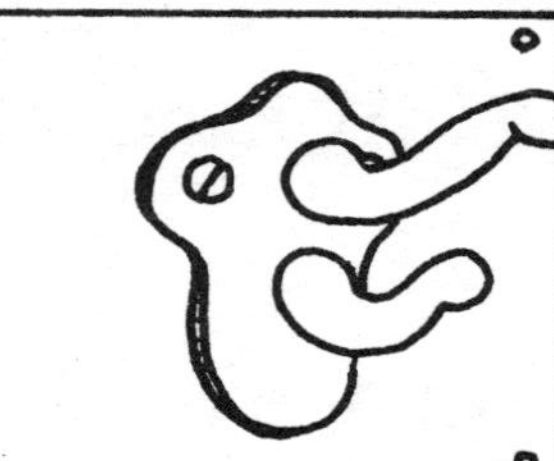

1 ____________________

2 ____________________

3 ____________________

4 ____________________

5 ____________________

6 ____________________

Glue the caps on the hooks to show your favorite arrangement.

Solve the word problem.

7 A peddler has 3 checked caps, 4 solid caps, and 5 striped caps. How many caps does the peddler have in all?

____

Math Mat 52

Name ______________________

ANALYZING CHARTS

A Fall Day

Answer the questions about the graph.

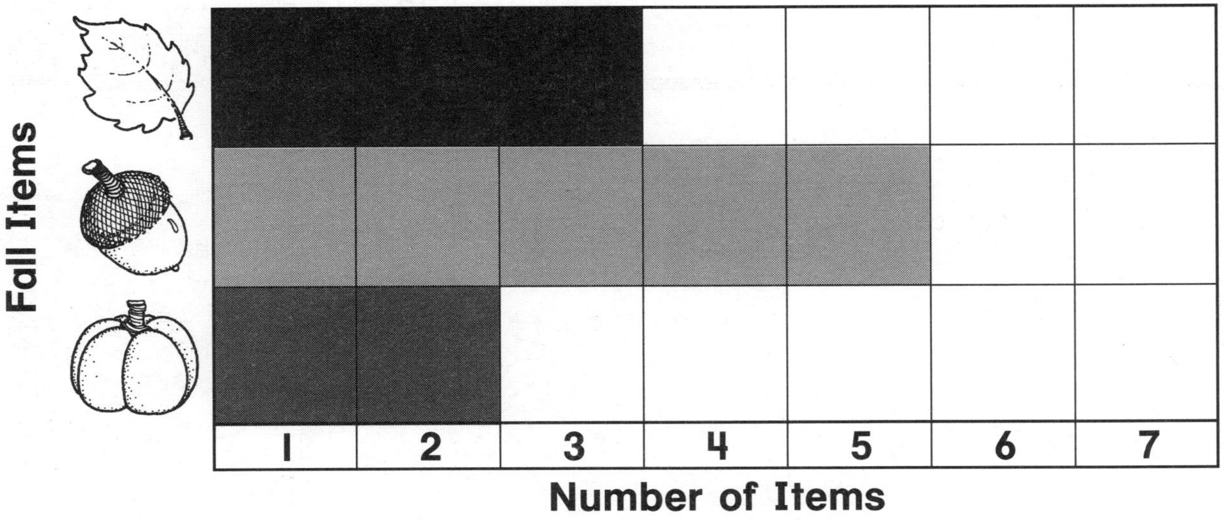

Fall Items

1 2 3 4 5 6 7

Number of Items

1 How many of each item are there?

______ ______ ______

2 Are there more leaves or pumpkins?

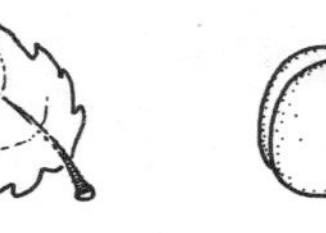

3 How many items are there in all? ______

Write the missing numbers.

4 0, 1, ___, 3,
4, ___, 6, 7

5 6, 7, ___, ___,
10, 11

6 11, ___, 13,
___, 15, 16

7 16, ___, 18,
___, 20

8 9, 10, ___, 12,
___, 14

Math Mat 53

Name ____________________

ANALYZING CHARTS

Favorite Ways to Eat an Apple

Mrs. Fletcher's class made a graph showing their favorite ways to eat an apple. Use the information shown on the graph to answer the questions.

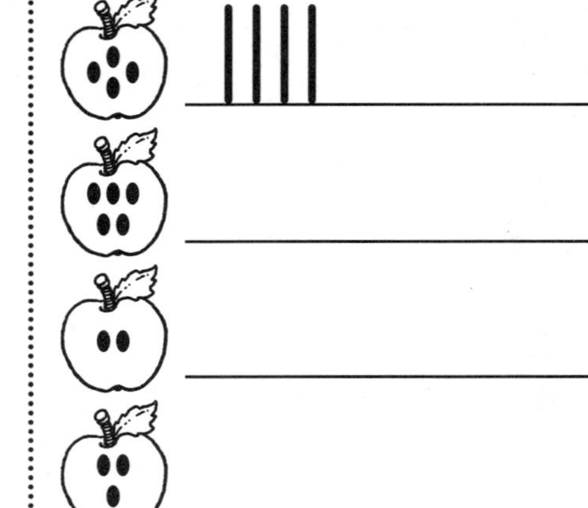

1 Which way did most of the students like to eat their apples? ____________________

2 Which way did the fewest number of students like to eat their apples? ____________________

3 How many students are in Mrs. Fletcher's class? ____________________

Use tally marks to show the number of seeds in each apple.

Ask ten friends how they like to eat an apple. Use tally marks to show how many.

____

____

____

Name ____________________

CREATING GRAPHS

A Roll of the Die!

Which number do you think the die will land on the most often? Record your guess at the right. Roll the die ten times. After each roll, record the number on the die by coloring the corresponding square.

Number Showing on Die

⚀								
⚁								
⚂								
⚃								
⚄								
⚅								
	1	2	3	4	5	6	7	8

Number of Rolls

My Guess

I think the die will land on the

number ______ the most often.

Results

1 Which number was rolled the most often?

____

2 Which number was rolled the least often?

____

3 Was your guess correct?

Circle one: **Yes** **No**

Math Mat 55 Name ____________

Jason's Classmates

Use the information to make a graph showing the first letter in each of Jason's classmates' names. Color a box for each classmate.

- 6 classmates have names that begin with the letter **D**.
- 3 classmates have names that begin with the letter **H**.
- 5 classmates have names that begin with the letter **Z**.

First Letters							
D							
H							
Z							
	1	2	3	4	5	6	7

Number of Classmates

1 Which letter did most of the students' names begin with? ________

2 Which letter did the fewest names begin with? ________

3 How many students are in Jason's class?

____

4 How many students in your class have names that begin with a **D**, an **H**, or a **Z**?

D ________

H ________

Z ________

Name ____________________

CREATING GRAPHS

Cowboys and Cowgirls

Glue the boots in the boots row, the hats in the hat row, and so on to make a graph.

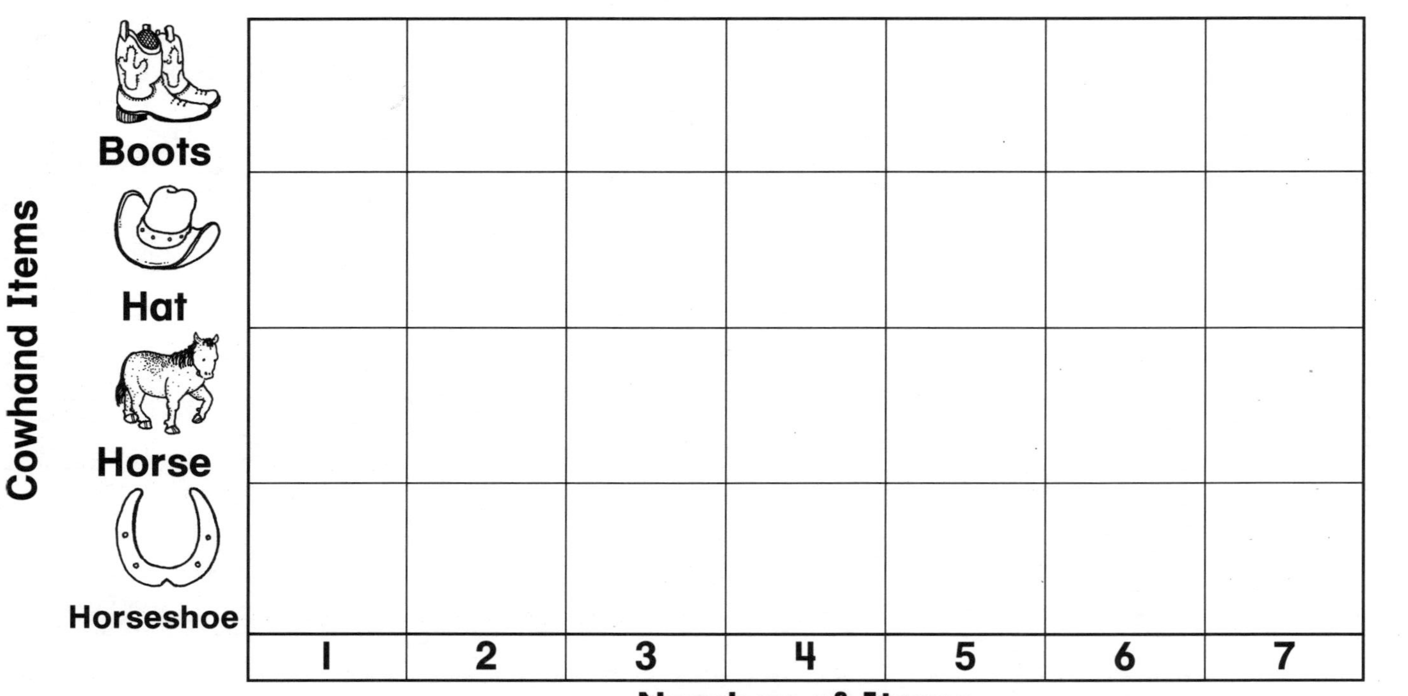

1 Are there more horses or horseshoes? ____________

2 Are there more hats or boots? ____________

3 Are there more horseshoes or hats? ____________

4 Which two items had the same number?

____________ and ____________

Math Mat 57 Name ______________________ CREATING GRAPHS

Maria's Gardening Equipment

Make a graph showing Maria's gardening equipment. Count the items in the box and fill in the graph. The first one has been done for you.

Garden Tools

rake	X	X	X				
shovel							
watering can							
wheelbarrow							
	1	2	3	4	5	6	7

Number of Items

Answer the questions.

1 How many of each item does Maria have?

rake ____________

shovel ____________

watering can ____________

wheelbarrow ____________

2 Does Maria have more rakes or more wheelbarrows?

____

3 Does Maria have more watering cans or more shovels?

____

Name ____________________ CREATING GRAPHS

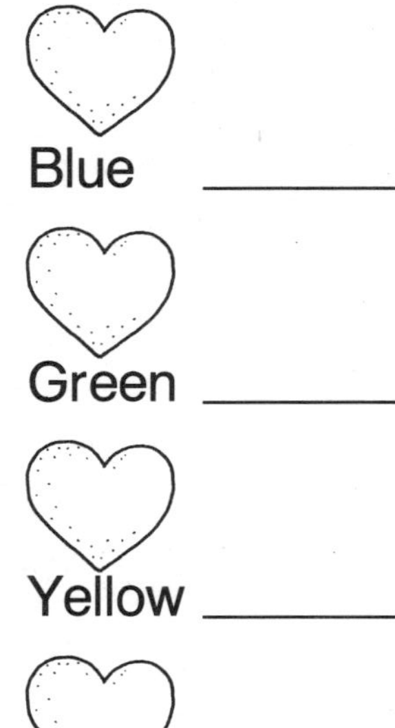

Favorite Hearts

Ask ten classmates which color heart they like best.
Draw hearts in each row to record each vote.

Color of Heart

blue										
green										
yellow										
purple										
red										
	1	2	3	4	5	6	7	8	9	10

Number of Students

How many votes did each heart receive?

Blue ____________

Green ____________

Yellow ____________

Purple ____________

Red ____________

Name ____________

Letters and Names

Write your first name by writing one letter in each box. Then write two of your classmates' names by writing a letter in each box. Answer the questions.

My name										
Classmate 1										
Classmate 2										

1 Count the number of letters in each name

My name ______ Classmate 1 ______ Classmate 2 ______

2 Which name is the longest? ____________

3 Which name is the shortest? ____________

4 Do any of the names have the same number of letters? ______

Write the three names used in the graph below. Write only one letter in each box. Then cut out the boxes. On the back of this page, sort the letters three different ways. Write a sentence telling about one of the ways you sorted the letters.

Name ____________________

Voting for Presidents

Ask ten classmates to vote for their favorite president.
Cut out the portraits and glue them in each box to record the votes.

George Washington	Abraham Lincoln
Total votes: ______	Total votes: ______

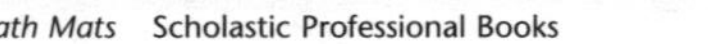

Name ______________________ **CREATING GRAPHS**

Penny Toss

Throw two pennies ten times. After each throw, record how the pennies landed.

1 I think the pennies will land most often on ______________________.

Both Heads										
Both Tails										
1 Heads, 1 Tails										

2 The pennies landed most often on ______________________.

If you reached into the bag of coins without looking, which coin do you think you would most likely pick? Use the back of this paper to explain your answer.

Name ______________________ **ANALYZING GRAPHS**

A Trip to the Orchard

Last Saturday, Mabel, Ray, Lee, and Arlene went cherry picking.
Use the graph to answer the questions.

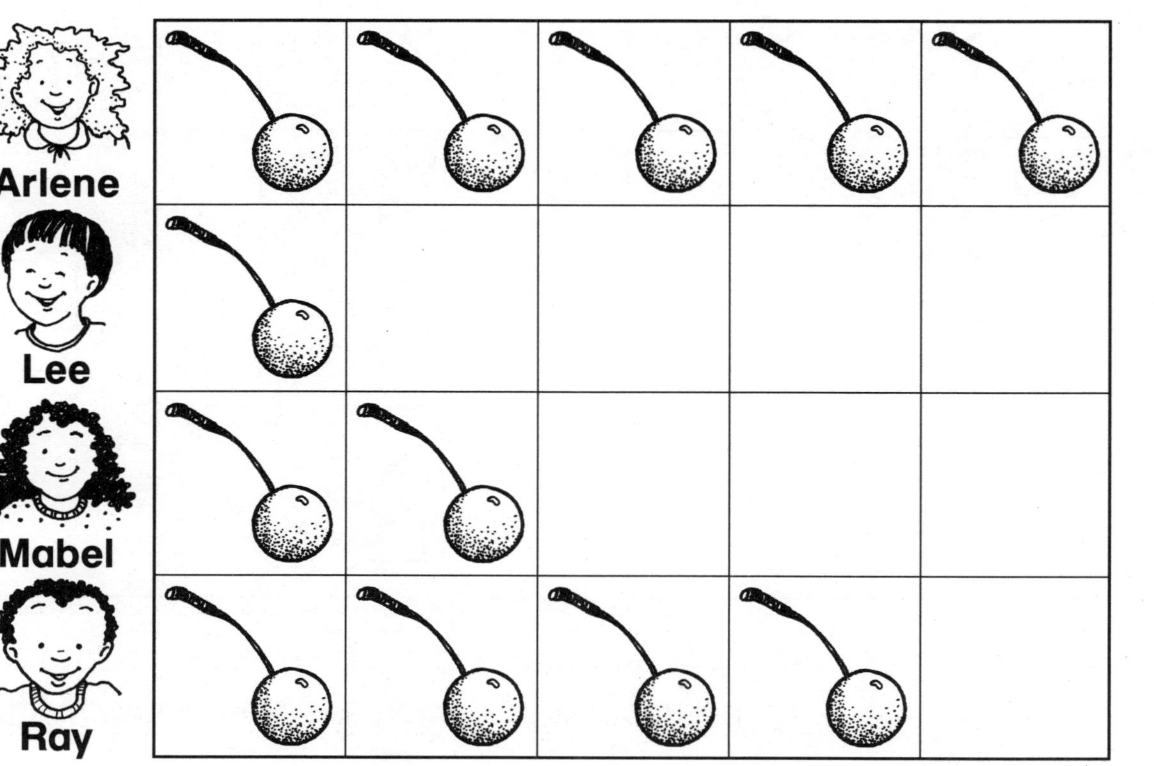

Legend:  = 2 cherries

1 How many cherries did each one pick?

Arlene ______________

Lee ______________

Mabel ______________

Ray ______________

2 Circle the pair that picked the most cherries.

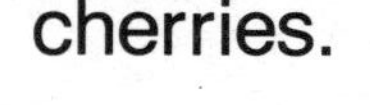

Arlene Ray   Lee Mabel

Math Mat 63 Name ____________

Flower Picking

Each day, Latrice picks the flowers in her garden.
Use the graph Latrice made to answer the questions.

Sunday	Monday	Tuesday	Wednesday	Thursday	Friday	Saturday
✿✿✿	✿	✿✿✿✿✿	✿	✿✿	✿✿✿✿	✿✿✿

Legend: ✿ = 5 flowers

1 How many flowers did Latrice pick each day?

Tuesday: ____________

Sunday: ____________

Friday: ____________

Monday: ____________

2 On which day did Latrice pick the most flowers?

____

3 On which days did Latrice pick the fewest flowers?

____

4 On which day did Latrice pick 10 flowers?

____

Name ____________________

Fair and Square

Use a paper clip and a pencil to work the spinners below. Spin each spinner ten times. After each spin, color in the corresponding square on the chart.

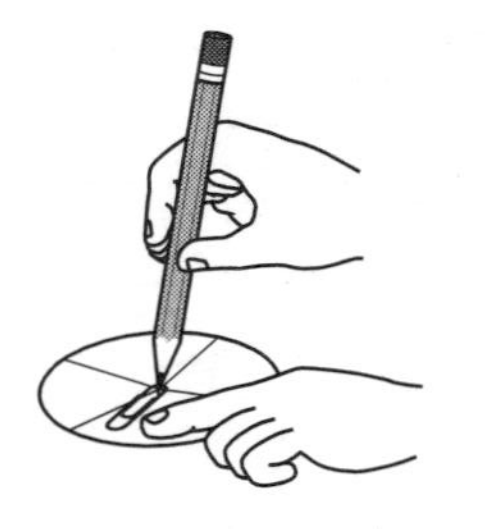

Which spinner is more fair? (*Fair* means that there is an equal chance that the spinner will land about the same number of times on the cat as on the dog.) Explain your answer on the back of this page.

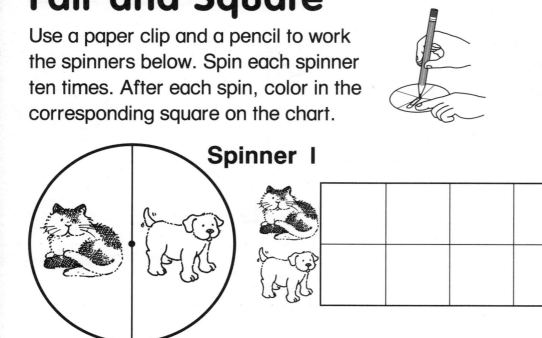

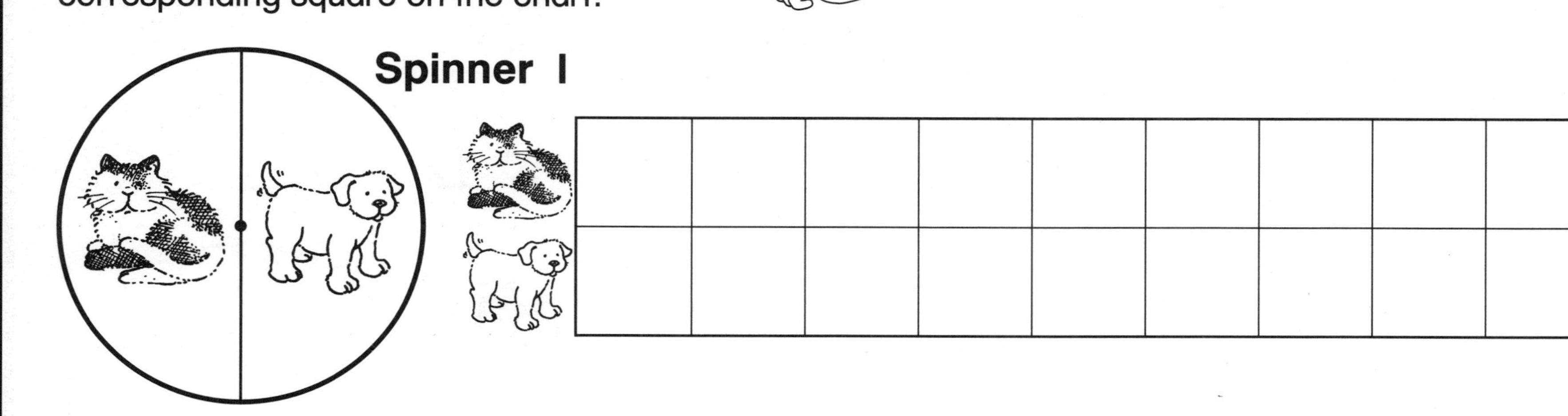

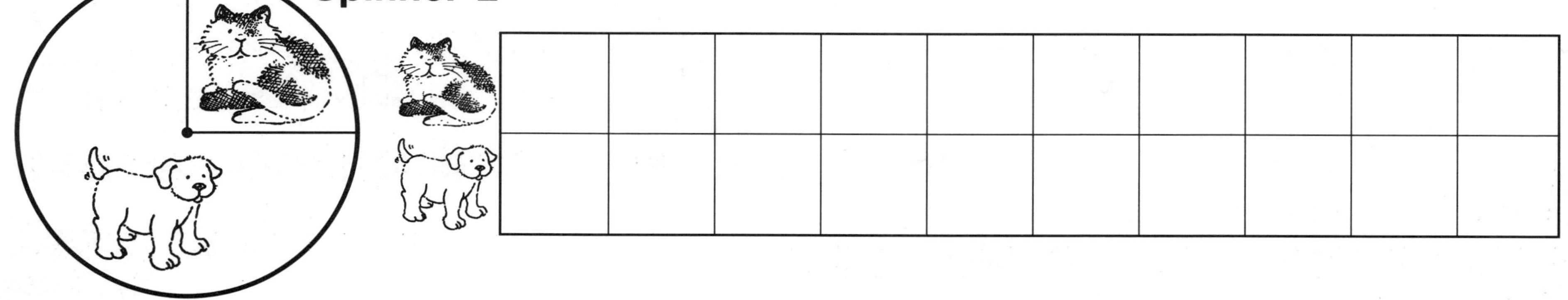

Math Mat 65 Name ______________________

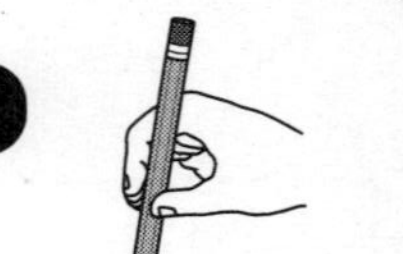

Circles and Squares

1 Draw a circle and square to make a spinner that will land mostly on circles. Use a paper clip and spin the spinner ten times. Record the results.

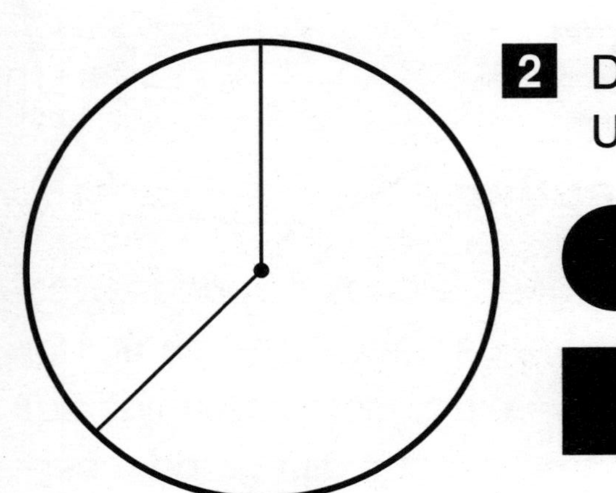

2 Draw a circle and square to make a spinner that will land mostly on squares. Use a paper clip and spin the spinner ten times. Record the results.

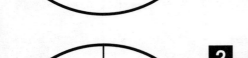

Did your spinners work like you thought they would? Why or why not? Use the back of this page to record your answer.

Name ______________________

Bear Buddies

1st ____ ____ 4th ____ ____ ____ 8th ____ ____

1. Finish numbering the bears from 1st to 10th.
2. Color the 2nd bear brown.
3. Draw a ○ around the 3rd bear.
4. Draw a line under the last bear.
5. Draw a ◇ around the 1st bear.
6. Draw a □ around the 5th bear.
7. Color all the bears with a bow tie blue.
8. Draw a ♡ on your favorite bear.

Name ______________________

USING COORDINATES

Animal Addresses

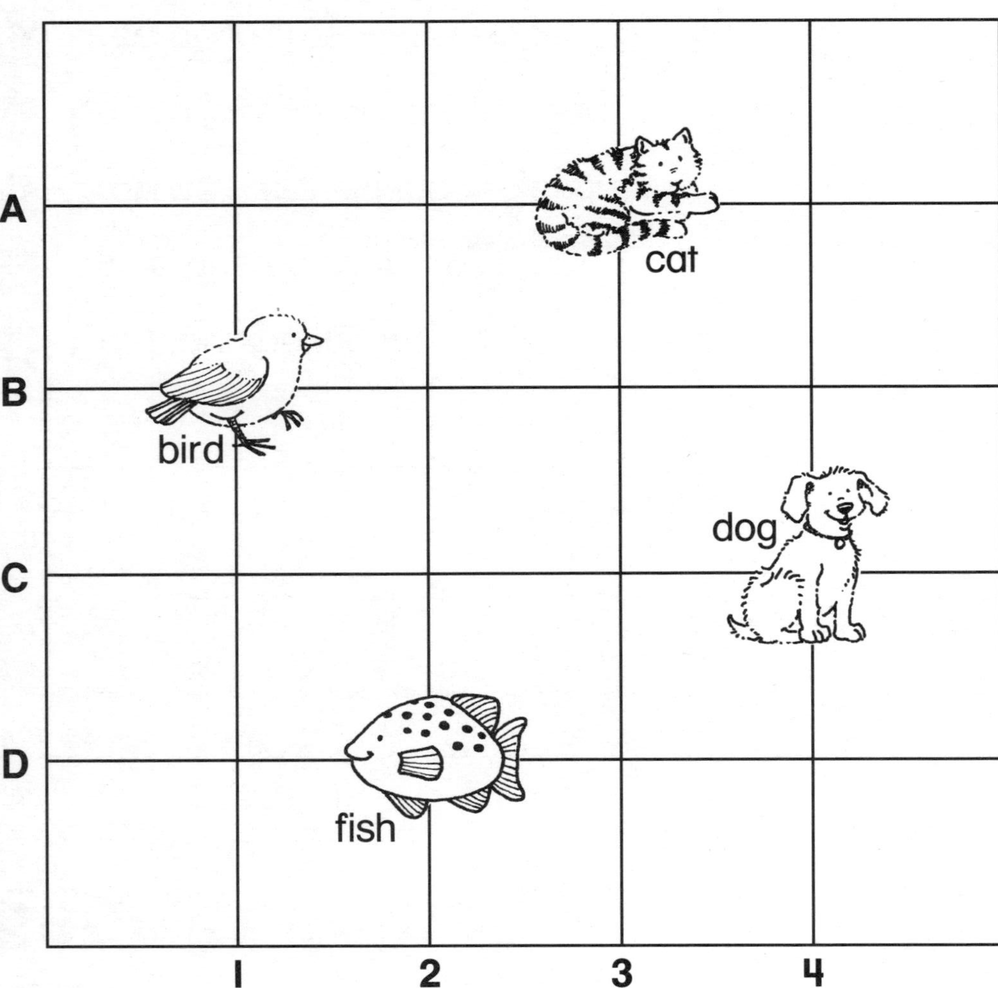

1 Write the name of each pet by its coordinates.

A3 ____________ **B1** ____________

C4 ____________ **D2** ____________

2 Draw a line matching each animal to its special place.

Which animal would you like to have for a pet? Explain your answer on the back of this page.

Name ____________________

DETERMINING COORDINATES

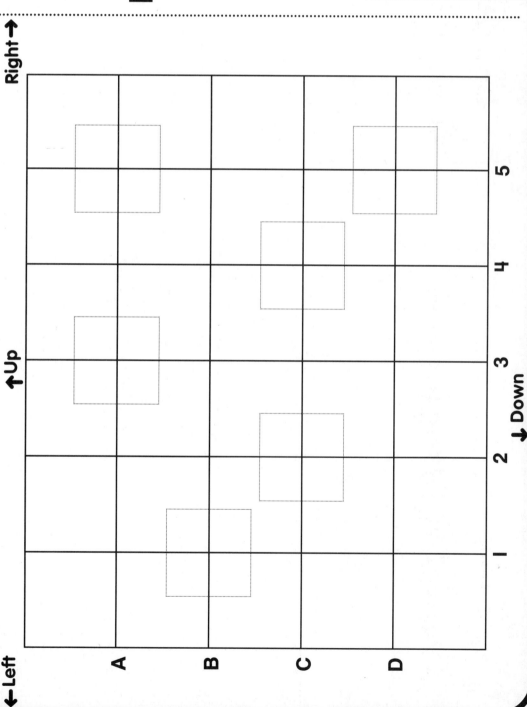

Creepy Crawlies

Cut out the creepy crawlies and glue them at the correct coordinates.

←Left ↑Up Right→

A					
B					
C					
D					
	1	2	3	4	5

↓Down

Find the creepy crawlies!

1 Start at A1.
Go right 3 coordinates.
Go down 2 coordinates.
Which creepy crawly am I?

____

2 Start at D1.
Go right 4 coordinates.
Go up 3 coordinates.
Which creepy crawly am I?

____

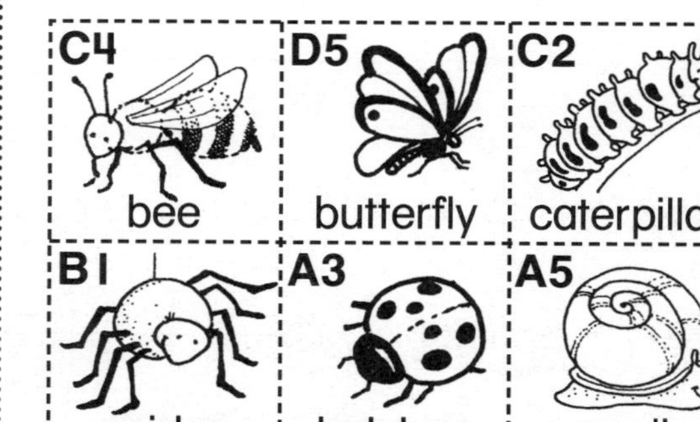

Math Mat 69 Name ____________ IDENTIFYING LEFT AND RIGHT

The Playground

Cut out the pictures and glue them in the correct places.

←Left Right→

1. The grass is <u>under</u> the school.
2. The sun is <u>over</u> the school.
3. The tree is to the <u>left</u> of the school.
4. The boy is to the <u>right</u> of the school.
5. The girl is to the <u>left</u> of the tree.
6. The swing set is to the <u>right</u> of the boy.

Name ____________________

IDENTIFYING COMPASS DIRECTIONS

Tiny Town

Use the information on the map to answer the questions.

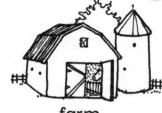

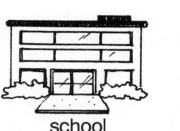

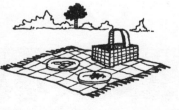

Read each question and circle the answer.

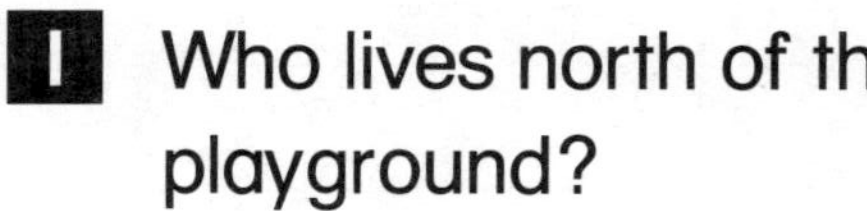

1 Who lives north of the playground?

Rachel Gwen

2 Whose house is east of the playground?

Henry's Zach's

3 What is south of the farm?

Henry's house

Rachel's house

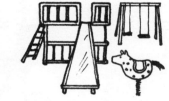

4 What is west of Gwen's house?

soccer field

picnic area

Name ______________________

A Trip to the Zoo

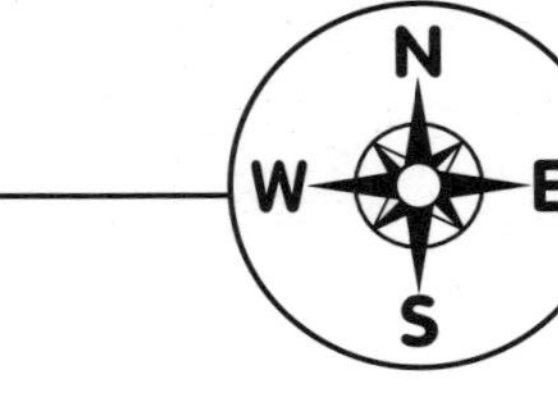
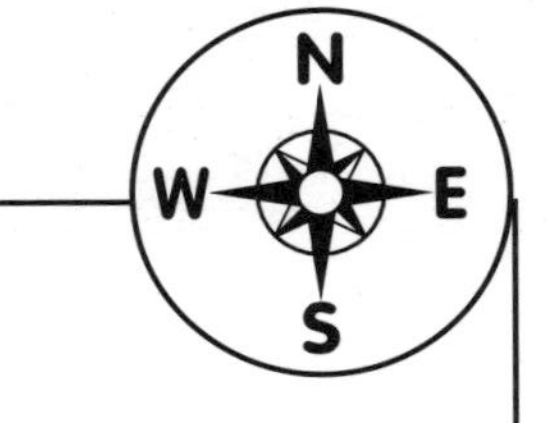

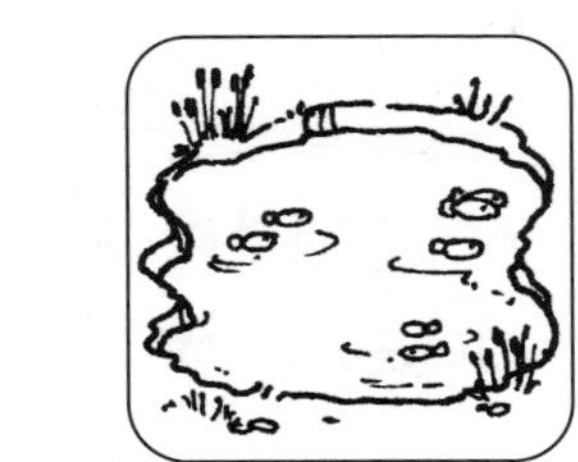

Cut out the animals. Read each direction and glue the animal in its correct home.

1. The giraffe is east of the ostrich.
2. The panda bear is to the west of the playground.
3. The polar bear is south of the duck pond.
4. The monkey is north of the panda.
5. The hippo is east of the playground.
6. The zebra is north of the hippo.

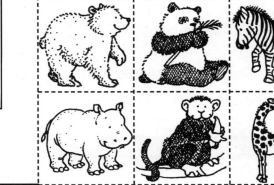

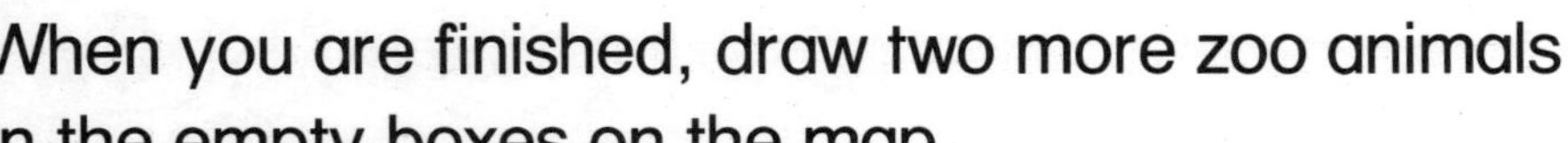

When you are finished, draw two more zoo animals in the empty boxes on the map.

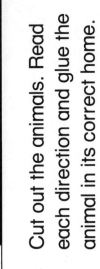

Name ____________________

CREATING MAPS

Our Classroom

Cut out the pictures and use them to make a map of your classroom. Add drawings of other items found in your classroom—windows, carpets, and so on.

How do you walk from the door to your desk? Use the back of this paper to explain.

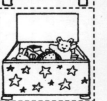

Math Mat 73 Name ____________________ CREATING MAPS

Design a Bedroom

Cut out the pictures and use them to design a bedroom.
Add drawings of other items you would like in a bedroom.

North

West

East

South

Write a sentence telling about the bedroom you designed on the back of this page.

Name ____________________

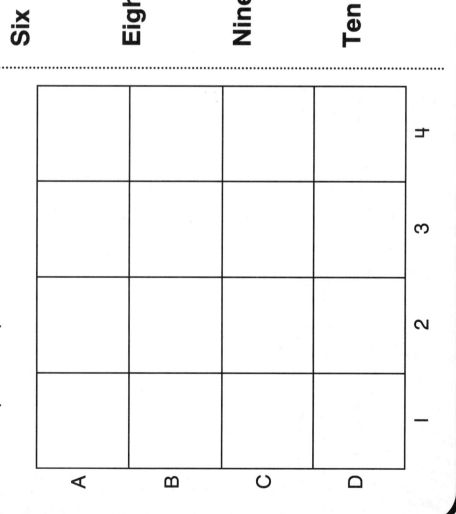

IDENTIFYING COORDINATES

Tasty Treat

Cut out the puzzle pieces.
Use the coordinates printed on the pieces to glue the puzzle pieces onto the grid.
What shape is the puzzle?

A				
B				
C				
D				
	1	2	3	4

Count the seeds in each apple. Draw a line from the number of apple seeds to the matching numeral and number word.

Six	  	**9**
Eight	 	**10**
Nine	 	**6**
Ten	 	**8**

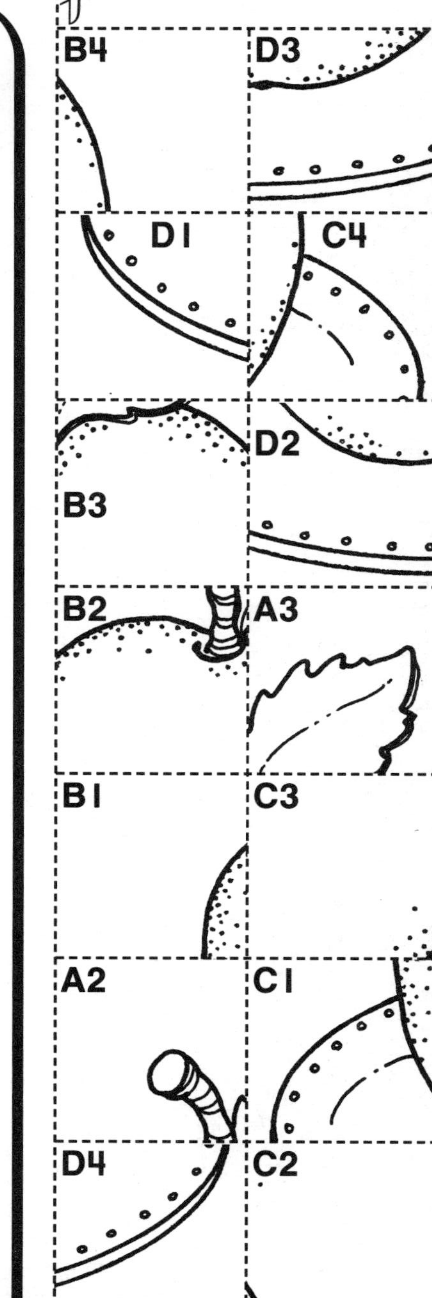

Name ____________________

IDENTIFYING COORDINATES

Furry Friend

Cut out the puzzle pieces. Use the coordinates printed on the pieces to glue the puzzle pieces onto the grid. What shape is the puzzle?

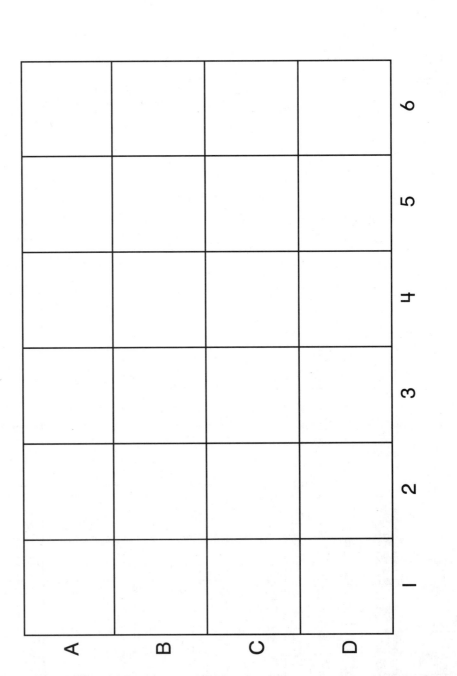

	1	2	3	4	5	6
A						
B						
C						
D						

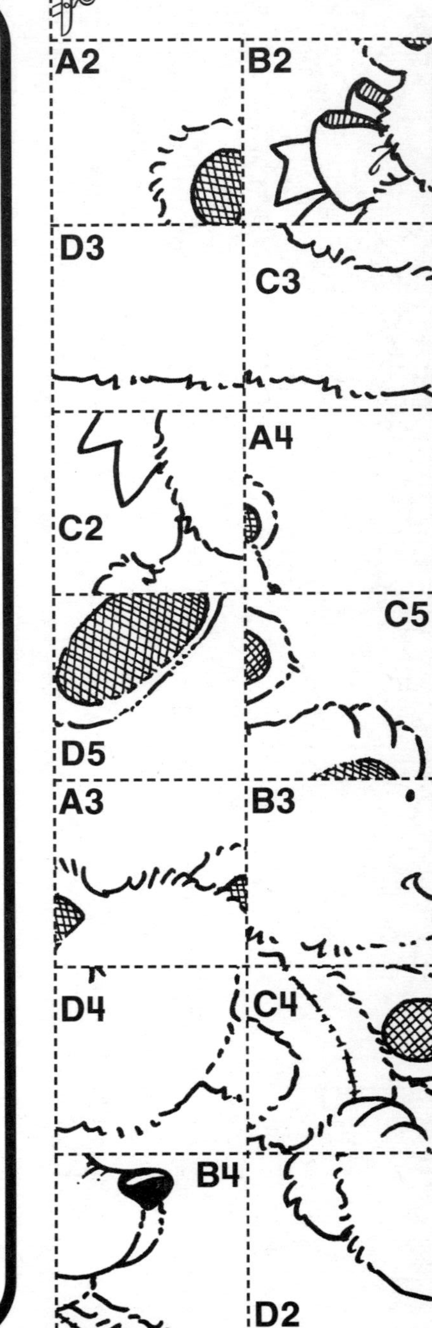

Name ______________________

IDENTIFYING COORDINATES

Me and My Big Trunk!

Cut out the puzzle pieces. Use the coordinates printed on the pieces to glue the puzzle pieces onto the grid. What shape is the puzzle?

	1	2	3	4	5	6	7
A							
B							
C							
D							
E							

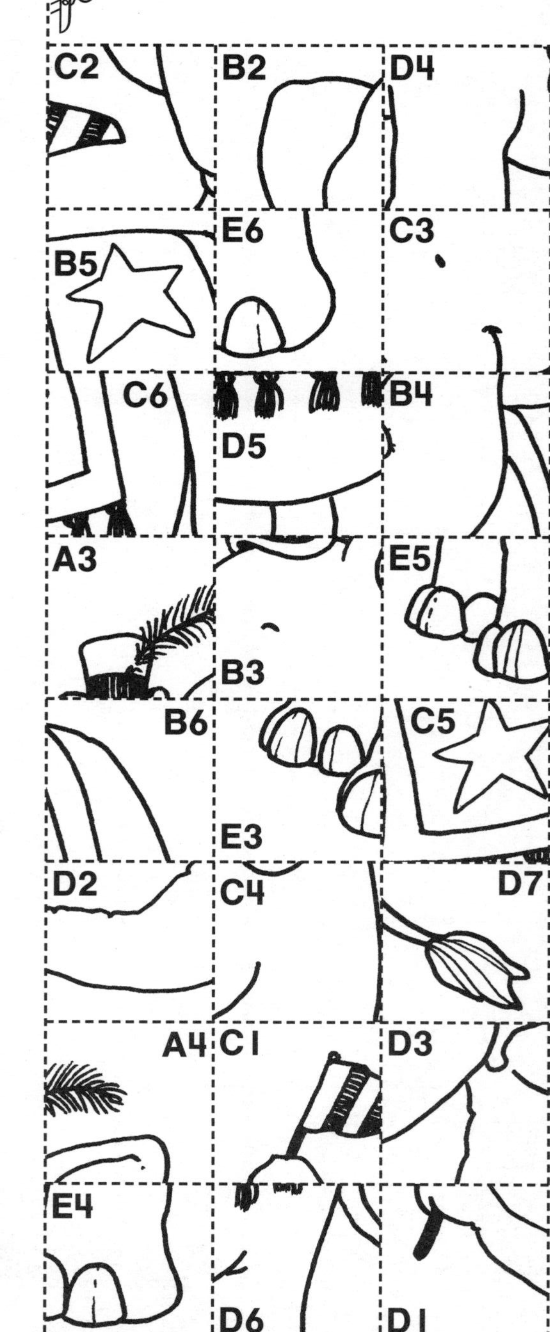

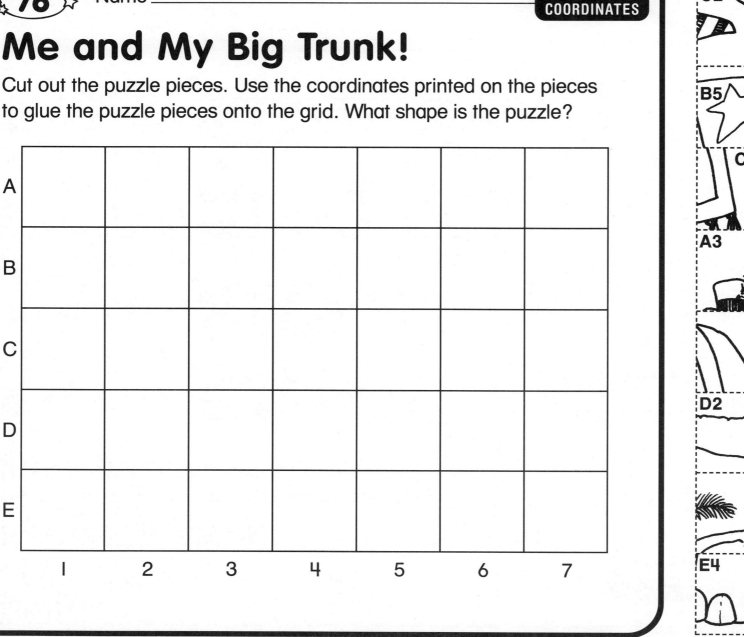

Name ______________________

Pencil Lengths

Cut out the apple ruler and use it to measure the pencils.
How many apples long is each pencil?

1 ________ apples

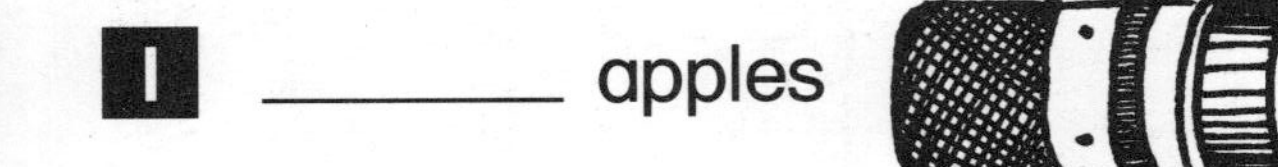
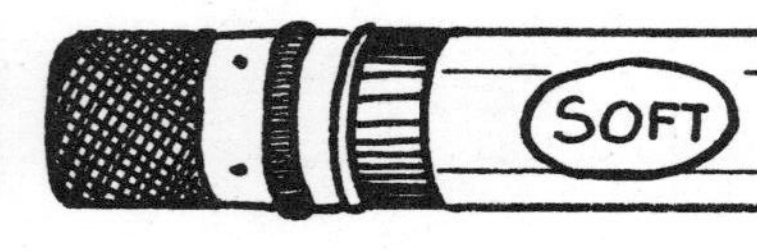

2 ________ apples

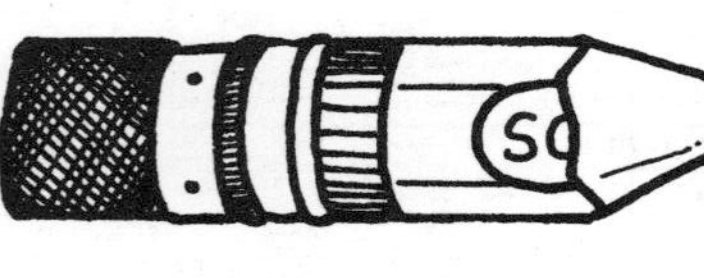

3 ________ apples

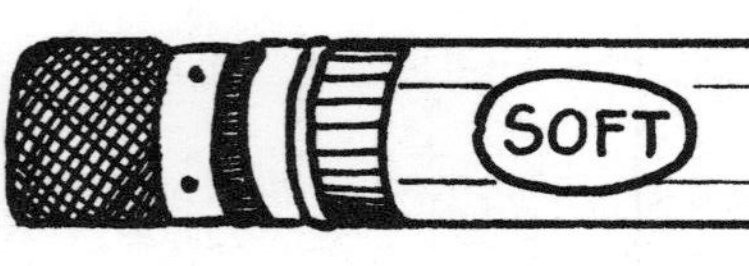

4 ________ apples

5 ________ apples

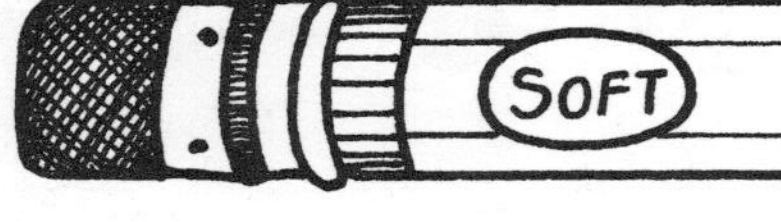

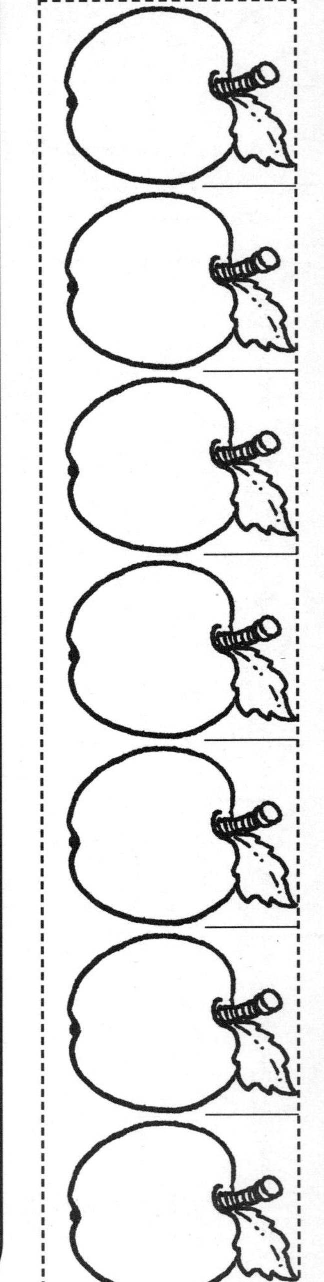

Name ____________________

MEASURING WITH INCHES

Ribbon Lengths

Cut out the inch ruler and use it to measure the ribbons.
Write the length of each ribbon to the nearest inch.

1. ______ inches long

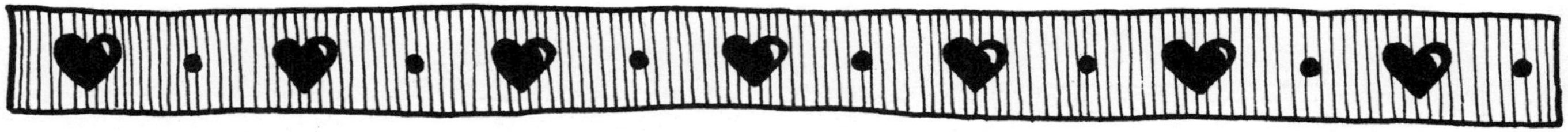

2. ______ inches long

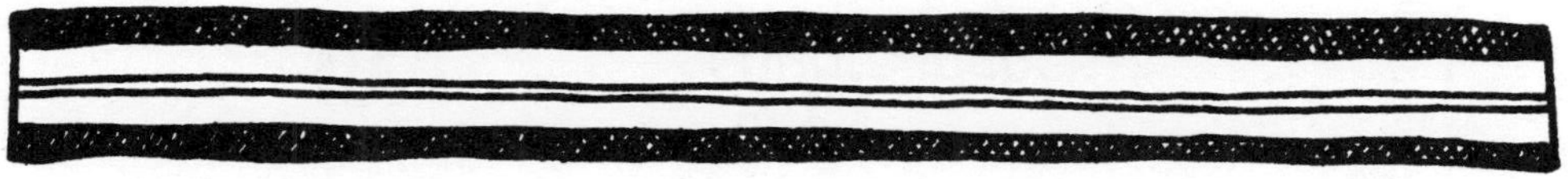

3. ______ inches long

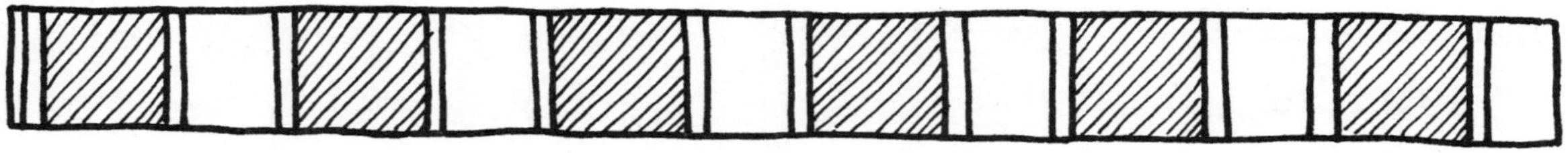

4. ______ inches long

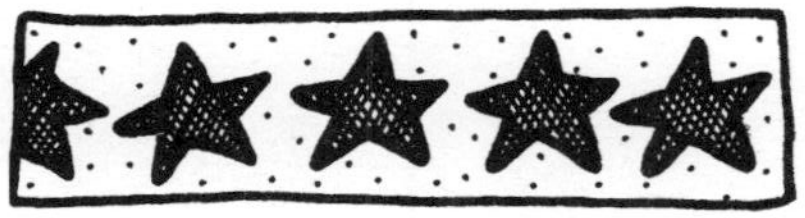

5. ______ inch long

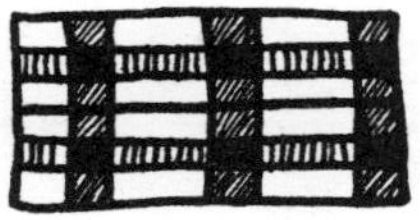

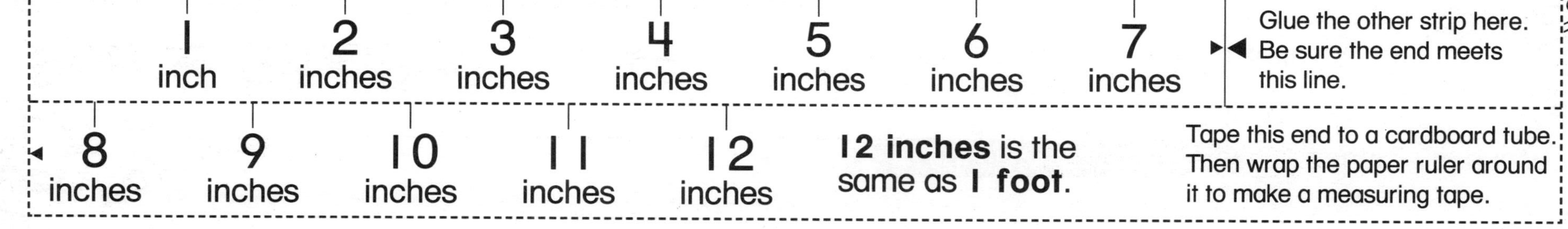

Math Mat 79 Name ____________________ **MEASURING AREA**

Shape Sizes

Count the number of square inches in each shape.

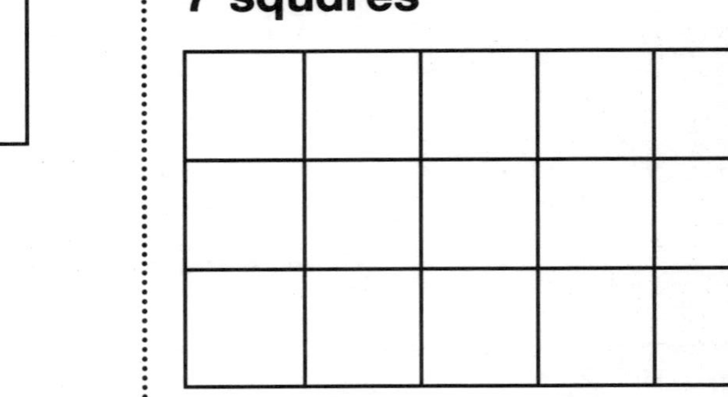

1 ________ square inches

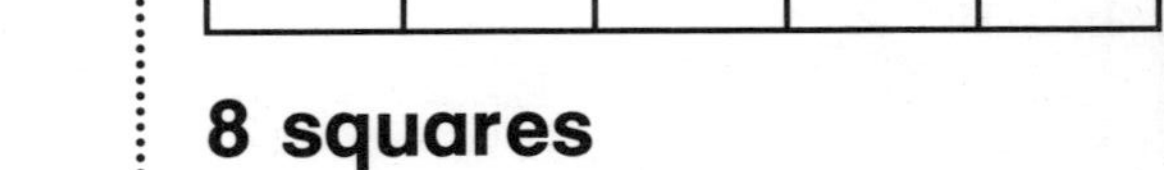

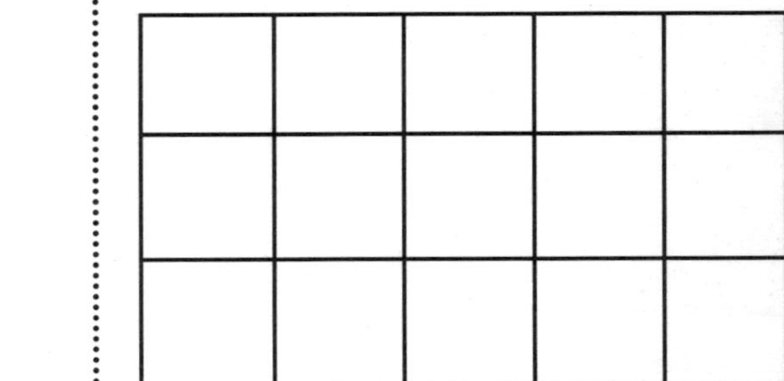

2 ________ square inches

3 ________ square inches

4 ________ square inches

Color the squares to show the area.

9 squares

7 squares

8 squares

Name ______________________

Estimating Weights

Cut out the pictures and sort them into groups of items weighing less than 1 pound and items weighing more than 1 pound.

Less Than 1 Pound	More Than 1 Pound

Math Mat 81 Name ________________ READING A THERMOMETER

What's the Temperature?

A thermometer is used to measure temperature.
Read each thermometer and write the temperature on the line.

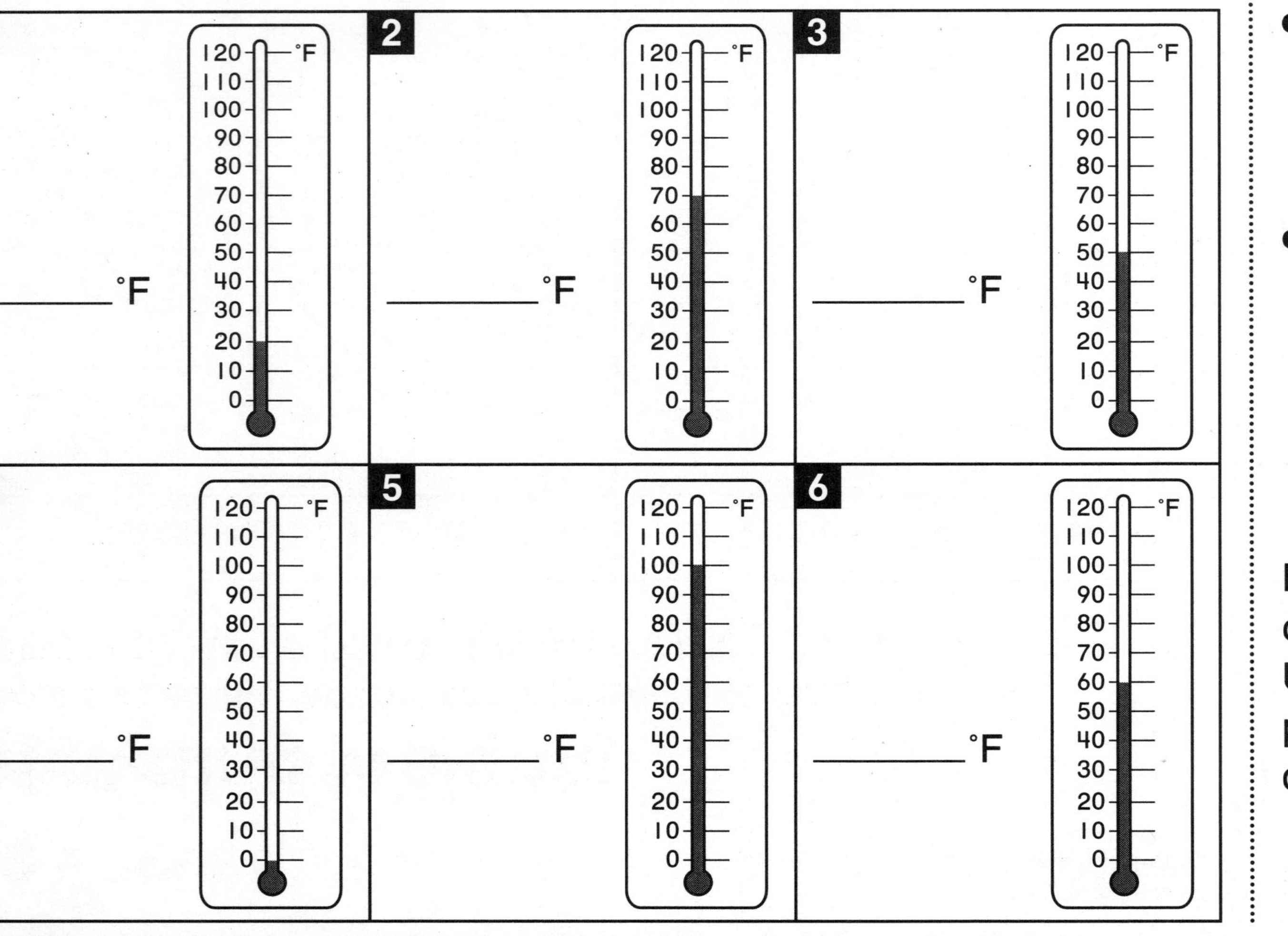

1 ________ °F

2 ________ °F

3 ________ °F

4 ________ °F

5 ________ °F

6 ________ °F

Weather Reports

Look for the local weather report to find the day's weather.

- Today's high:

  ________ °F

- Today's low:

  ________ °F

Do you like hot weather or cold weather? Why? Use the back of this paper to write your answer.

Name ______________________ **ESTIMATING VOLUME**

More or Less Water

Circle the object that would hold **more** water.

1 **2**

Circle the one that would hold **less** water.

3 **4**

Circle the answer.

5 Which one would you carry water in at the beach?

6 Which one would you use to measure a cup of water for cooking?

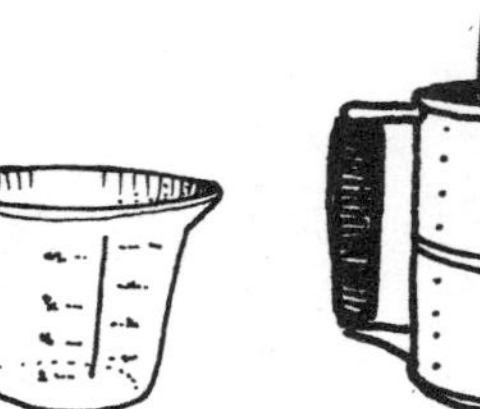

Math Mat 83 Name ______________________ ESTIMATING VOLUME

About a Cup

Cut out the pictures. Decide whether each item holds **less than** 1 cup, **about** 1 cup, or **more than** 1 cup of water. Place each picture in the correct category.

Less Than 1 Cup	About 1 Cup	More Than 1 Cup

Name ______________________

MEASURING VOLUME

Ways to Measure Volume

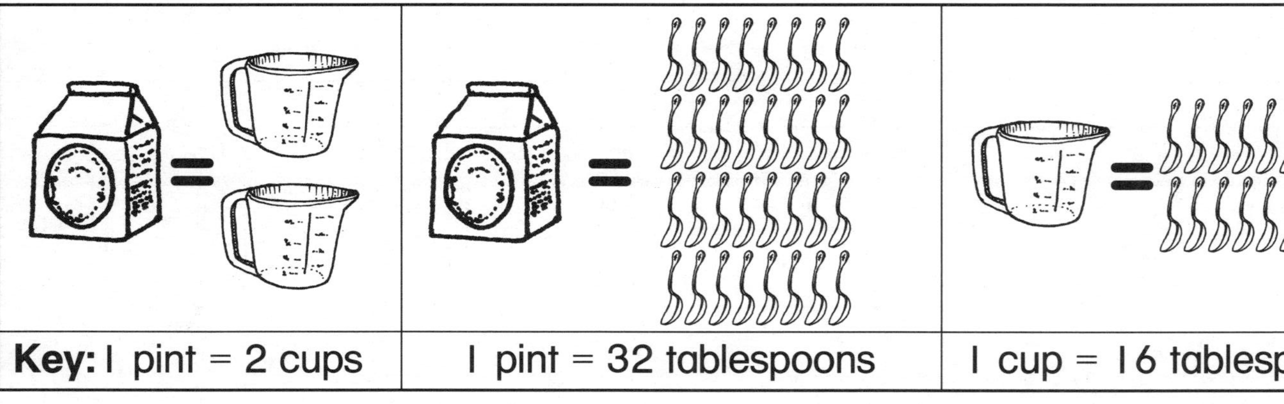

Key: I pint = 2 cups	I pint = 32 tablespoons	I cup = 16 tablespoons

Circle the one that holds more.

Number the containers in order from least to greatest using the numbers 1, 2, and 3.

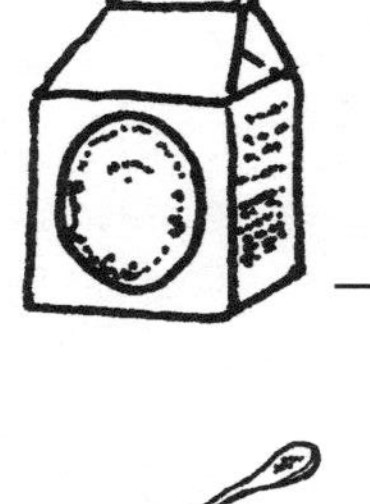
______

______

______

Would you rather have a **tablespoon** or **pint** of hot cocoa? Use the back of this page to explain your answer.

Math Mat 85

Name ____________________

MEASURING VOLUME

More Ways to Measure Volume

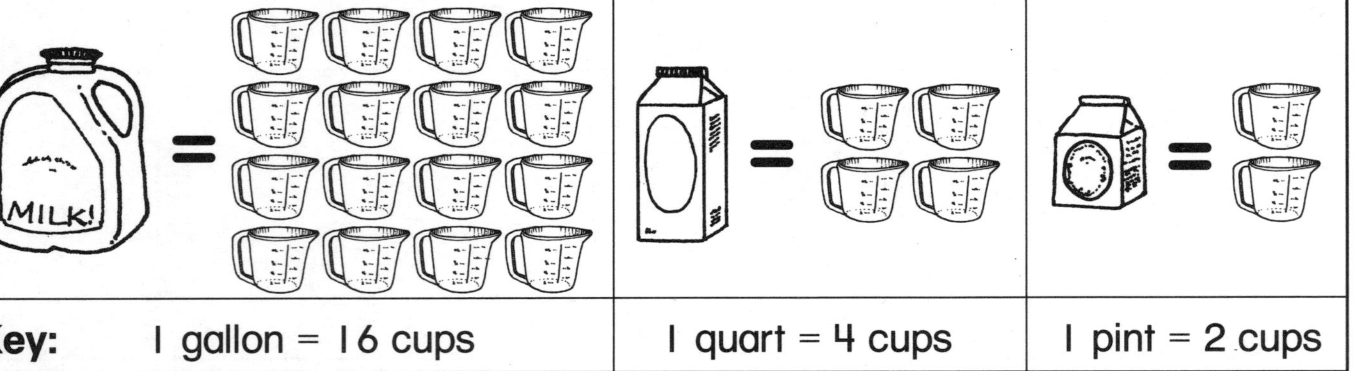

Key: 1 gallon = 16 cups	1 quart = 4 cups	1 pint = 2 cups

Cut out the pictures. Glue each picture next to its equivalent measurement.

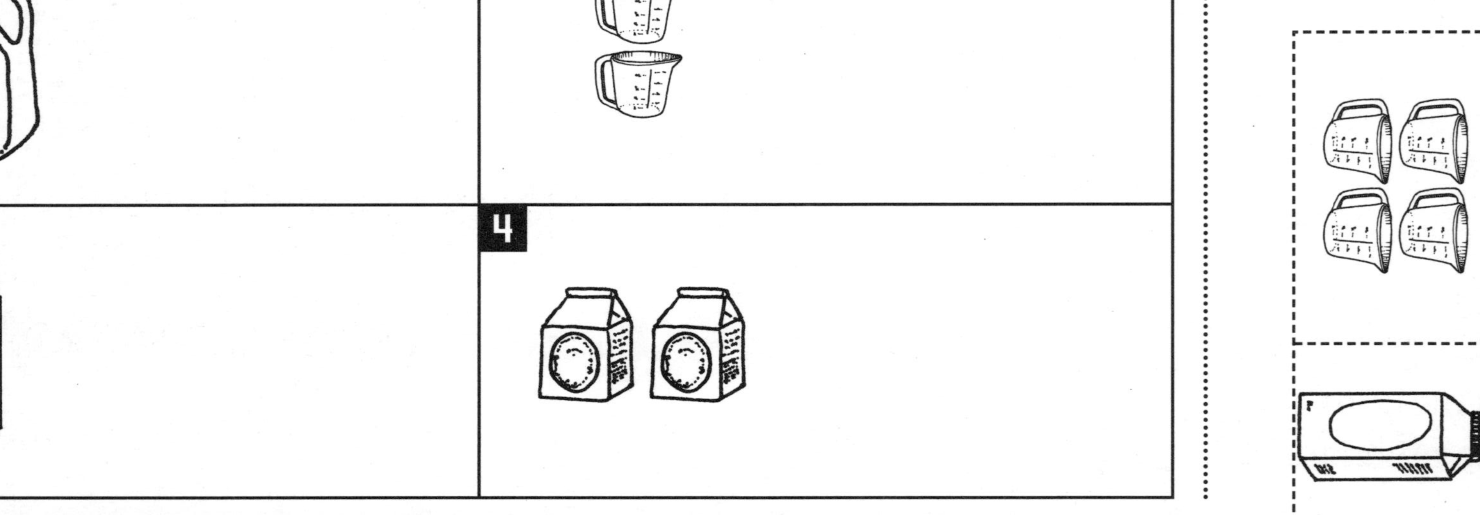

Find and circle each word.

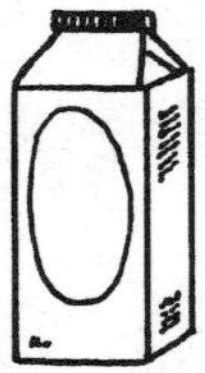

measure	cup
tablespoon	pint
gallon	quart

M T M E N G D
E A T K H A F
A B O R T L E
S L S M D L K
U E J Q A O Q
R S C U P N R
E P N A I C T
Y O X R N M S
A O P T T N G
W N I L H Z A

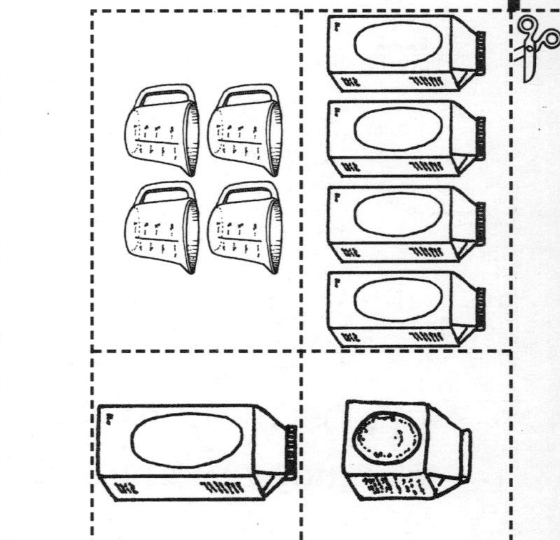

Math Mat 86 Name ______________________

MEASURING PERIMETER

Animal Pens

The perimeter is the boundary of an area.
Use the ruler to find the perimeter for each animal's pen.

1 ____ + ____ + ____ = ____ inches

2 ____ + ____ + ____ + ____ = ____ inches

3 ____ + ____ + ____ + ____ = ____ inches

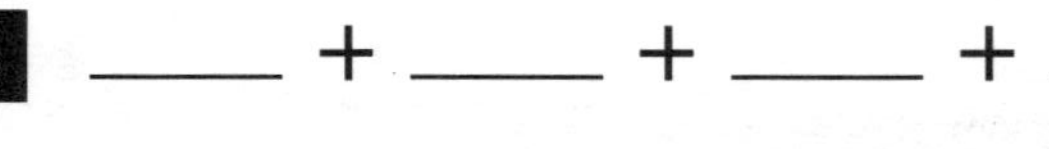

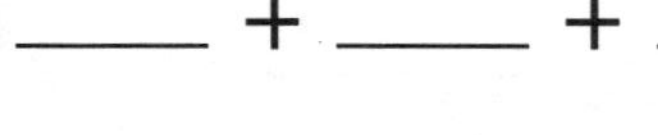

1 2 3 4 5 6

This is an inch ruler. A short way to write **inches** is **in.**

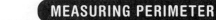

Name ______________

Measuring Me

Cut out and put together the paper measuring tape. Measure each part of your body and record the measurement below.

My ear is ______ inches long.

My nose is ______ inches long.

My smile is ______ inches wide.

My wrist is ______ inches around.

My ankle is ______ inches around.

My foot is ______ inches long.

inches

1 2 3 4 5 6 7

Glue strip with 7 here.

8 9 10 11 12 13 14

Glue strip with 14 here.

15 16 17 18 19 20 21

Name ______________________

Our Classroom

Take a piece of adding machine paper and mark off the following segments: 1 inch, 1 foot, and 1 yard.

1 inch	1 foot = 12 inches	1 yard = 3 feet = 36 inches

Then measure the items to the nearest mark (inch, foot, or yard) and record your answer below.

book ______ flag ______ desk ______ bookshelf ______ door ______

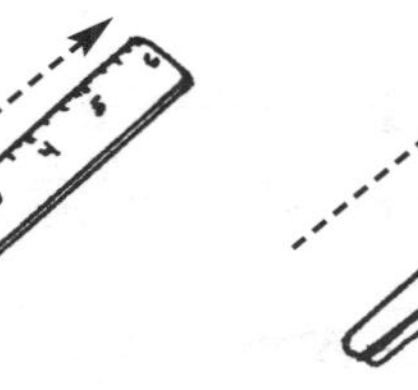

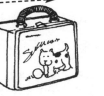

crayon ______ lunchbox ______ ruler ______ scissors ______ window ______

Circle the longest one.

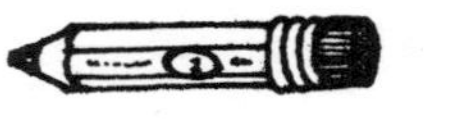
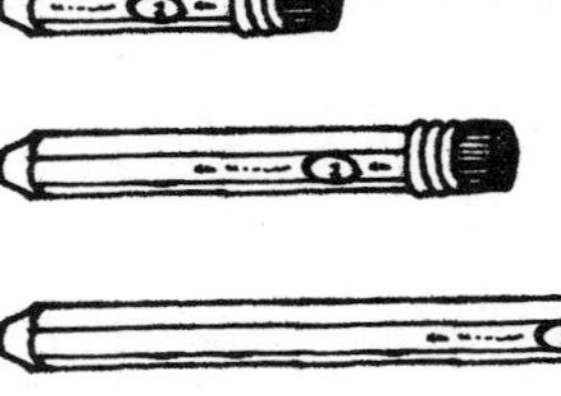
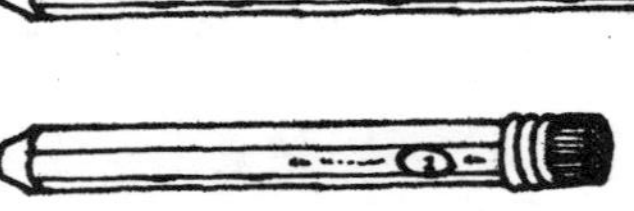

Circle the shortest one.

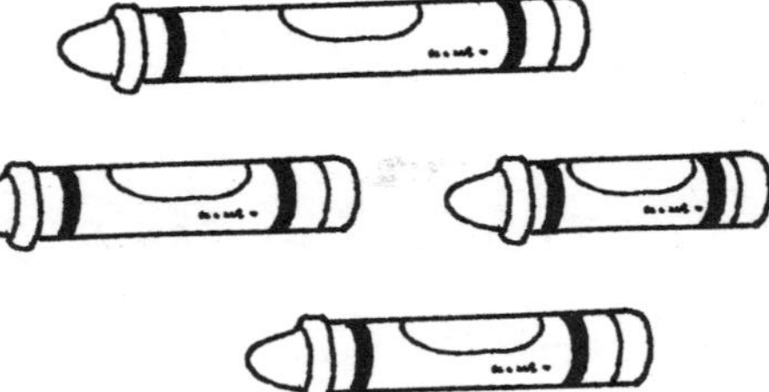

Circle the two that are the same size.

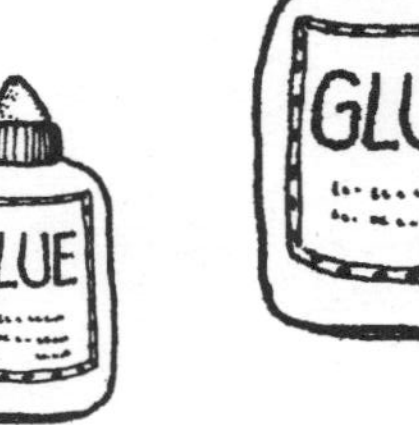

Math Mat 89 Name ____________________ MEASURING DISTANCE

Campground Map

Use a ruler to measure the number of miles from one area of the campground to another area of the campground. Use the legend to convert inches to miles.

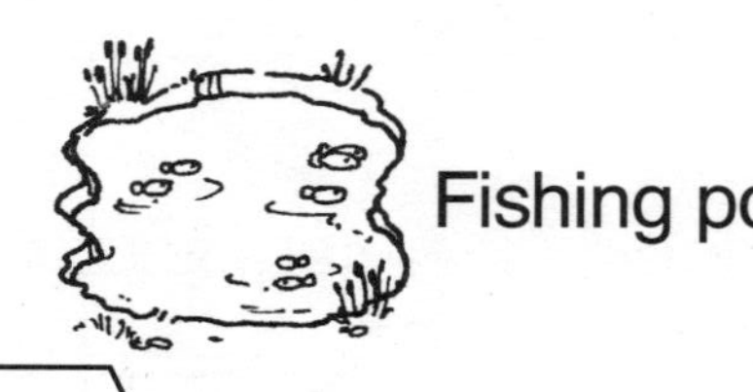

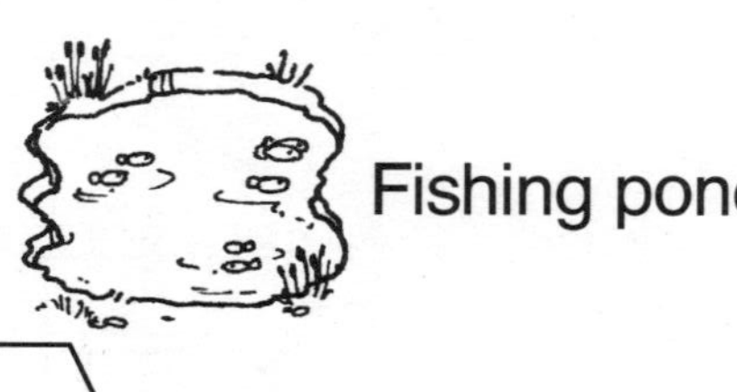
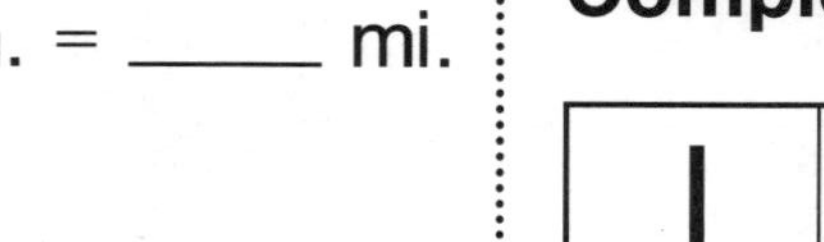
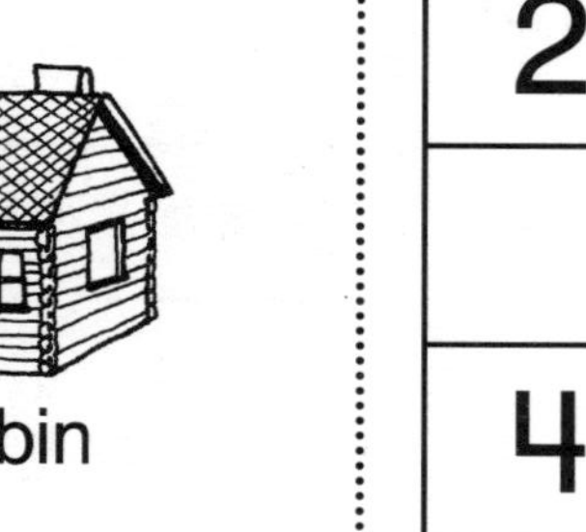

Campsite

_____ in. = _____ mi.

Fishing pond

_____ in. = _____ mi.

_____ in. = _____ mi.

Canoes

_____ in. = _____ mi.

Cabin

Legend
1 inch (in.) = 2 miles (mi.)

Figure the Miles

1. Cabin to Fishing pond = _____ mi.
2. Fishing pond to Campsite = _____ mi.
3. Campsite to Canoes = _____ mi.
4. Canoes to Cabin = _____ mi.

Complete the table.

1	2
2	4
	6
4	
	10
6	

How did you figure out which numbers were missing? Use the back of this paper to explain.

Name ______________________

MEASURING WITH CENTIMETERS

Camping Out

Cut out the centimeter ruler and measure the items. Write each answer on the line.

1 The canoe is ____________ cm long.

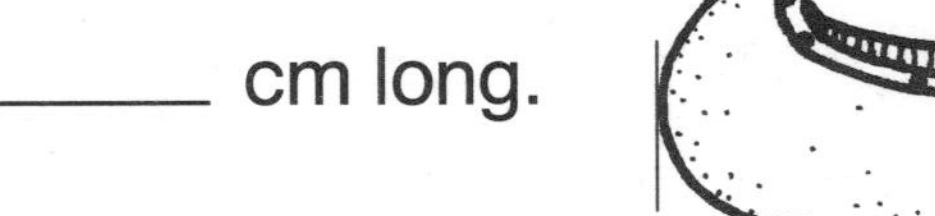

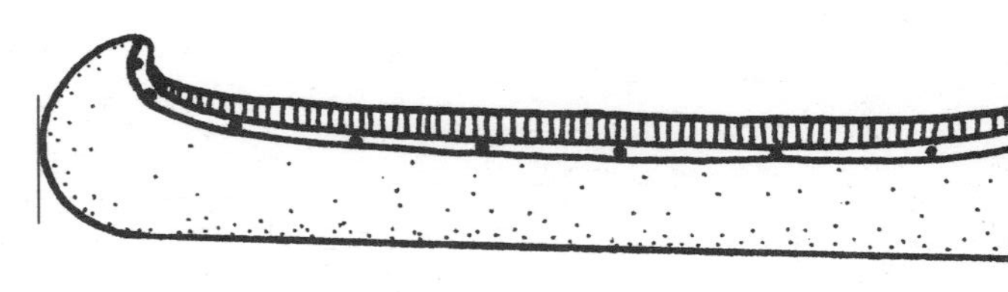

2 The paddle is ____________ cm long.

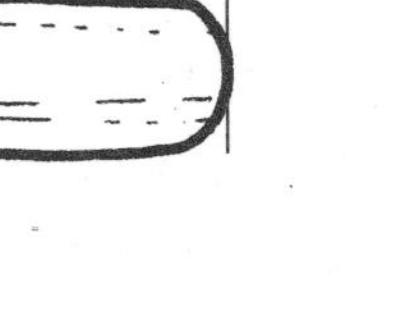

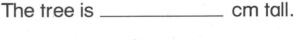

3 The tent is ____________ cm tall.

4 The branch is ____________ cm long.

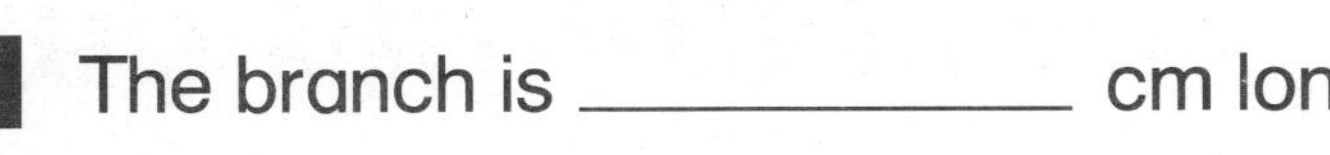

5 The tree is ____________ cm tall.

1 2 3 4 5 6 7 8 9 10 11 12 13 14 15 16 17

This is a centimeter ruler. A short way to write **centimeters** is **cm**.

Name ____________________

MEASURING WITH CENTIMETERS

Find the Area

Count the number of square centimeters in each shape.

1

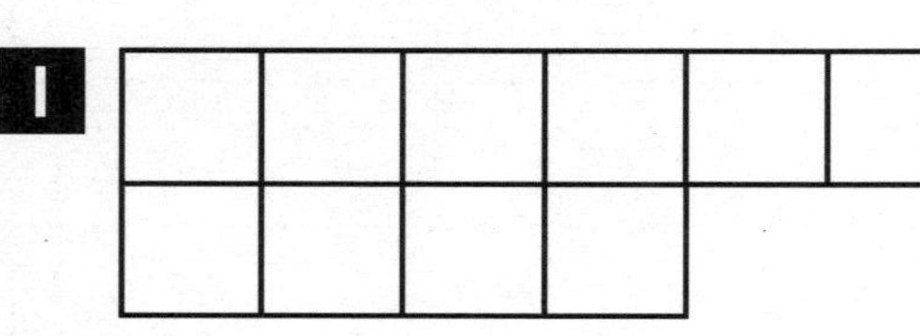

_______ square centimeters

2

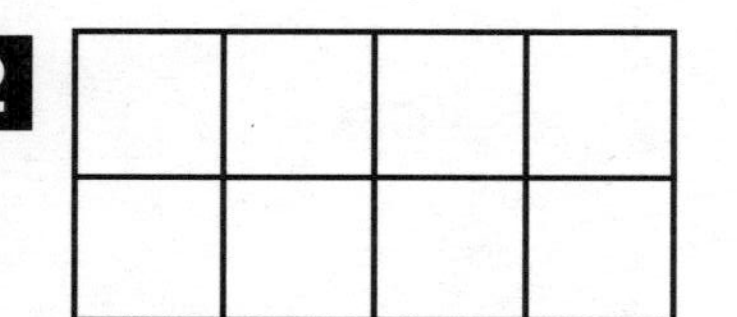

_______ square centimeters

3

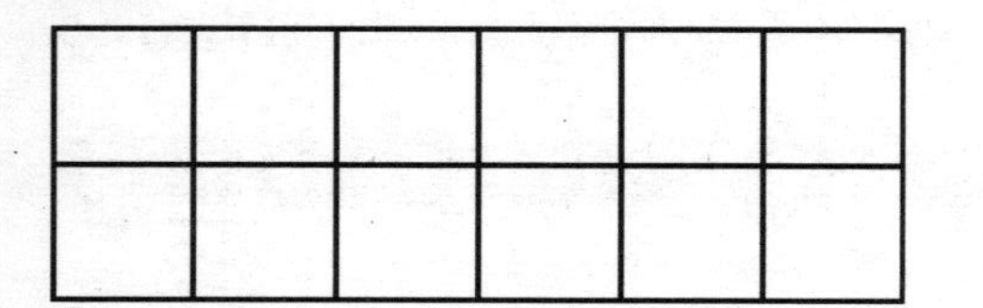

_______ square centimeters

4

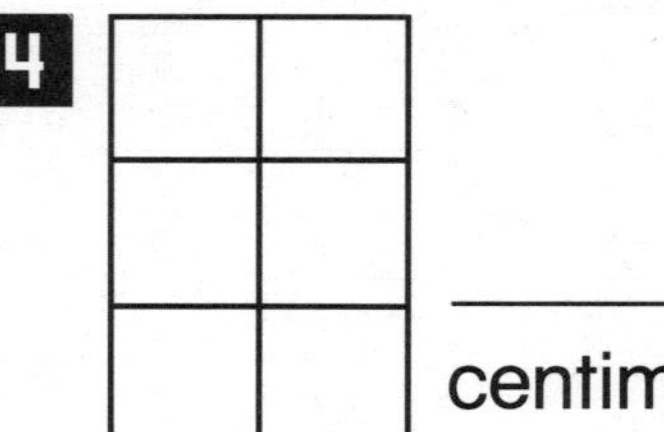

_______ square centimeters

5

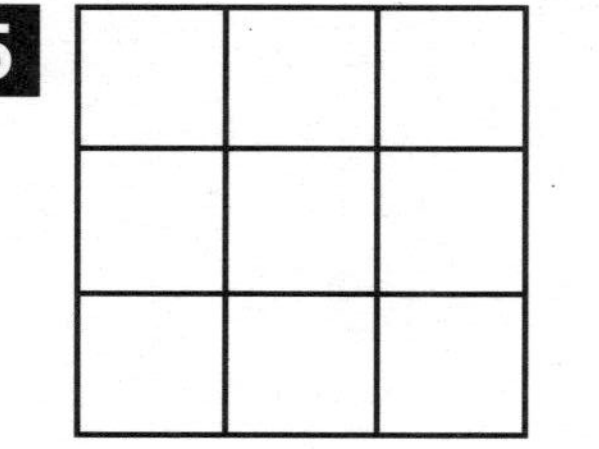

_______ square centimeters

6

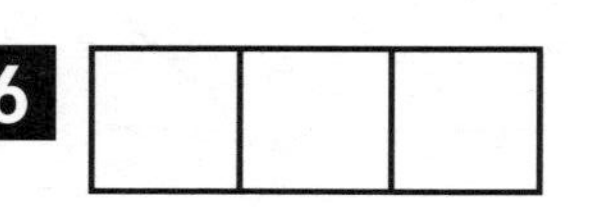

_______ square centimeters

7

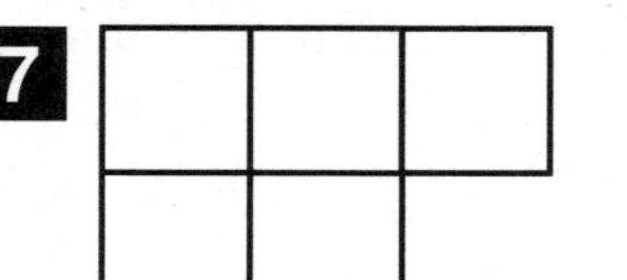

_______ square centimeters

Color the squares to show the area.

11 square centimeters

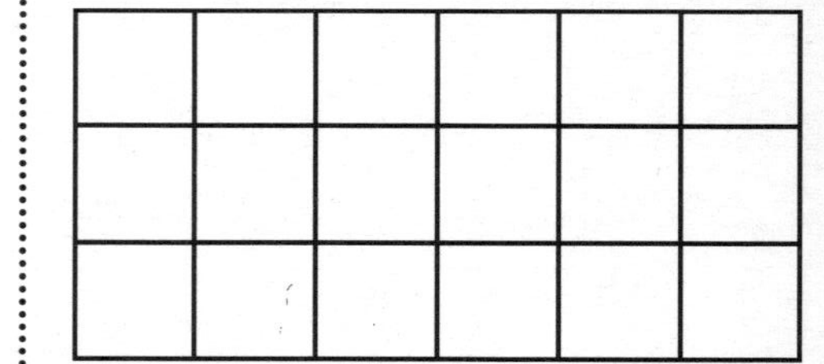

14 square centimeters

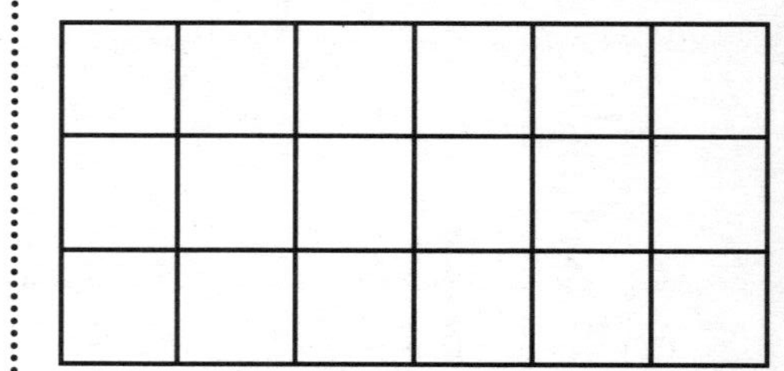

16 square centimeters

Name ____________________

ESTIMATING LENGTH

About Meters

A meter is 100 centimeters. Cut a piece of string 1 meter long. Use the string to measure the items found in the classroom. Record each item's measurement by making an **X** in the correct column.

	scissors	football	window	yardstick	student	bookshelf
Less Than a Meter						
About a Meter						
More Than a Meter						

List three items in the classroom that are about a meter long.

1 ____________________

2 ____________________

3 ____________________

Cut out and use the numbers to complete the subtraction square.

9	5	
6	4	
		2

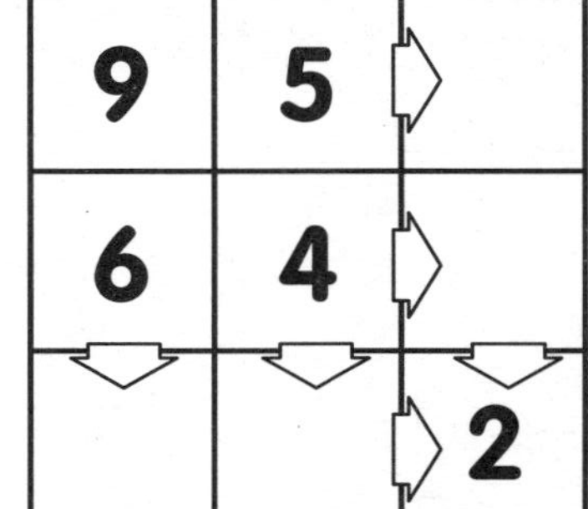

1	2
3	4

Math Mat 93 Name ____________

CONVERTING KILOMETERS TO MILES

Kilometers

A kilometer is 1,000 meters.
A kilometer is 0.6 of a mile.

To Change Kilometers to Miles:

____ (km) [x] [.] [6] [=] ____ (mi.)

Read the sign.
Use a calculator to change the kilometers (km) to miles (mi.).

1 **Bear Valley** **7 km = ________ mi.**

2 **Honeyville** **12 km = ________ mi.**

3 **Busy Bee Town** **14 km = ________ mi.**

4 **Sugar Valley** **22 km = ________ mi.**

5 **Fish Camp** **25 km = ________ mi.**

Find the difference in kilometers from one town to the next.

6 Sugar Valley to Bear Valley

________ **km**

7 Fish Camp to Honeyville

________ **km**

8 Sugar Valley to Busy Bee Town

________ **km**

Name ______________________ ESTIMATING WEIGHT

Grams and Kilograms

A kilogram weighs about 2 pounds. It takes 1,000 grams to equal 1 kilogram. Look at each picture and decide if it should be weighed in grams or kilograms. Circle the answer.

1 grams kilograms	**2** grams kilograms	**3** grams kilograms
4 grams kilograms	**5** grams kilograms	**6** grams kilograms

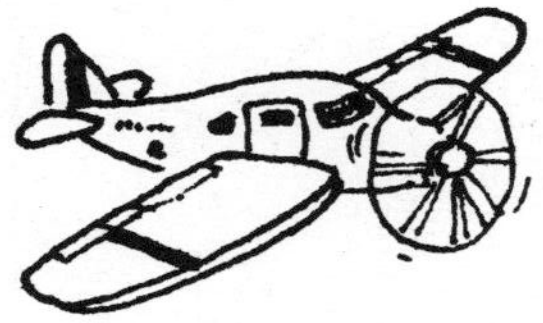

Use a calculator to figure out each item's weight in kilograms.

To Change Pounds (lb.) to Kilograms (kg):

____ (lb.)

____ (kg)

7 Bat

1 lb. x 2.2 = ______ kg

8 Dog

8 lb. x 2.2 = ______ kg

Name ______________________

ESTIMATING VOLUME

Liters

Color the items that would hold about 1 liter.

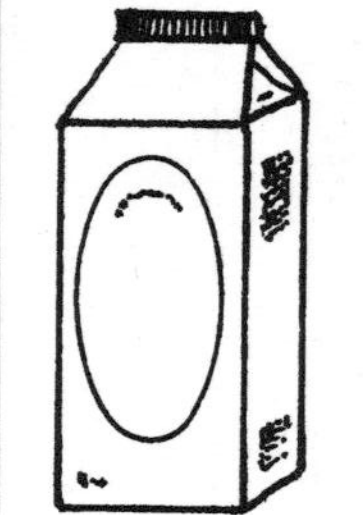

A liter holds a little bit more than 1 quart or 4 cups.

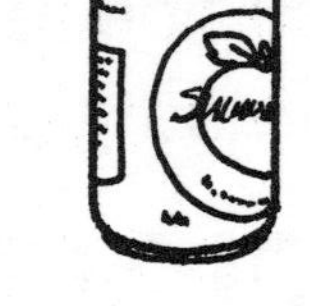

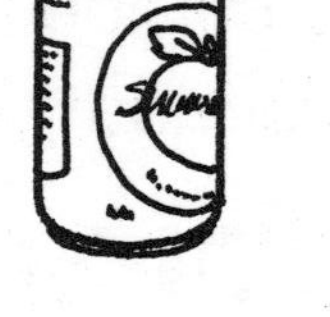

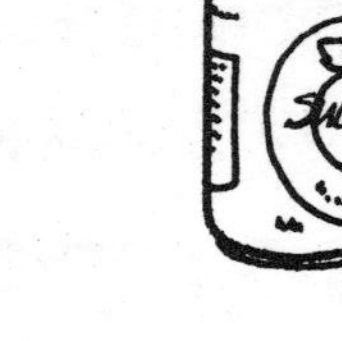
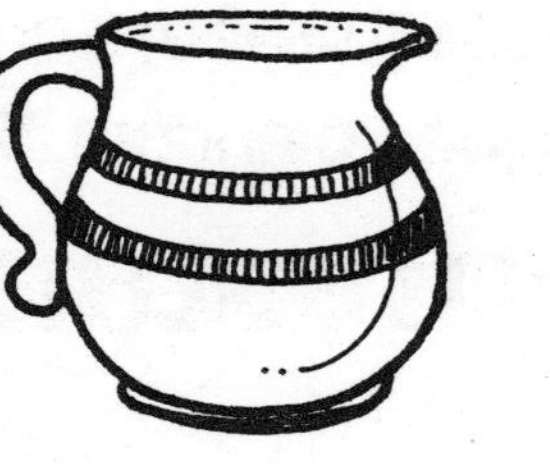

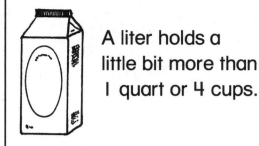

Use the words in the box to complete the sentences.

thermometer	cup
clock	ruler

1 To measure an object, use a ____________.

2 To measure temperature, use a ____________.

3 To measure ingredients, use a ____________.

4 To measure time, use a ____________.

Name ______________________

SORTING WEATHER-RELATED ACTIVITIES

°Celsius

Celsius is another way to tell the temperature. Read each thermometer and write the temperature on the line. Cut out the pictures and sort them into the correct temperature category.

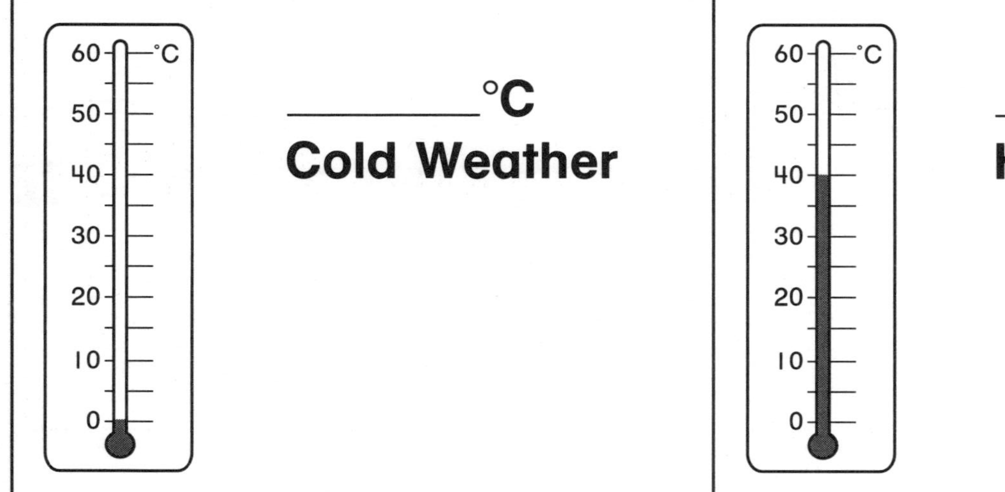

_______ °C **Cold Weather**	_______ °C **Hot Weather**

Math Mat 97 Name ____________________ IDENTIFYING COINS

Coin Values

Cut out the coins. Glue each coin below its name and value.

Penny 1 cent 1¢	Nickel 5 cents 5¢	Dime 10 cents 10¢	Quarter 25 cents 25¢

1 Circle the coin with the highest value.

2 Circle the coin with the lowest value.

Count the pennies.

3 ________¢

4 ________¢

Name ____________________

COUNTING PENNIES

Making Cents

Count the number of pennies. Write the answer on the line.

1 ________¢

2 ________¢

3 ________¢

Buy some fruit. Cut out and glue the correct number of the pennies.

4 **5**

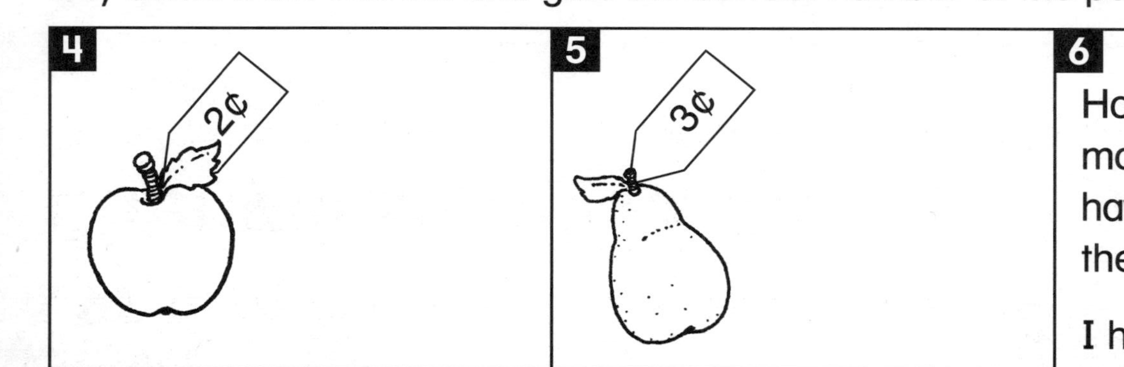

6 How much money do you have left? Glue the change here.

I have ________¢ left.

7 If you bought the apple and the pear, how much money would you spend?

I would spend

________¢.

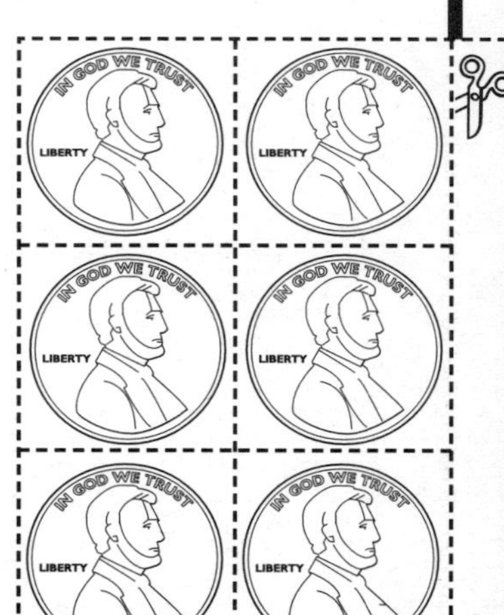

Math Mat 99 Name ____________________ **ADDING COINS**

Change for a Nickel

Show two ways to make 5¢. Glue the coins in the boxes.
Then complete the sentences.

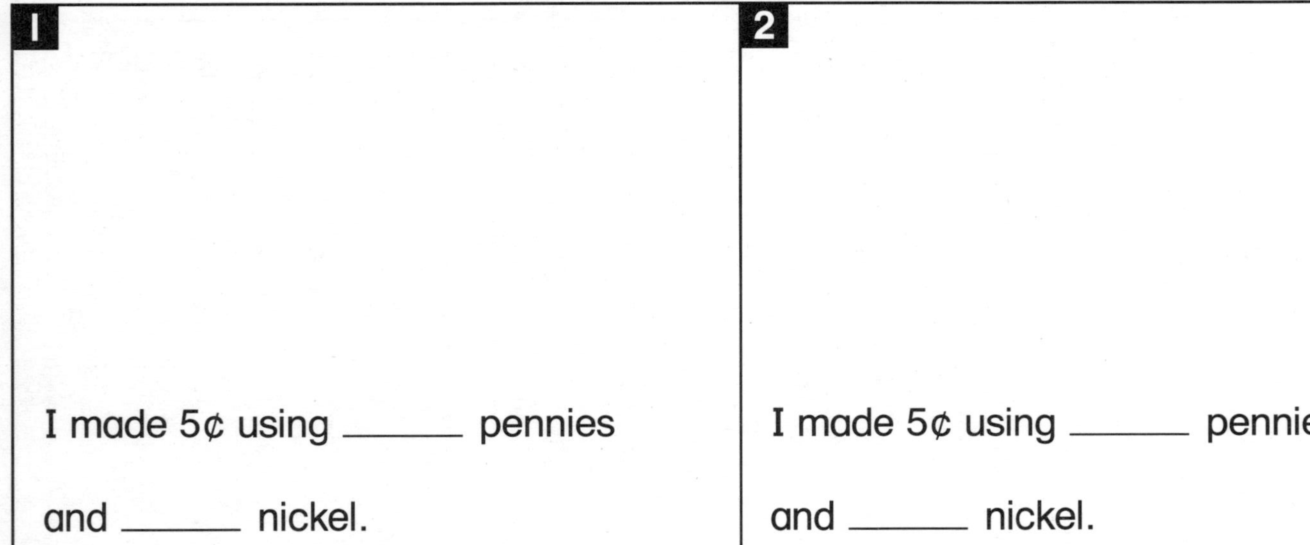

1

I made 5¢ using ______ pennies

and ______ nickel.

2

I made 5¢ using ______ pennies

and ______ nickel.

Count the coins.

3 __________¢

4 __________¢

Name ____________________

Change for a Dime

Cut out the coins. Make 10¢ five different ways.

1 10¢	**2** 10¢	**3** 10¢
4 10¢	**5** 10¢	**6** Count the money. ________¢

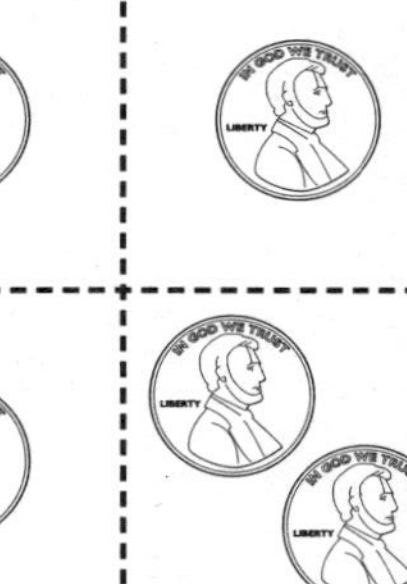

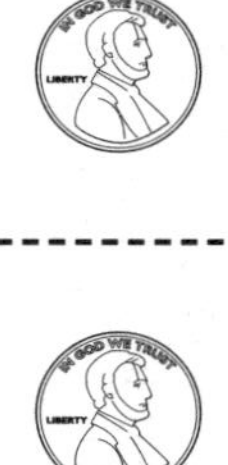

Math Mat 101 Name ____________________ ADDING COINS

The School Store

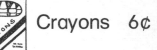

Cut out the pennies. Use the pennies to solve each word problem.

1 Jessica had 10¢. She bought a pencil. How much money does Jessica have left? Jessica has ________ ¢ left.	**2** Taylor had 9¢. He bought glue. How much money does Taylor have left? Taylor has ________ ¢ left.
3 Brianna had 7¢. She bought crayons. How much money does Brianna have left? Brianna has ________ ¢ left.	**4** Emilio had 8¢. He bought a notepad. How much money does Emilio have left? Emilio has ________ ¢ left.

Notepad 4¢

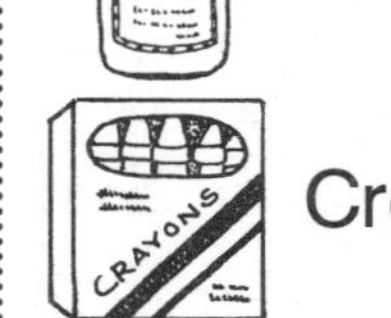

Pencil 3¢

Glue 5¢

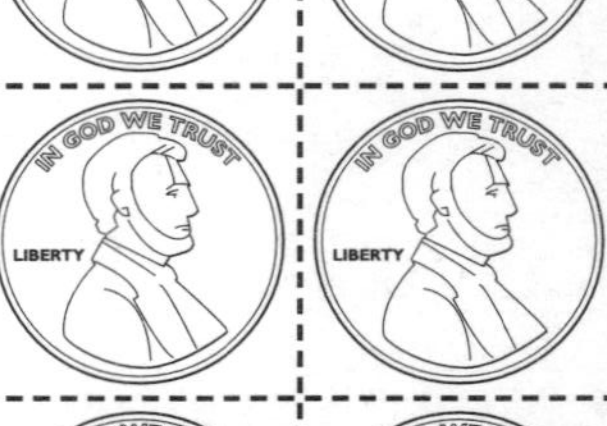

Crayons 6¢

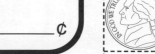

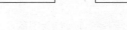

Name ____________________

SKIP-COUNTING BY 5s

Counting With Nickels

Cut out the nickels and glue one nickel in each box.

Count by 5s to complete the number pattern.

_____¢ _____¢ _____¢ _____¢ _____¢

_____¢ _____¢ _____¢ _____¢ _____¢ _____¢ _____¢

_____¢ _____¢ _____¢ _____¢ _____¢ _____¢ _____¢

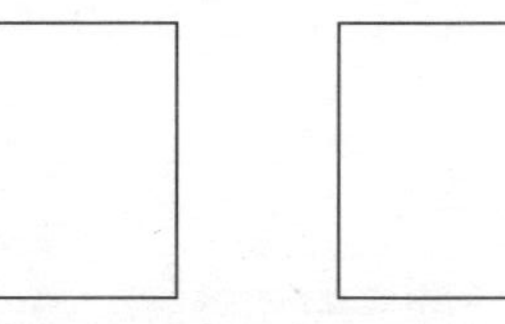

Write the number of nickels needed to make each amount of money.

1. 35¢ _____
2. 10¢ _____
3. 50¢ _____
4. 5¢ _____

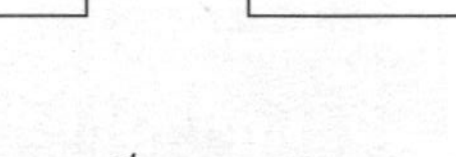

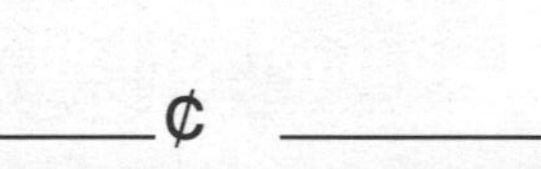

Math Mat 103

Name ____________________

SKIP-COUNTING BY 10s

Counting With Dimes

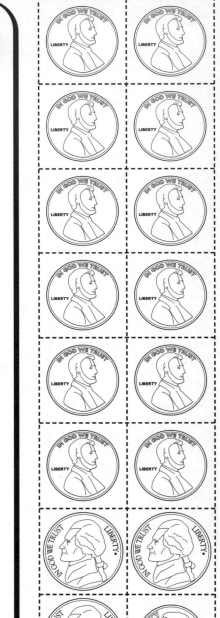

Show two ways to make 10¢. Complete the sentences. Glue the coins in each box.

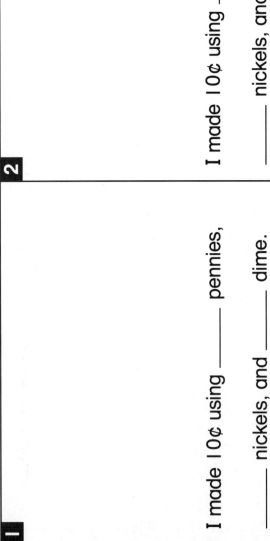

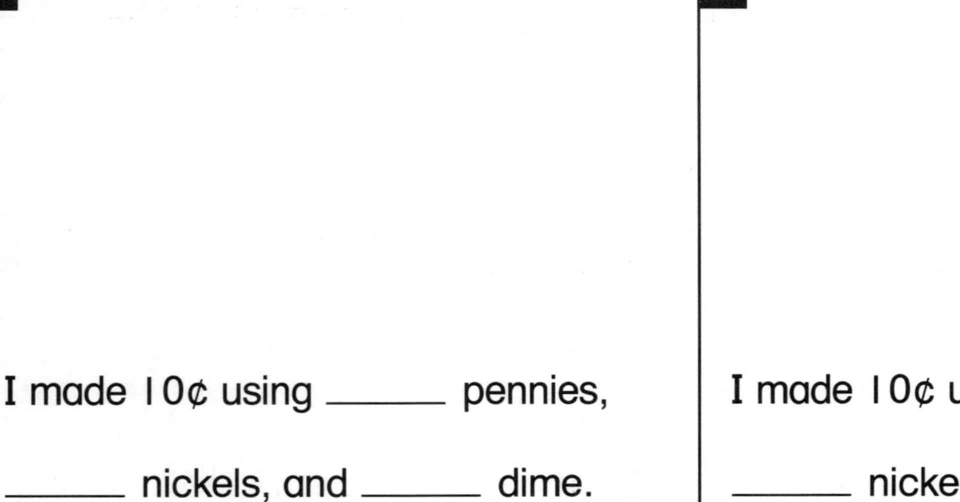

1

I made 10¢ using _____ pennies,

_____ nickels, and _____ dime.

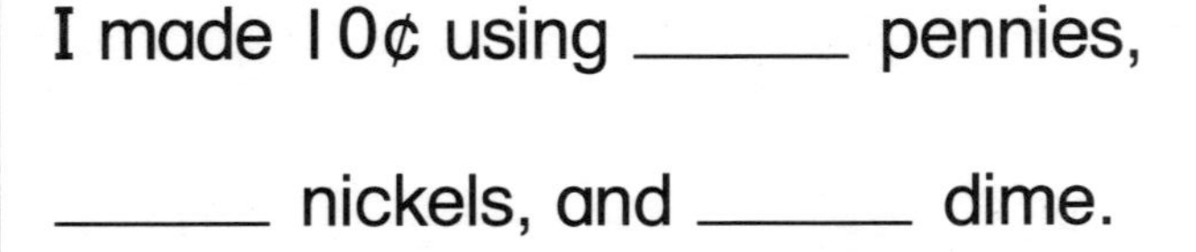

2

I made 10¢ using _____ pennies,

_____ nickels, and _____ dime.

3 Count by 10s. Write the numbers below each dime.

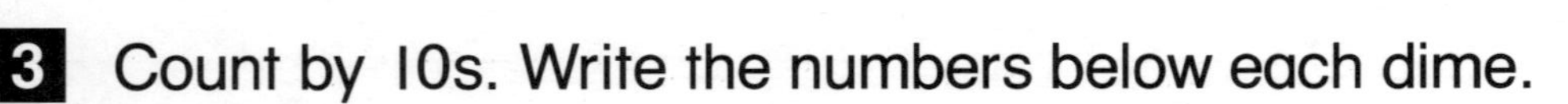

_____¢ _____¢ _____¢ _____¢ _____¢ _____¢ _____¢ _____¢ _____¢ _____¢

4 Complete the number pattern.

10, _____, 30, _____, _____, 60, _____, _____, _____, 100

Name ____________________

SKIP-COUNTING BY 25s

Counting With Quarters

Cut out the quarters. Glue the correct number of quarters by each amount of money.

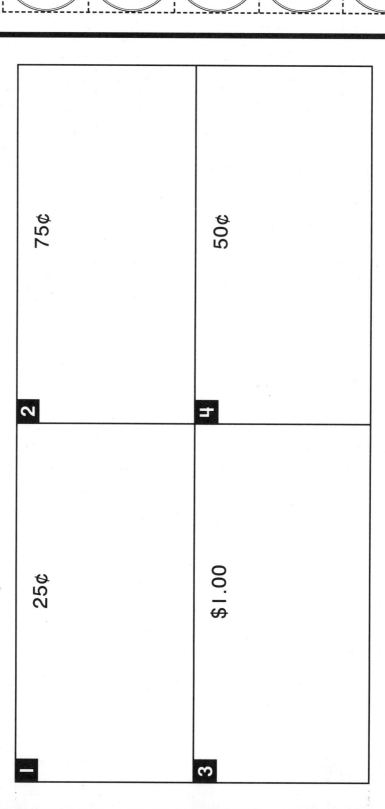

1 25¢	**2** 75¢
3 $1.00	**4** 50¢

5 How many quarters are left? ____________________

6 What is the total value of the quarters? ____________________

Math Mat 105 Name ____________________ ADDING COINS

Counting Loose Change

Cut out each set of coins. Glue them next to their total value.

1 3¢	5 10¢
2 5¢	6 11¢
3 7¢	7 12¢
4 9¢	8 15¢

Name ____________________

Sweet Shop

You have 15¢ to spend at the snack shop. Make a list of what you will buy and how much money you will have left. (Hint: Use the coins!)

I will buy: It costs:

____________________ ________¢

____________________ ________¢

____________________ ________¢

____________________ ________¢

Total amount spent: ________¢

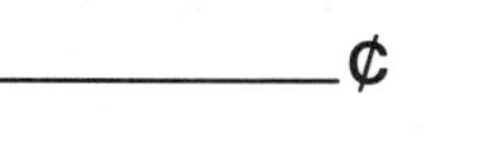

I will have ________¢ left.

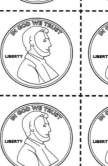

lollipop 2¢

pie 10¢

cupcake 7¢

popcorn 3¢

ice cream cone 4¢

cookie 5¢

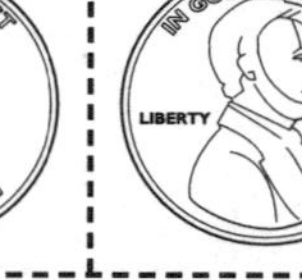

Math Mat 107 Name ____________

Pennies and Dimes

Cut out the coins. Glue the coins in each box to show the amount of money.
Write the number of tens (dimes) and ones (pennies) used to make each number.

1 32¢		2 25¢		3 54¢		4 43¢	
Tens	Ones	Tens	Ones	Tens	Ones	Tens	Ones

Use the remaining number cards to show the following numbers.

5 More than 17¢	6 Less than 39¢	7 More than 50¢	8 Less than 46¢

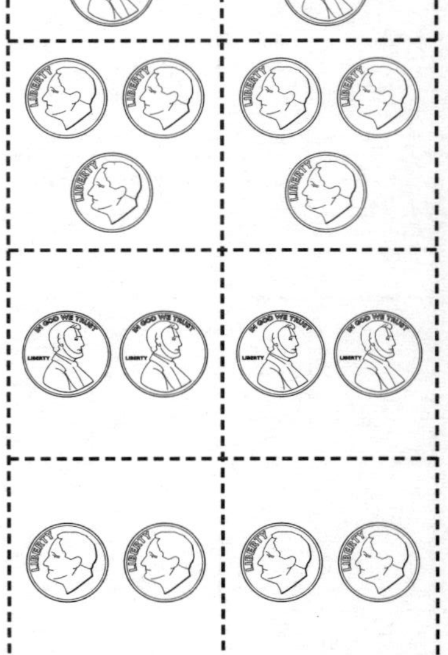

Name ____________________

SOLVING WORD PROBLEMS

Frisbee Dog

Miguel loves to play Frisbee with his dog, Bart. On Saturday, Miguel threw 10 Frisbees to Bart. Bart brought back only 7 of the Frisbees. How many Frisbees were not brought back to Miguel?

Write the math problem and the sentence telling about the answer.

____

____

If Bart earns 1¢ for every Frisbee returned, how many Frisbees will he need to return to earn $1.00?

____

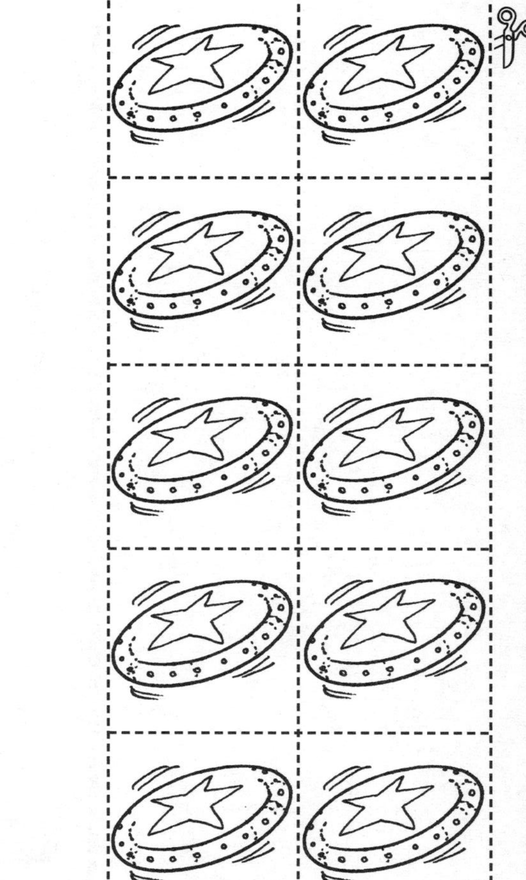

Math Mat 109 Name ____________ **ADDING MONEY**

Dollars and Cents

Cut out the dollars and cents. Glue the correct amount of money in each box.

1 $1.50	**2** $2.20
3 $2.03	**4** $1.05

Look at the boxes above.

5 Which is the largest amount of money? ____________

6 Which is the smallest amount of money? ____________

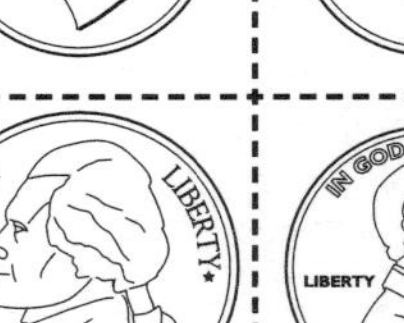

Name ____________________

SOLVING WORD PROBLEMS

Bait and Tackle Shop

Solve each word problem.

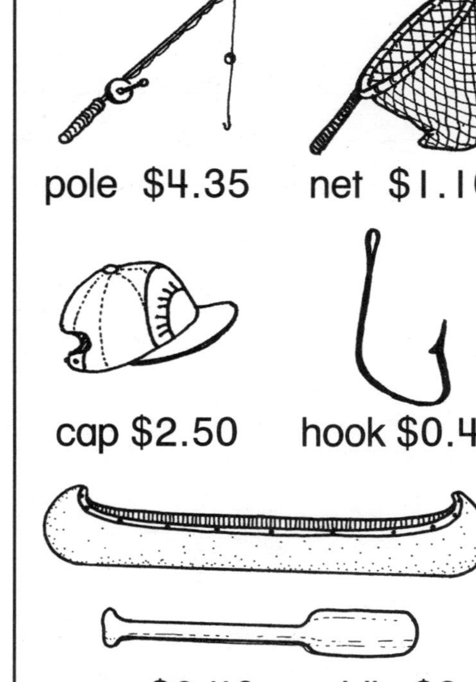

1 Jason bought a fishing pole and a hook. How much money did Jason spend?

Jason spent $__________.

2 Alice bought a cap and a paddle. How much money did Alice spend?

Alice spent $__________.

3 Use the numbers 1–6 to put the fishing equipment in order from least expensive to most expensive.

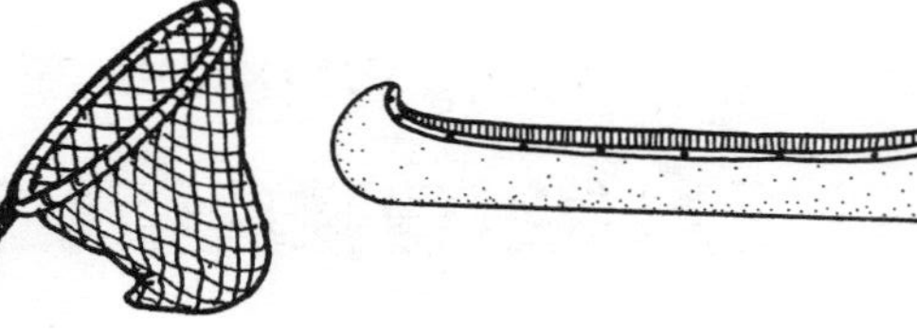

_____ _____ _____ _____ _____ _____

4 Circle the more expensive item.

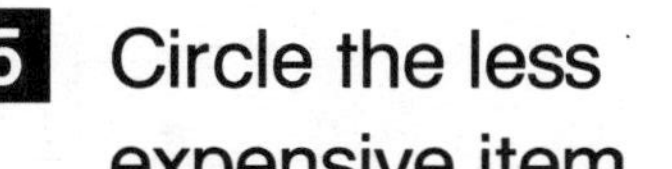

5 Circle the less expensive item.

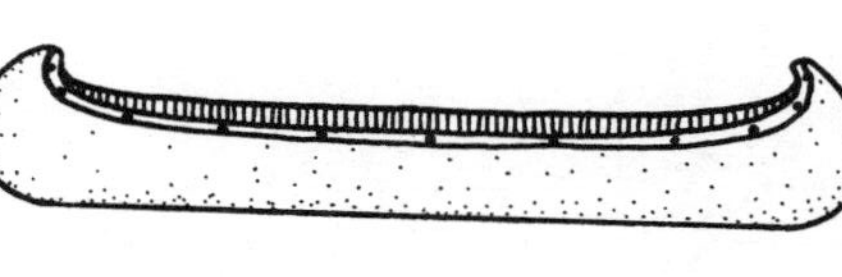

6 Circle the least expensive item.

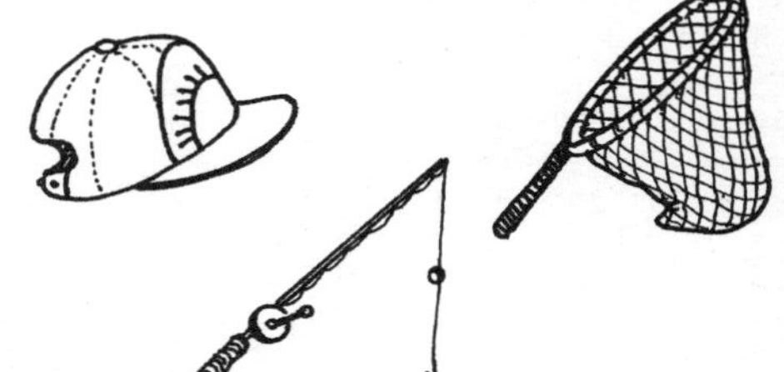

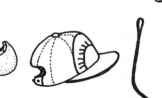

Name ____________________ COUNTING MONEY

Matching Money

Cut out the bills and count them. Glue each set of bills next to its dollar amount.

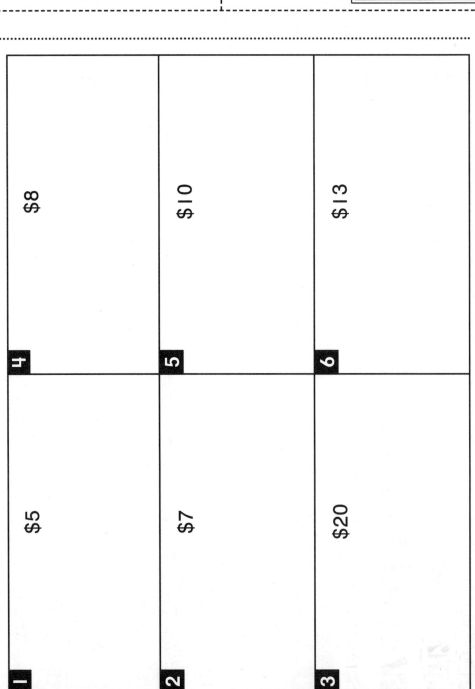

1 $5	**4** $8
2 $7	**5** $10
3 $20	**6** $13

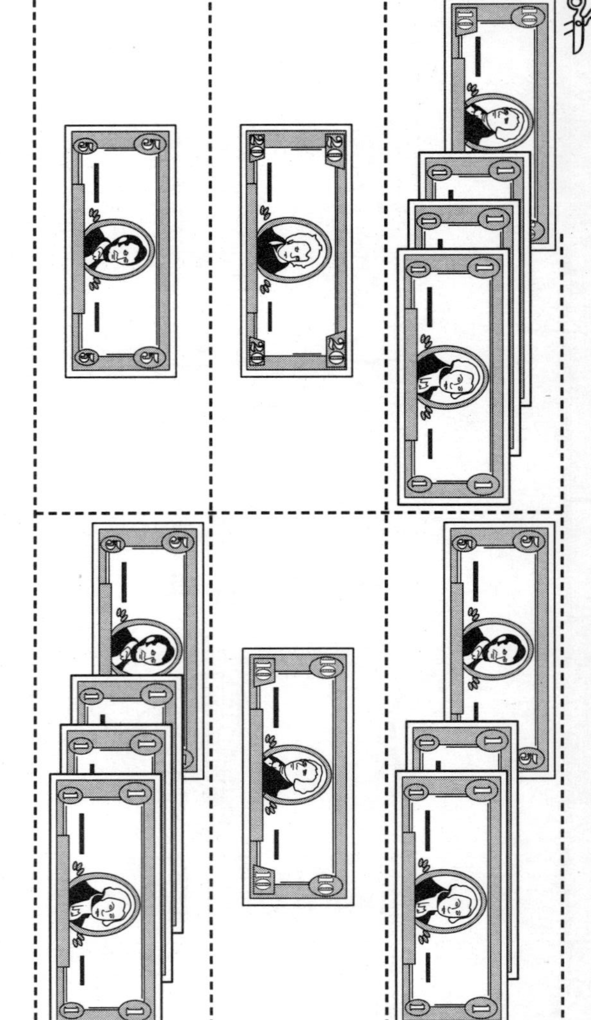

Name ______________________

ADDING MONEY

Money Review

Write the value of each coin.

______¢ ______¢ ______¢ ______¢

Use the coins to make the correct amount of money needed to buy each item.

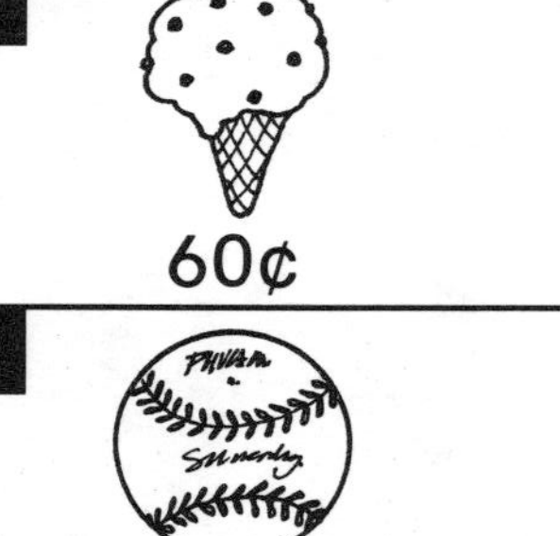

1 60¢

2 1.40¢

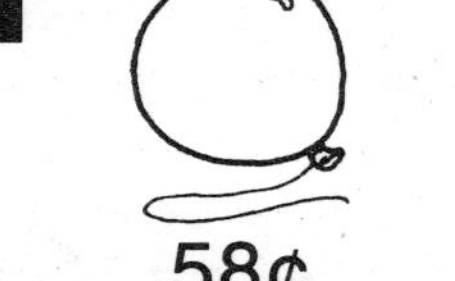

3 58¢

What have you learned about money?
Write your answer on the back of this paper.

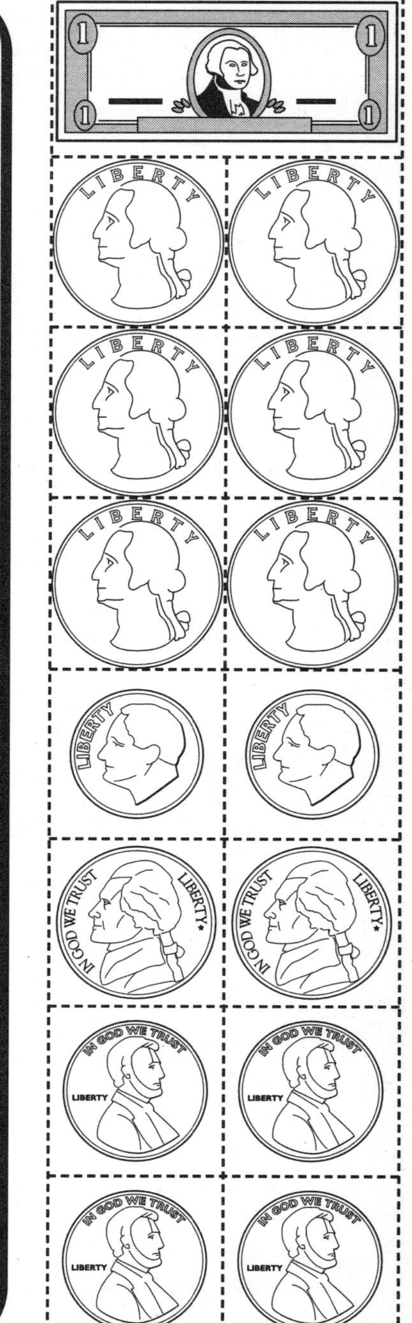

Name ____________________

Plenty of Penguins

About Multiplication

I × 2

I × 2 means there is I set with 2 items in the set.

2 × I

2 × I means there are 2 sets with I item in each set.

Multiplication is a quick way of adding sets of items.
Write the multiplication problem for each set of penguins.

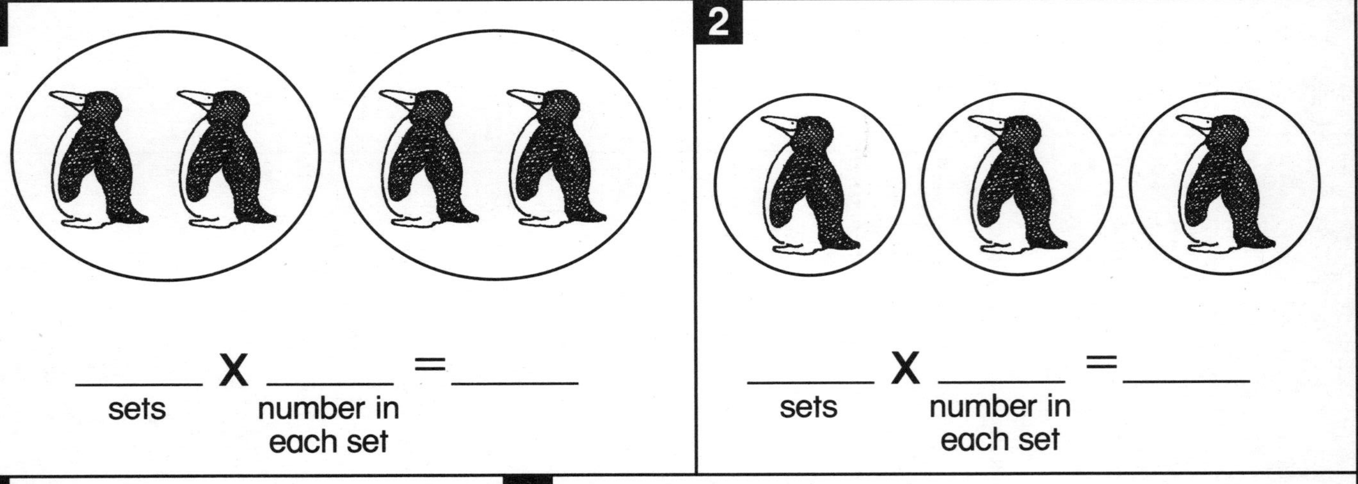

I

_____ X _____ = _____
sets — number in each set

2

_____ X _____ = _____
sets — number in each set

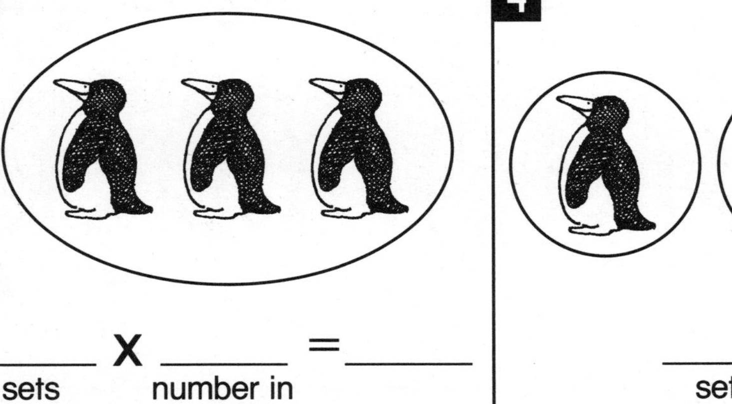

3

_____ X _____ = _____
sets — number in each set

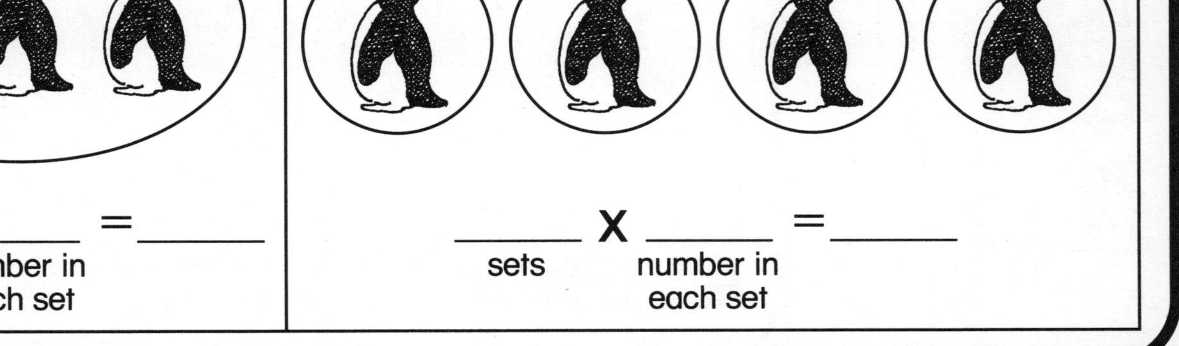

4

_____ X _____ = _____
sets — number in each set

Name ____________________

SOLVING MULTIPLICATION SENTENCES

Fabulous Fish

Cut out each group of fish. Match each fish group to the multiplication problems. Glue in place.

Multiplication Tip: When multiplying a number by 1, the answer is always the same as the number!

		1 — 1 × 1
2 — 2 × 1	3 — 8 × 1	4 — 1 × 9
5 — 7 × 1	6 — 1 × 10	7 — 1 × 3
8 — 5 × 1	9 — 1 × 6	10 — 4 × 1

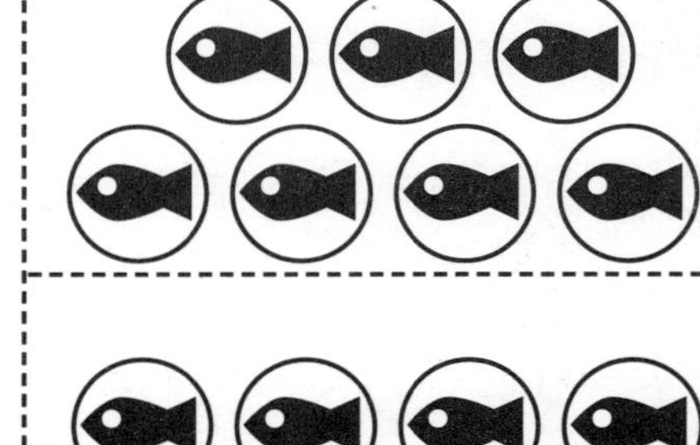

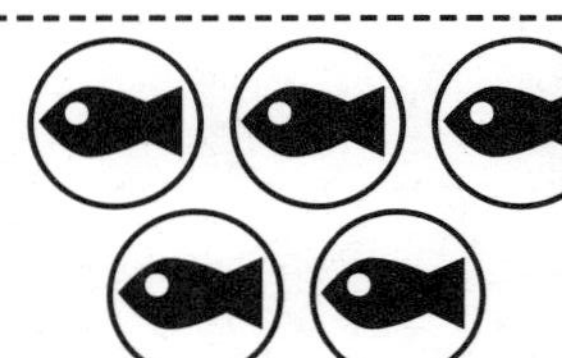

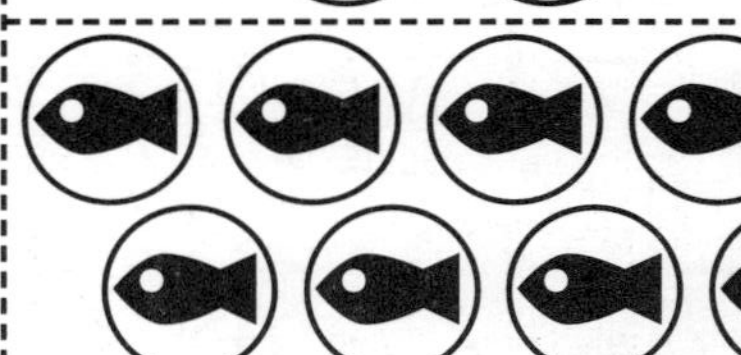

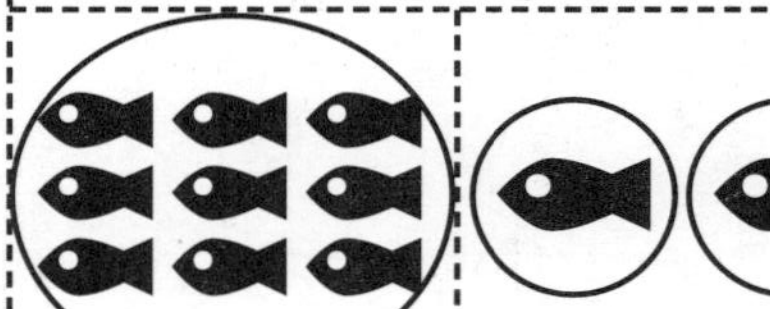

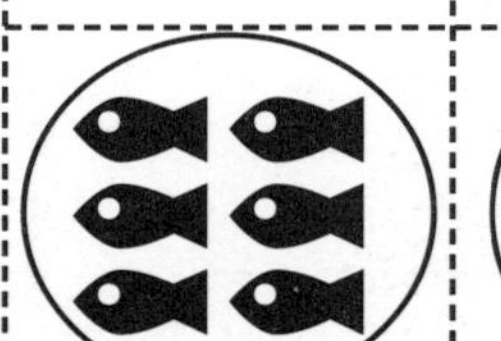

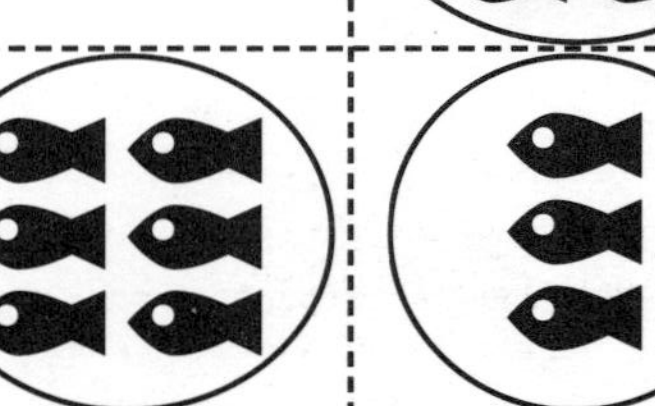

Math Mat 115 Name ____________

SOLVING MULTIPLICATION SENTENCES

Busy Bees

Cut out the sets of bees.
Use the bee sets to help you solve each multiplication problem.

2×2
(2 sets × 2 bees in each set)
$2 \times 2 = 4$

1. $1 \times 2 =$ ______
2. $2 \times 2 =$ ______
3. $3 \times 2 =$ ______
4. $4 \times 2 =$ ______
5. $5 \times 2 =$ ______
6. $6 \times 2 =$ ______
7. $7 \times 2 =$ ______
8. $8 \times 2 =$ ______
9. $9 \times 2 =$ ______
10. $10 \times 2 =$ ______

Name ____________________

SOLVING MULTIPLICATION SENTENCES

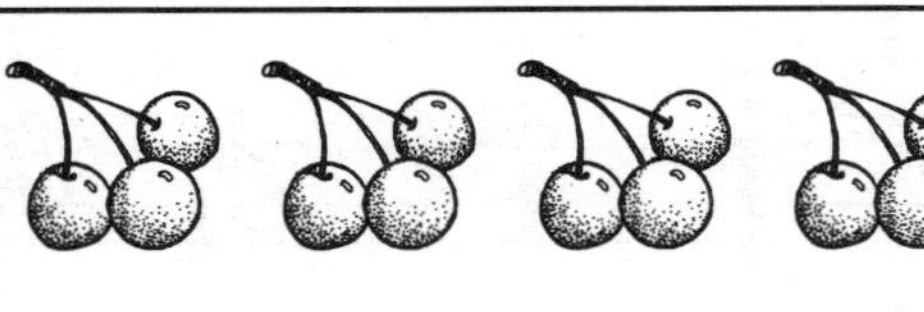

Fresh Fruit

Count the cherries and complete the chart.

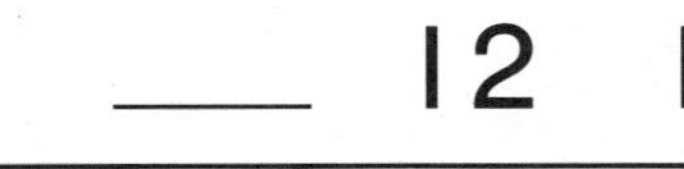
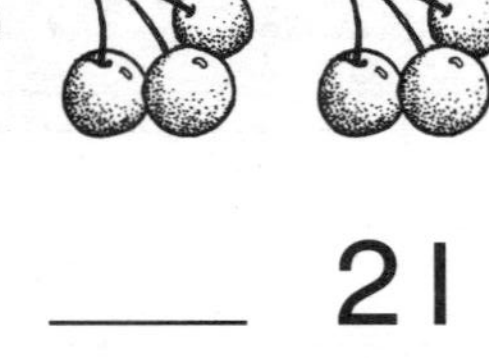
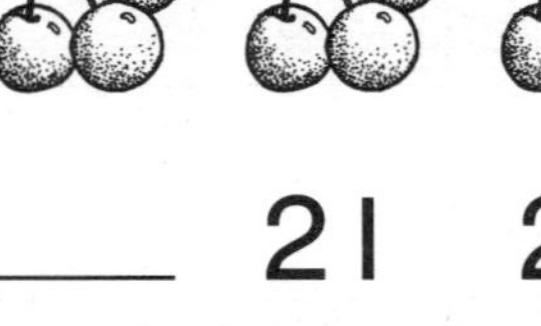

3	6	___	12	15	___	21	24	___	___

Use the chart to solve the multiplication problems.

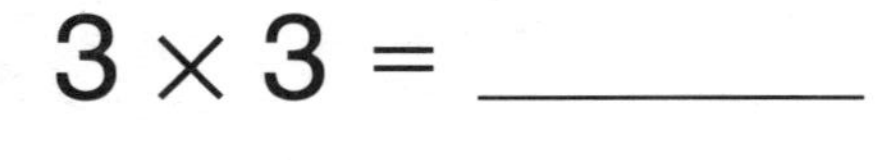

1. $3 \times 3 =$ ________
2. $3 \times 1 =$ ________
3. $3 \times 5 =$ ________
4. $3 \times 2 =$ ________
5. $3 \times 9 =$ ________

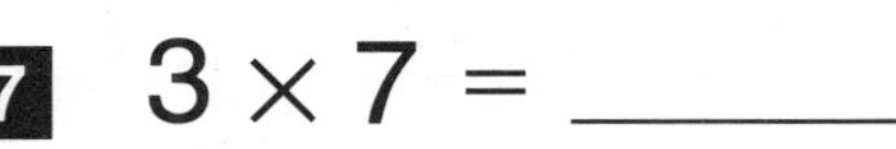
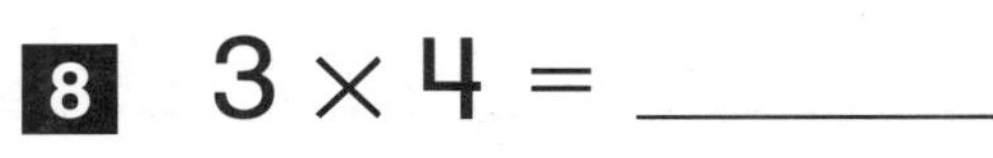

6. $3 \times 6 =$ ________
7. $3 \times 7 =$ ________
8. $3 \times 4 =$ ________
9. $3 \times 10 =$ ________
10. $3 \times 8 =$ ________

Write the multiplication problem.

11. 

____ × ____ = ____

12. ____ × ____ = ____

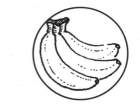

13. ____ × ____ = ____

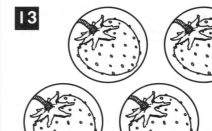

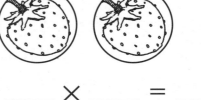

Math Mat 117 Name ____________________

RECOGNIZING PATTERNS

Multiplication Chart

Complete the chart.

×	0	1	2	3	4	5
0	0		0			0
1	0	1	2	3	4	5
2			4		8	
3	0			9		15
4		4		12	16	
5			10			25

Multiplication Tip: When multiplying any number by 0, the answer is always 0!

Read and solve each word problem. (Hint: Make a picture to solve each word problem.)

1. Carmen had 2 dogs. Each dog had 3 bones. How many bones were there in all?

   $2 \times 3 =$ ________

2. Travis had 1 bag of marbles. There were 4 marbles in the bag. How many marbles did Travis have?

   $1 \times 4 =$ ________

Math Mat 118 Name ____________

SOLVING WORD PROBLEMS

Apple Division

Divide each group into equal sets. Then draw a circle around each set and complete the sentences.

1 Make 2 equal sets.

Each set will have ______ apple(s).

2 (apples) ÷ 2 (sets) = ______ apple(s) in each set

2 Make 4 equal sets.

Each set will have ______ apple(s).

12 (apples) ÷ 4 (sets) = ______ apple(s) in each set

3 Make 3 equal sets.

Each set will have ______ apple(s).

6 (apples) ÷ 3 (sets) = ______ apple(s) in each set

4 Make 1 set.

Each set will have ______ apple(s).

5 (apples) ÷ 1 (sets) = ______ apple(s) in each set

Math Mat 119 Name ________

WRITING DIVISION PROBLEMS

In the Woods

Write the division problem for each set of pictures.

1 4 acorns in 2 groups

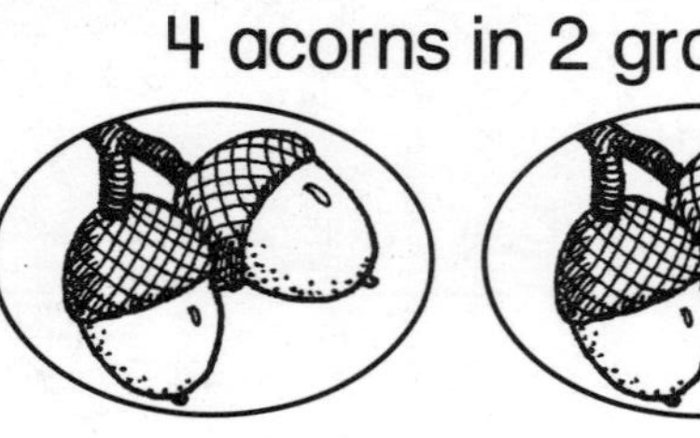

$4 \div 2 =$ ______

There are ______ acorns in each group.

3 3 leaves in 3 groups

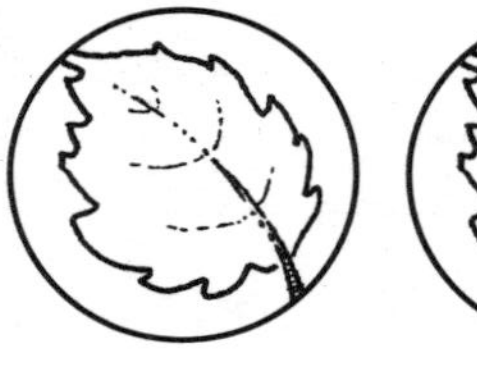

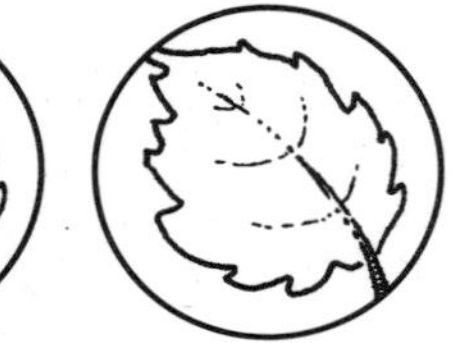
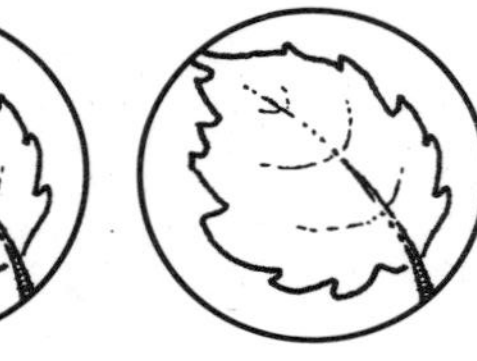

$3 \div 3 =$ ______

There is ______ leaf in each group.

2 9 pinecones in 3 groups

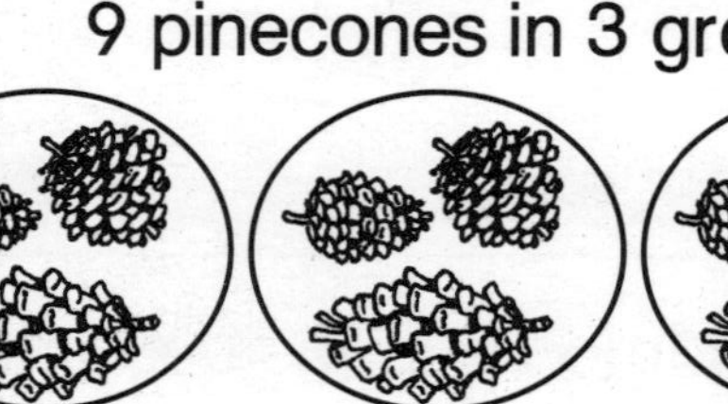

$9 \div 3 =$ ______

There are ______ pinecones in each group.

4 10 flowers in 2 groups

$10 \div 2 =$ ______

There are ______ flowers in each group.

Read each word problem. Circle the correct math problem.

5 6 acorns were divided into 3 groups. How many were in each group?

$6 \div 3 = 2$

$6 \div 2 = 3$

6 The 8 pinecones were divided among the 4 friends.

$8 \div 2 = 4$

$8 \div 4 = 2$

Name ____________________

MATCHING FRACTIONS

Pizza Parlor

How much pizza was eaten? Draw a line matching fractions and pizzas.

1 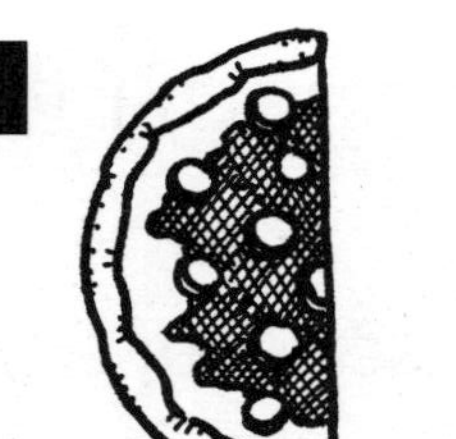

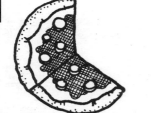

$\frac{1}{3}$

2

$\frac{1}{5}$

3

$\frac{1}{2}$

4

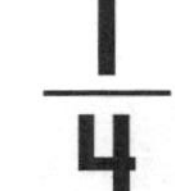
$\frac{1}{4}$

What is your favorite kind of pizza?

____

____

What is your least favorite pizza topping?

____

____

Why don't you like it? Use the back of this paper to write your answer.

Math Mat 121 Name ______

DIVIDING WHOLE NUMBERS

Division Review

Solve each division problem.

1 $3 \div 3 =$ ______ **2** $5 \div 1 =$ ______ **3** $2 \div 2 =$ ______

4 $2 \div 1 =$ ______ **5** $3 \div 1 =$ ______ **6** $7 \div 1 =$ ______

7 $4 \div 4 =$ ______ **8** $1 \div 0 =$ ______ **9** $6 \div 6 =$ ______

Write the missing number.

10 $1 \div$ ______ $= 1$ **11** $5 \div$ ______ $= 0$ **12** ______ $\div 8 = 1$

13 ______ $\div 1 = 2$ **14** $3 \div$ ______ $= 1$ **15** $4 \div$ ______ $= 4$

16 $2 \div$ ______ $= 2$ **17** ______ $\div 1 = 9$ **18** ______ $\div 1 = 6$

Division Tips!

- When dividing a number by 1, the answer is always the same as the number.
  $4 \div 1 = 4$
- When dividing a number by the same number, the answer is always 1.
  $3 \div 3 = 1$
- When dividing a number by 0, the answer is always 0.
  $5 \div 0 = 0$

Brain Teaser!

Solve each problem.

$100 \div 1 =$ ______

$100 \div 0 =$ ______

Name ____________________

IDENTIFYING ODD AND EVEN

Pencil Pairs

How can you tell if the number of pencils is **odd** or **even**?

- If one pencil is not part of a pair, the number is **odd**.
- If all the pencils are in pairs, the number is **even**.

Circle pairs of pencils and then circle **odd** or **even**.

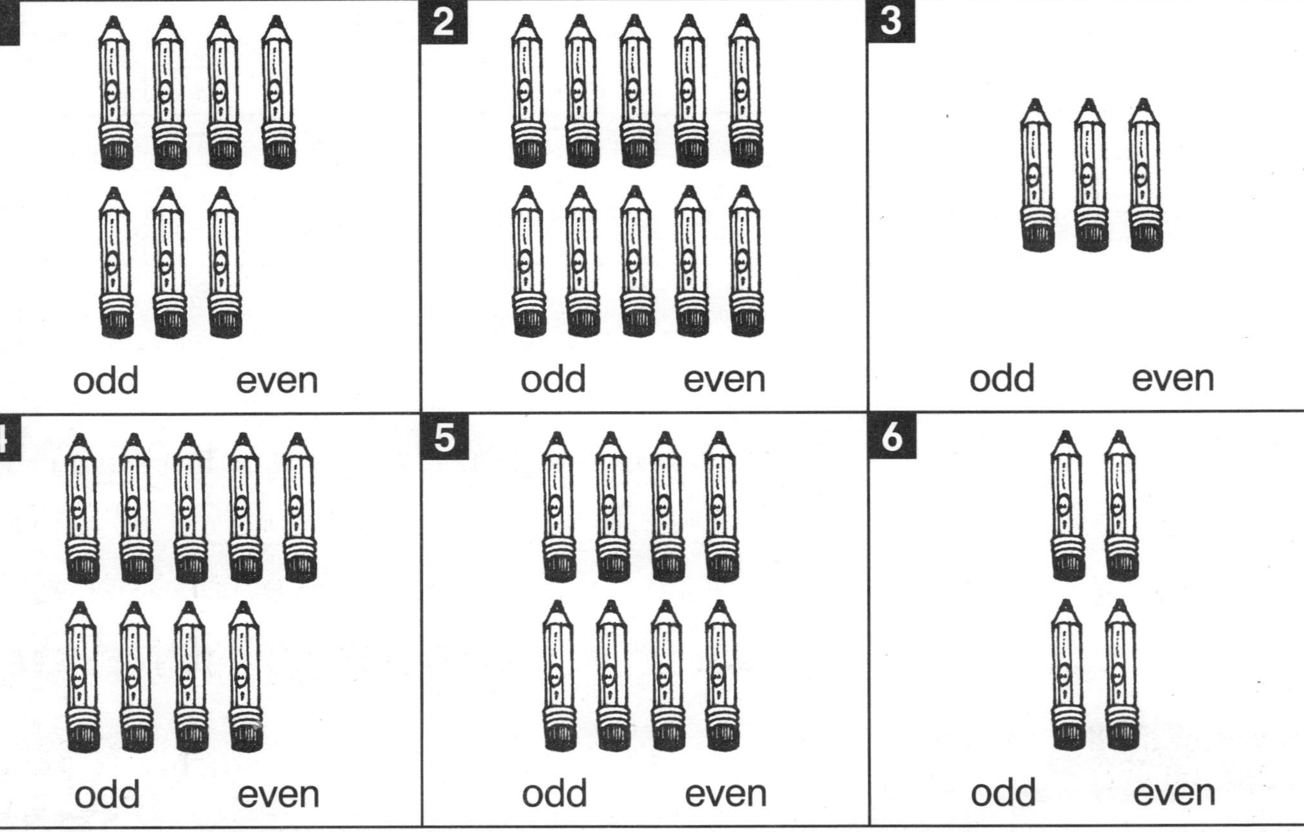

Write the missing numbers to count to 10.

____, ____, 3,

____, 5, ____, 7,

____, ____, 10

- Circle the odd numbers with a red crayon.
- Circle the even numbers with a blue crayon.

1 5 9

8 2 6 3

4 10 7

Name ____________________

APPLYING CONCEPTS OF PROBABILITY

Odd or Even?

Do you think a die will land more often on odd numbers or even numbers?

Record your guess. Roll a die ten times. After each roll, record the number by coloring the corresponding square.

I think the die will land more often on __________ numbers.

Odd Numbers							
Even Numbers							

Write the numbers 1 to 10.

- Draw a **circle** around the **even** numbers.
- Draw a **square** around the **odd** numbers.

____, ____, ____, ____, ____, ____, ____, ____, ____, ____

When sorting numbers with two or more digits into groups of odd or even numbers, look at the number in the ones place.

- If the digit in the ones place is odd, then the number is odd.
- If the digit in the ones place is even, then the number is even.

Look at each number. Write **odd** or **even** on the line.

74 ____________________

61 ____________________

28 ____________________

17 ____________________

123 ____________________

249 ____________________

Name ______

COUNTING PAIRS

Lost Mittens

1 3 children lost their mittens.
How many mittens did they lose?
(Hint: Each child wears two mittens.)

1 child + 1 child + 1 child = ______ children

______ mittens + ______ mittens + ______ mittens = ______ mittens

The 3 children lost ______ mittens.

2 Read the clues to discover which pair of mittens belongs to each child. Make an **X** in the box if the answer is **no**. Make an **O** in the box if the answer is **yes**.

- Ted wears only green mittens.
- Lia never wears red or green mittens.
- Nick never wears blue or green mittens.

	Blue	**Green**	**Red**
Ted			
Lia			
Nick			

Which child wears the red mittens?

______

Math Mat 125

Name ____________________

COUNTING BY 2s

What's the Pattern?

Cut out and arrange the numbers to make the pattern. Glue the numbers down. Write more numbers to complete the pattern to 36.

Write a sentence describing the pattern.

____

10	20
14	2
22	8
4	28
26	16
32	24
18	30
12	6

Name ____________________

COUNTING BY 5s

What's the Pattern?

Cut out and arrange the numbers to make the pattern. Glue the numbers down. Write more numbers to complete the pattern to 100.

Write a sentence describing the pattern.

____

30	45
60	10
70	20
5	55
40	65
50	25
75	80
15	35

Math Mat 127 Name ____________________ COUNTING BY 10s

What's the Pattern?

1 Cut out and arrange the numbers to complete the pattern to 100. Glue the numbers in place.

10

Write a sentence describing the pattern.

____

Write the missing numbers.

2 10, 20, ___, ___, 50, ___, ___, ___, 90, ___

3 ___, ___, 30, 40, ___, 60, 70, ___, ___, 100

4 Write a number greater than 10 but less than 25.

____

5 Write a number greater than 50 but less than 100.

____

40	60	30
100	90	80
20	50	70

Math Mat 128

Name ______________________

REPRESENTING NUMBERS

Planes and Trains

Count the number of planes and trains and write the number word on the line.

1	2	3	4
______	______	______	______

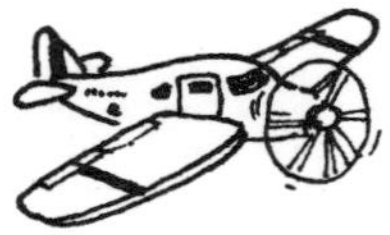

5	6	7	8
______	______	______	______

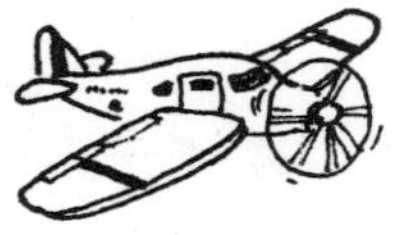

Trace each number word.

one

one

two

two

Circle the words **one** and **two**.

```
T W O Q R U D O W X
O N E P S B R Z I O
H T W O E C W W T E
I C B Q V O L K H M
N O N E D I T I V Y
W S H Y O N E D B U
N T W O P Y B W R I
C N F H T W O X O R
T W O C M O N E J M
U N J R O N E N P K
```

Math Mat 129 Name ____________________

Counting Apples

Draw the correct number of apples on each tree.

1 3 apples

2 4 apples

3 4 apples

4 3 apples

5 4 apples

6 3 apples

Trace each number word.

three

three

four

four

Circle the apple that does not belong.

Name ____________________

MATCHING NUMBERS AND NUMERALS

Snack Food

Cut out the pennies and glue them next to the piece of food to show the price.

apple 5¢

2

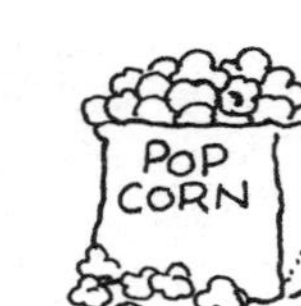

popcorn 6¢

3

strawberry 5¢

banana 6¢

Trace each number word.

five

five

six

six

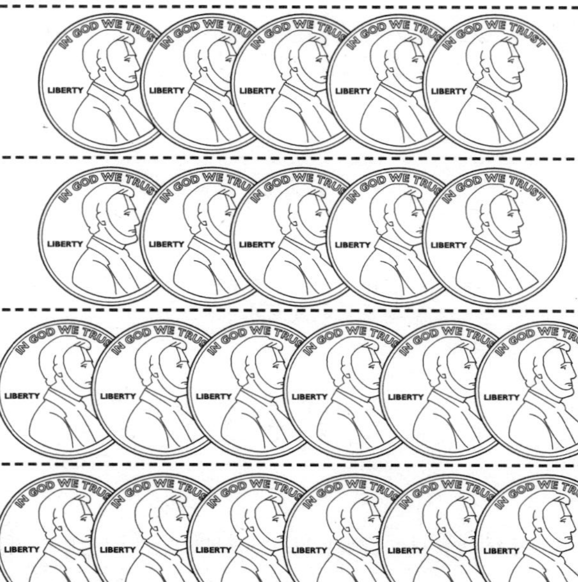

Math Mat 131

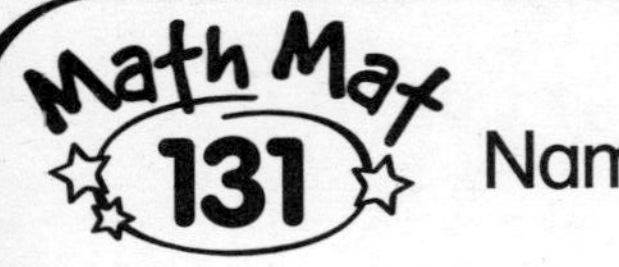

Name ______________________

REPRESENTING NUMBERS

How Many Shoes?

Count the number of shoes on each spider.
Write the number on the line.

1
______

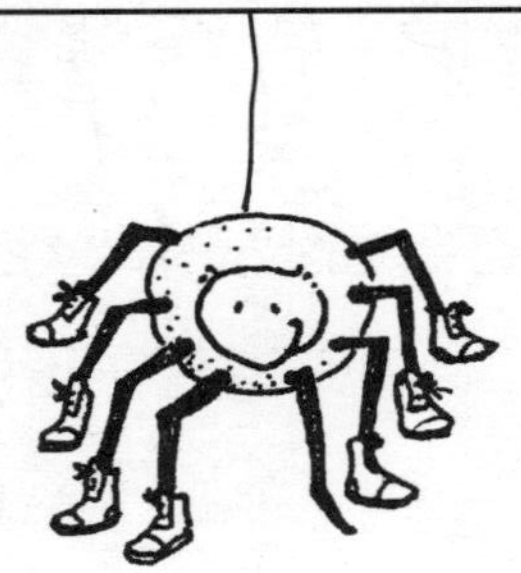

2
______

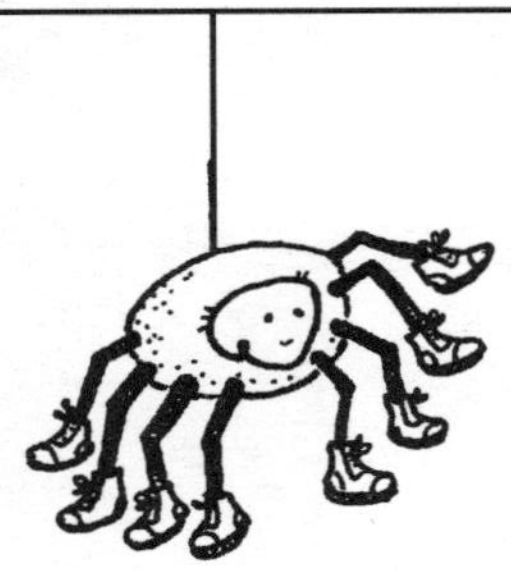

3
______

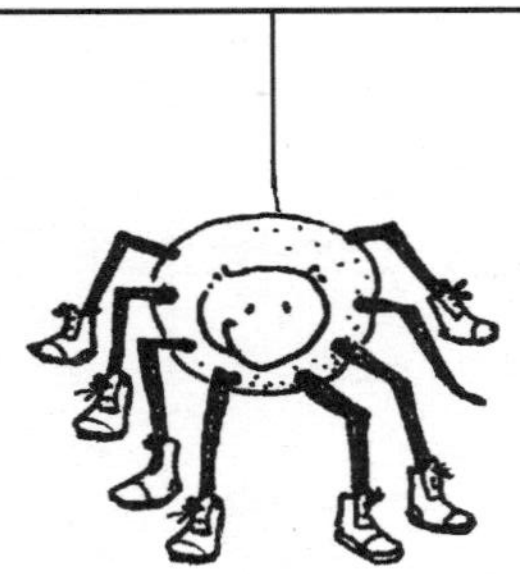

4
______

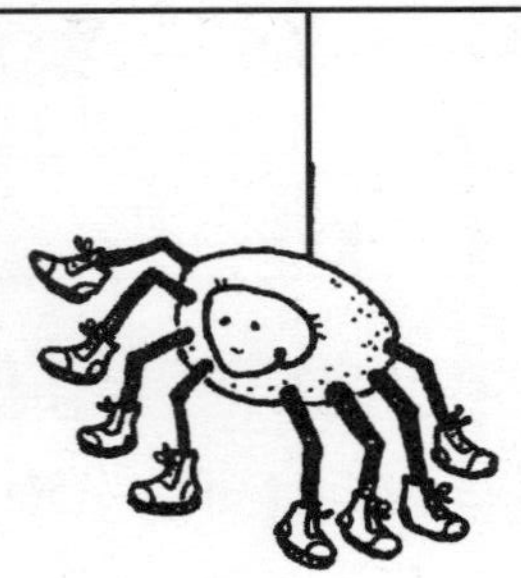

5
______

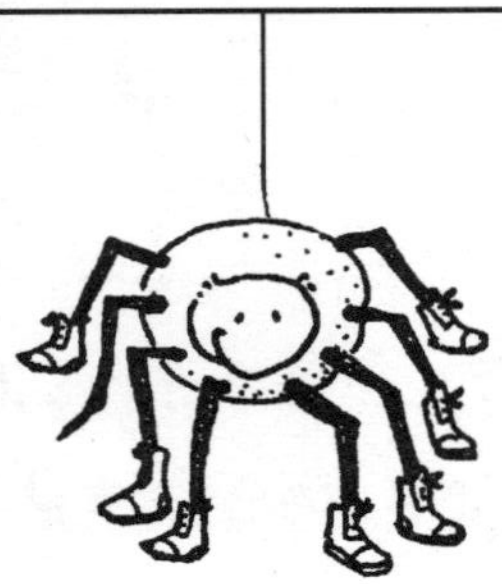

6
______

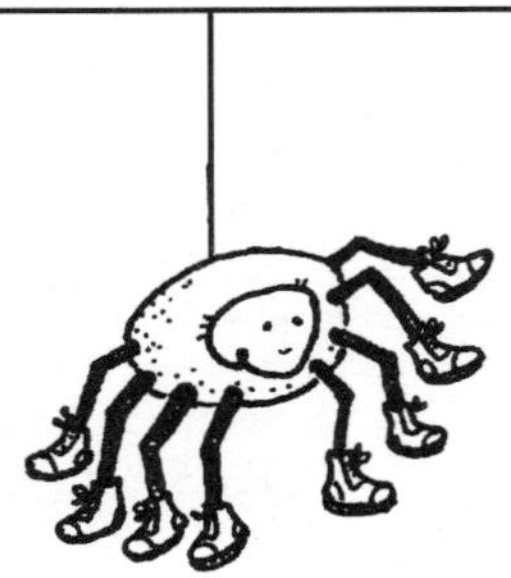

Trace each number word.

seven

seven

eight

eight

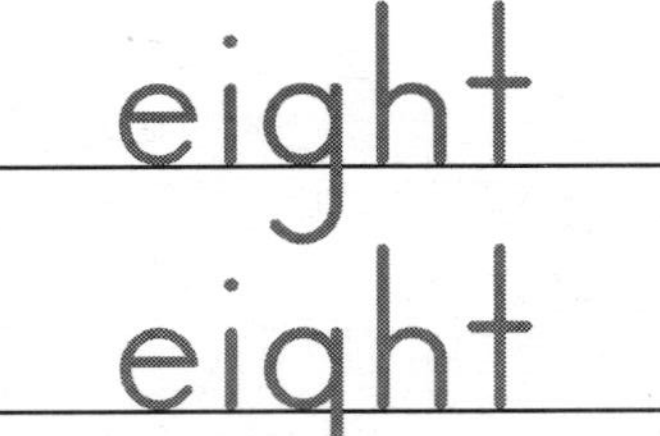

Start at the spider. Draw a line from 1 to 8 in order.

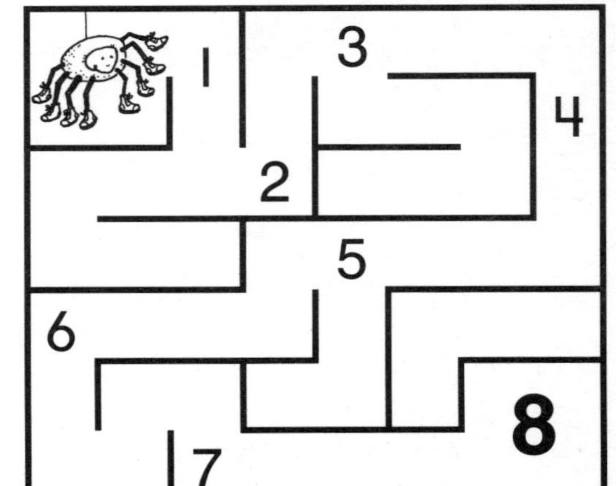

Name ____________________

MATCHING NUMBERS WITH NUMERALS

School Supplies

Cut out the number word cards. Count the school supplies.
Glue the correct number word card in each box.

1	2	3
4	**5**	**6**

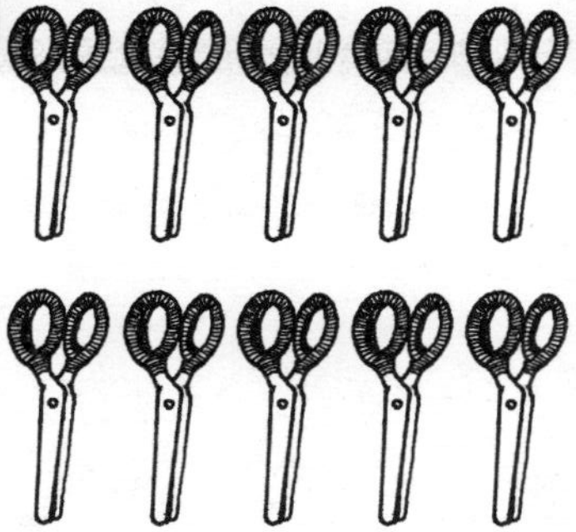

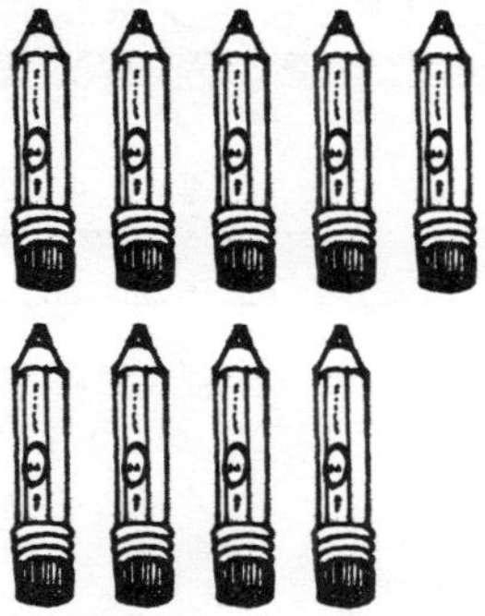

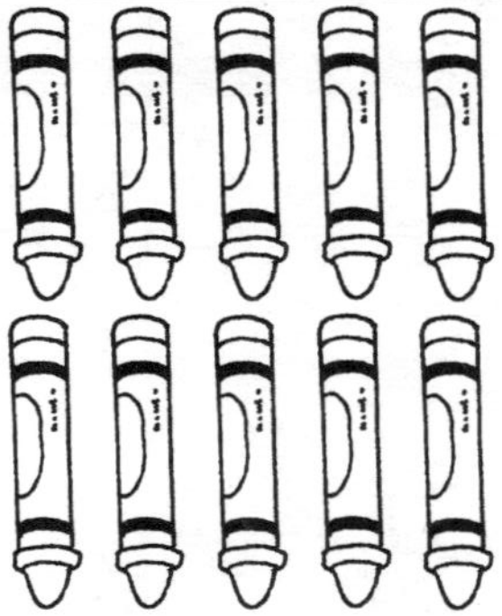

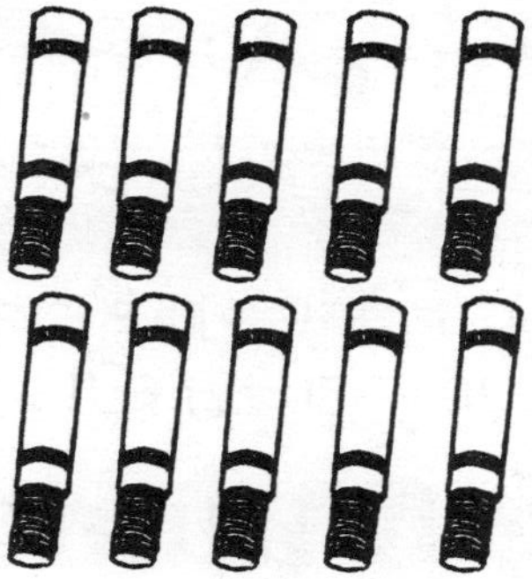

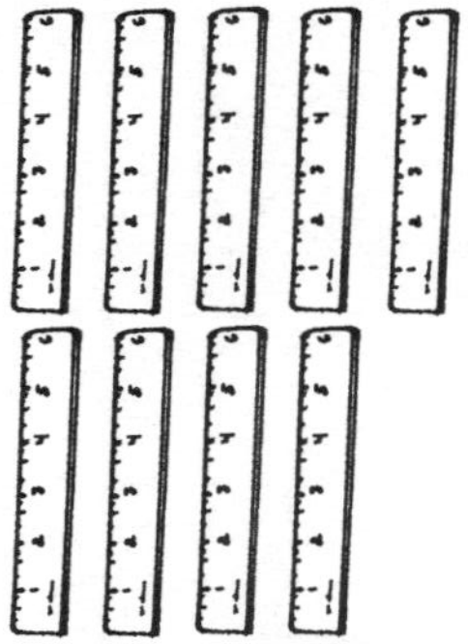

Trace each number word.

nine

nine

ten

ten

What do you have ten of?

____

nine	ten
nine	ten
nine	ten

Math Mat 133

Name ____________________

MATCHING ARRAYS WITH NUMERALS

Counting Books

Count the books. Use the words in the Word Bank to write the number on the line.

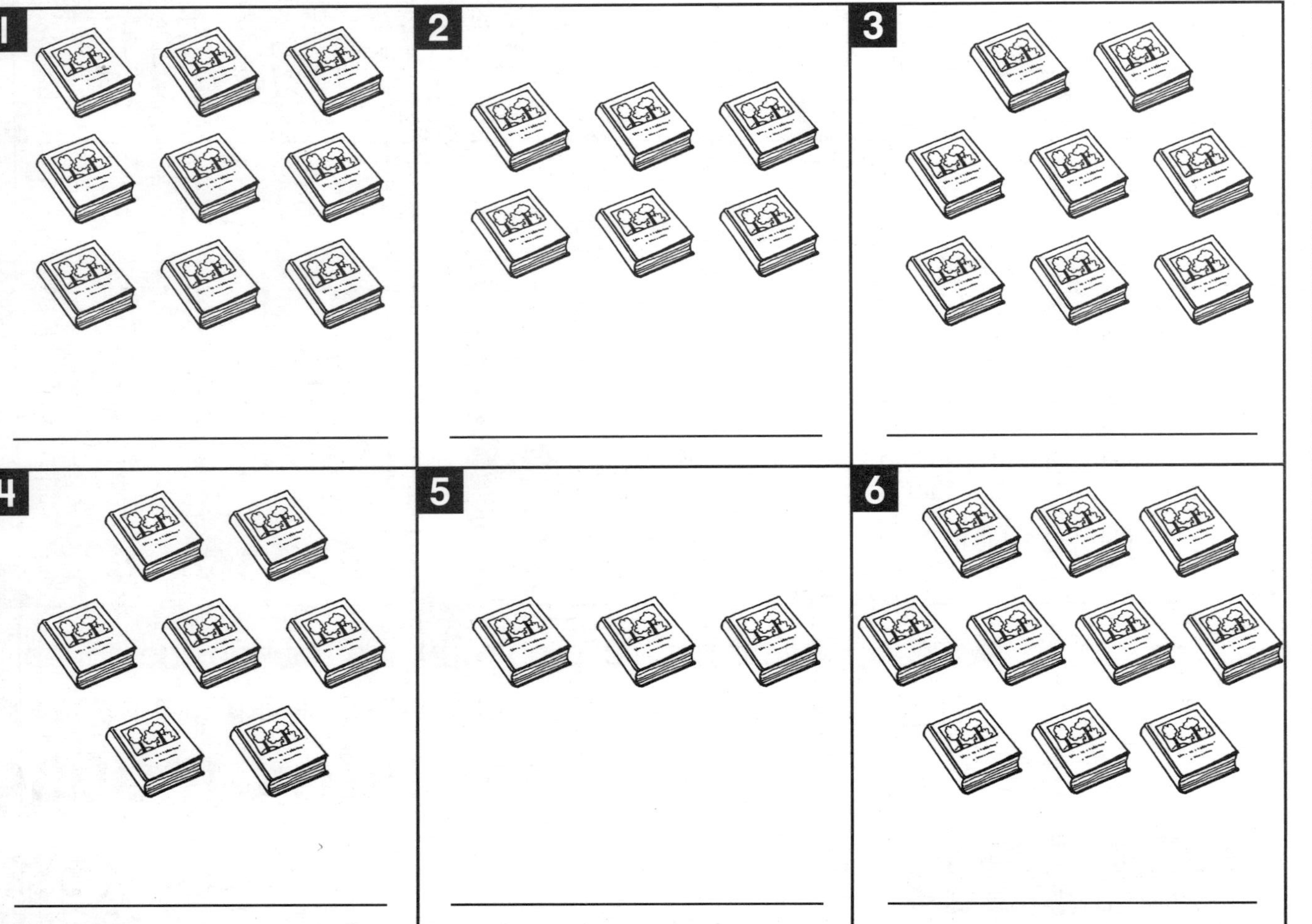

Word Bank

nine	seven	six
ten	three	eight

Trace each number word.

zero

zero

Word Problem

Ben read 2 books.
Jen read 3 books.
How many books did Ben and Jen read in all?

$2 + 3 =$ ______

Name ____________________

MATCHING ARRAYS WITH NUMERALS

Mice Count

Count the number of mice. Circle the answer.

1	2	3
11 12	11 12	11 12

4	5	6
11 12	11 12	11 12

Trace each number word.

eleven

eleven

twelve

twelve

Color the words **eleven** and **twelve** in the word search.

T W E L V E V K N
E L E V E N A Z O
N F V T W E L V E
R T W E L V E F V
E L E V E N H I D
V T W E L V E S P
O B D E L E V E N

Math Mat 135 Name ____________

FINDING THE MISSING ADDEND

Seeing Stars

Draw more stars to make each number. Complete the math problem.

1 ☆☆☆☆ 4 + ____ = 13	2 ☆☆☆☆☆☆☆ 7 + ____ = 14	3 ☆☆☆☆☆ 5 + ____ = 13
4 ☆☆☆ 3 + ____ = 13	5 ☆☆☆☆☆☆☆☆☆ 9 + ____ = 14	6 ☆☆ 2 + ____ = 14

Trace each number word.

thirteen

thirteen

fourteen

fourteen

Mystery Number

Read the clues to find the mystery number. The number line will help you.

1 2 3 4 5 6 7 8 9 10 11 12 13 14 15

- It's greater than 5.
- It's less than 12.
- When you count by 3s, you say its name.
- It's an odd number.

Mystery number: ____

Name ______________ **REPRESENTING NUMBERS**

Pennies

Count the pennies. Write how many cents.

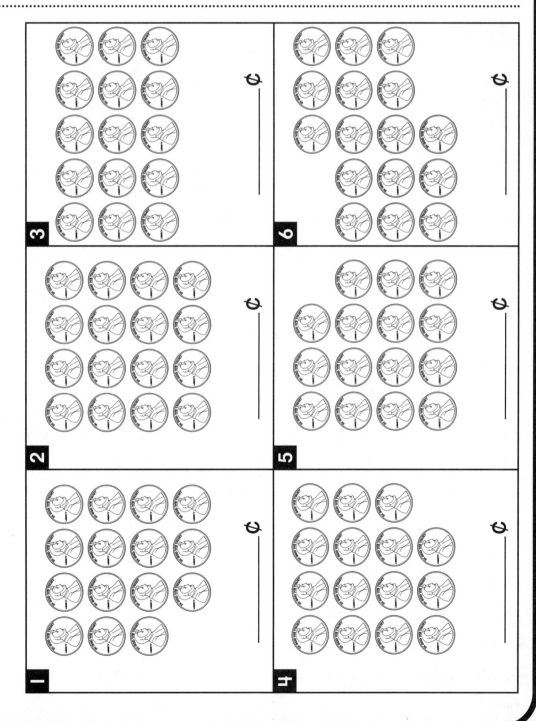

1 ________¢

2 ________¢

3 ________¢

4 ________¢

5 ________¢

6 ________¢

Trace each number word.

fifteen

fifteen

sixteen

sixteen

Lisa has 8 pennies in one pocket and 7 pennies in another pocket. How many pennies does Lisa have in all?

____

Name ______________________

COUNTING ITEMS IN AN ARRAY

Pet Math

Read and solve each word problem.

1

Vivian had 9 mice. She bought 8 more mice. How many mice does Vivian have?

Vivian has ________ mice in all.

2

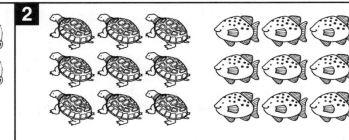

Charlie has 9 turtles and 9 fish. How many pets does Charlie have in all?

Charlie has ________ pets in all.

3

Chester saw 10 cats in the morning and 8 cats in the afternoon. How many cats did Chester see in all?

Chester saw ________ cats in all.

4

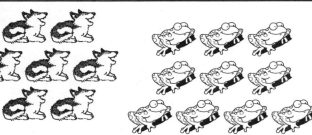

Molly has 7 dogs and 10 frogs. How many pets does Molly have in all?

Molly has ________ pets in all.

Trace each number word.

seventeen

seventeen

eighteen

eighteen

To find how many pets Molly and Charlie have in all, do you need to add or subtract? Circle one.

add   subtract

Math Mat 138

Name ____________

SEQUENCING NUMERALS

Missing Numbers

Write the missing numbers in each row.

1 1, ____, 3, 4, ____, 6, 7, 8, ____, 10, 11

2 11, 12, ____, 14, 15, ____, 17, ____, 19

3 10, ____, ____, ____, 14, ____, ____, 17

Write the number that comes **before**.

4 ____, 6 ____, 14 ____, 10

Write the number that comes **after**.

5 7, ____ 11, ____ 15, ____

Write the number that comes **between**.

6 3, ____, 5 8, ____, 10 16, ____, 18

Trace each number word.

nineteen

nineteen

twenty

twenty

Find and circle each number word.

fourteen	fifteen
twenty	seventeen
eighteen	nineteen

S E V E N T E E N
E I G H T E E N K
N I N E T E E N H
F O U R T E E N A
C T W E N T Y R B
A F I F T E E N P

Math Mat 139 Name ____________________

MATCHING NUMBERS AND NUMERALS

Teddy-ominoes

Cut out the teddy bear cards and place them faceup in order 1 to 12.

Spin the spinner 12 times. After each spin, turn over the matching teddy bear card.

Were you able to turn over all of the teddy bear cards?

Use a paper clip as the spinner and a pencil to hold the spinner in place.

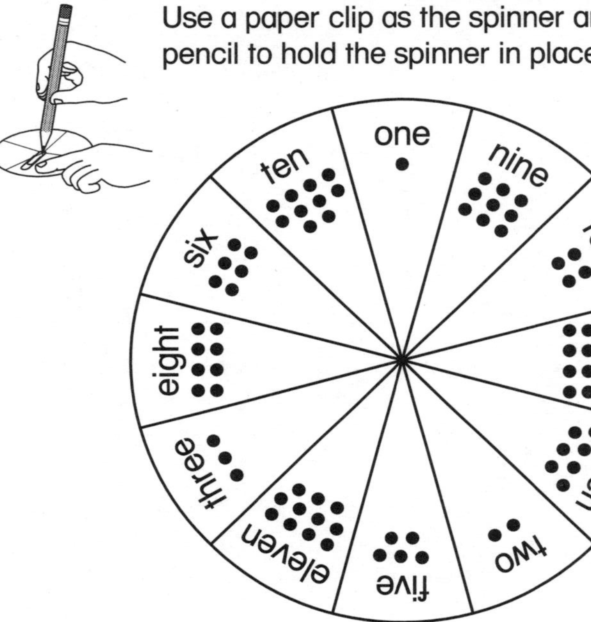

Extension Idea

Play the game with a partner. The first player to turn over all 12 teddy bear cards wins the game!

Name ______________________

RECOGNIZING NUMERALS

Partners Bingo

1. Play with a partner. Each partner gets a game board and writes the numbers 1 to 16 randomly in the boxes.
2. Cut out the numbers on the side of the page. Shuffle the cards and place them in a stack facedown.
3. Taking turns, turn over the top card and say the number. Both players use a crayon to color the number on their game boards. The first player to color 4 numbers in a row (vertically, horizontally, or diagonally) wins the game.
4. After playing, glue the number cards in order on the back of this page.

1	2
3	4
5	6
7	8
9	10
11	12
13	14
15	16

Name ____________________

Naming Shapes

1 Draw a line matching each shape to its name.

triangle

circle

square

rectangle

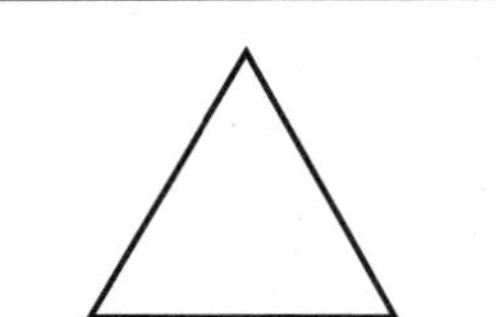

2 Make an **X** on the shape that does not belong in the row.

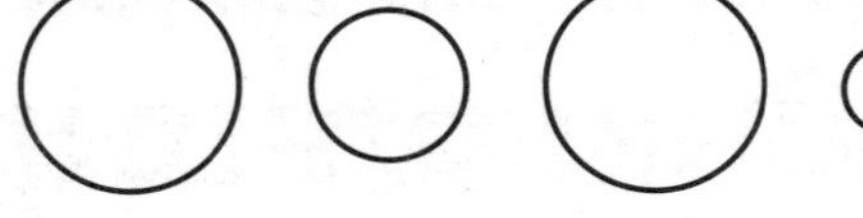

3 Why doesn't the shape belong in the row? Use the back of this paper to write your answer.

Circle the answer.

4 Which shape looks like a balloon?

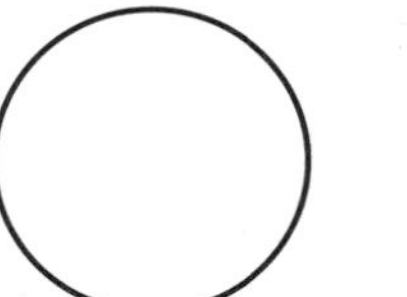

5 Which shape has four corners?

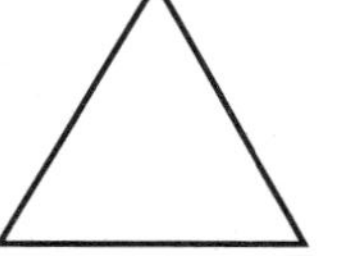

6 Which shape looks like an egg?

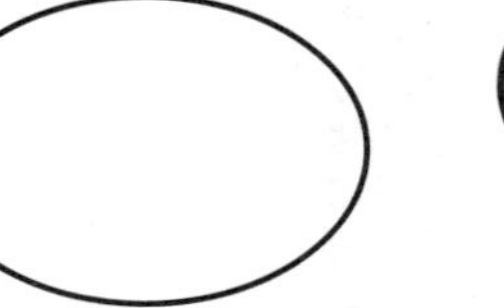

7 Draw your favorite shape.

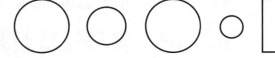

Name ____________________

IDENTIFYING PATTERNS

What Comes Next?

Cut out the shapes. Use the shapes to complete each pattern.

1

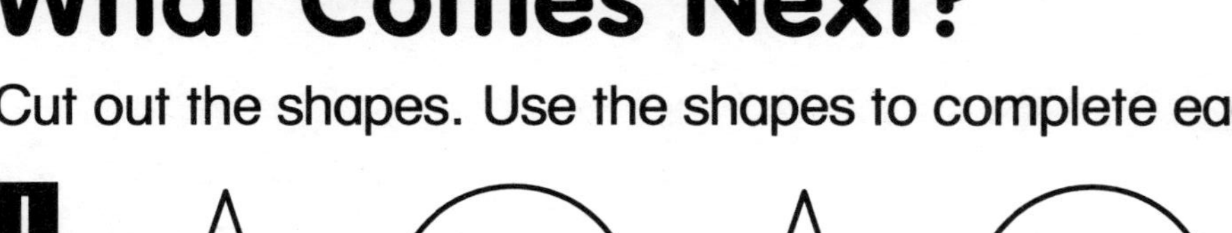

2

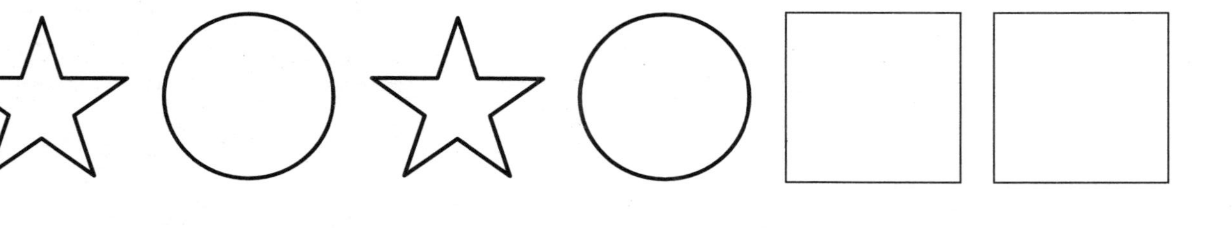

3

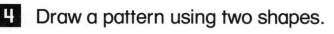

4 Draw a pattern using two shapes.

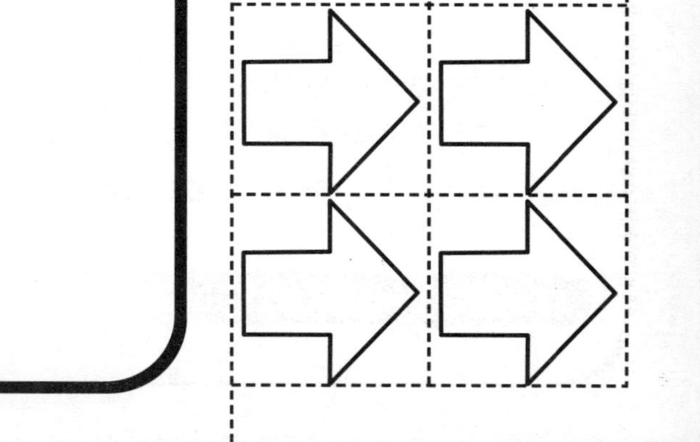

Name ______________________

Button Patterns

Finish labeling each pattern.

1

A B A B ___ ___

2

A A B A ___ ___

3

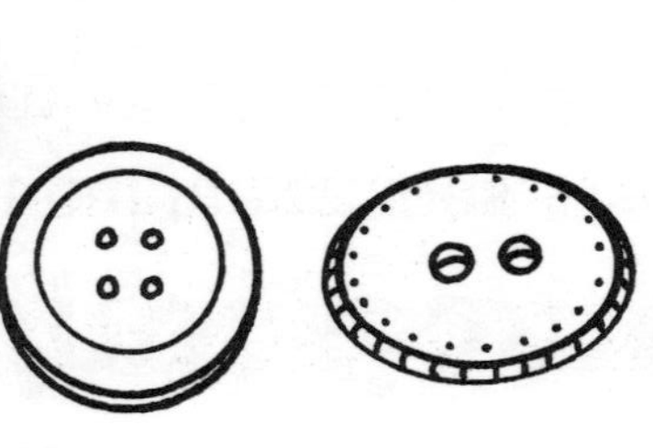      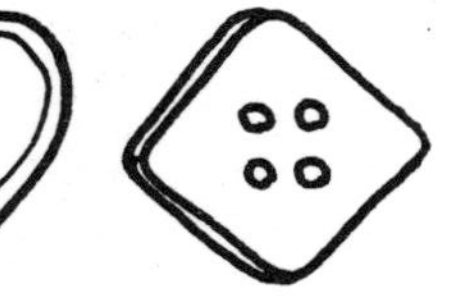  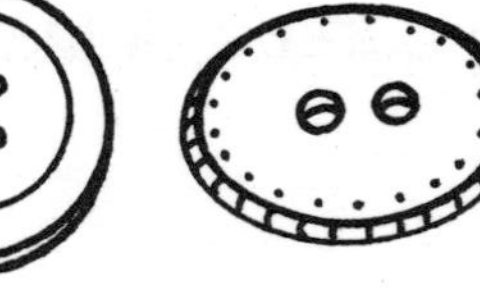 

A B C A ___ ___

Look at each pattern. What kind of pattern is it? Circle the answer.

4

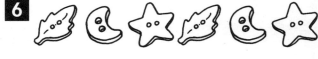

AAB **AB**

5

ABC **ABB**

6

ABC **ABBC**

Make an AABC pattern using your favorite button shapes.

Name ______________________

IDENTIFYING PATTERNS

Seeing Patterns

Use numbers to label each pattern. Always begin numbering each pattern with the number 1.

1

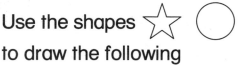

1 2 3 ___ ___ ___ ___ ___ ___

2

___ ___ ___ ___ ___ ___ ___ ___ ___

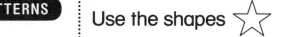

3

___ ___ ___ ___ ___ ___ ___ ___ ___

Use the shapes 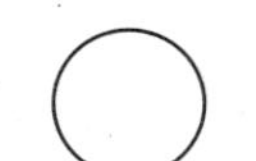 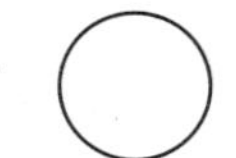 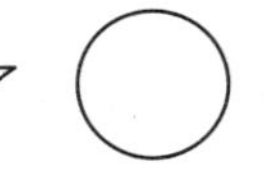 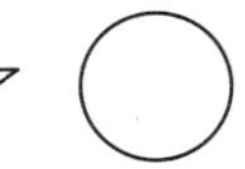   to draw the following patterns below.

4 **12** pattern

5 **1122** pattern

Math Mat 145 Name ____________________

IDENTIFYING ATTRIBUTES

Shapes, Sides, and Corners

Complete the sentences about shapes.

1

This is a ____________________.

This shape has ________ sides.

This shape has ________ corners.

2

This is a ____________________.

This shape has ________ sides.

This shape has ________ corners.

3

This is a ____________________.

This shape has ________ sides.

This shape has ________ corners.

4

This is a ____________________.

This shape has ________ sides.

This shape has ________ corners.

Follow the directions.

5 Draw a square. Then draw a line through it to divide it in half to make two rectangles.

6 Draw a square. Then draw a line through it to divide it in half to make two triangles.

7 Draw a diamond. Then draw a line through it to divide it in half to make two triangles.

Math Mat 146 Name ____________ SORTING BY ATTRIBUTE

Seeing Shapes

Cut out the shapes. Record the different ways the shapes can be sorted. Glue the shapes down to show your favorite way.

How many of these shapes have only straight lines? ______

What is your favorite way to sort the shapes?
Use the back of this paper to write your answer.

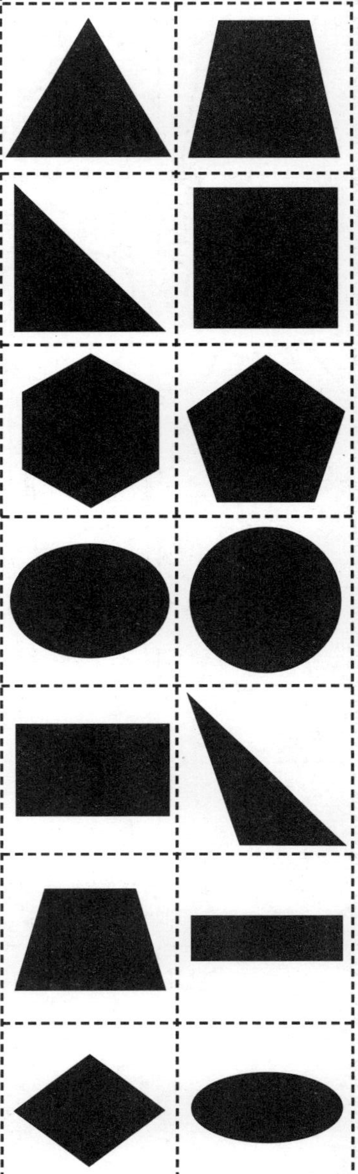

Math Mat 147 Name ____________ CATEGORIZING OBJECTS

Sorting Shapes

Cut out each shape and place it in the correct category.

Sphere	Cone

Cube	Cylinder

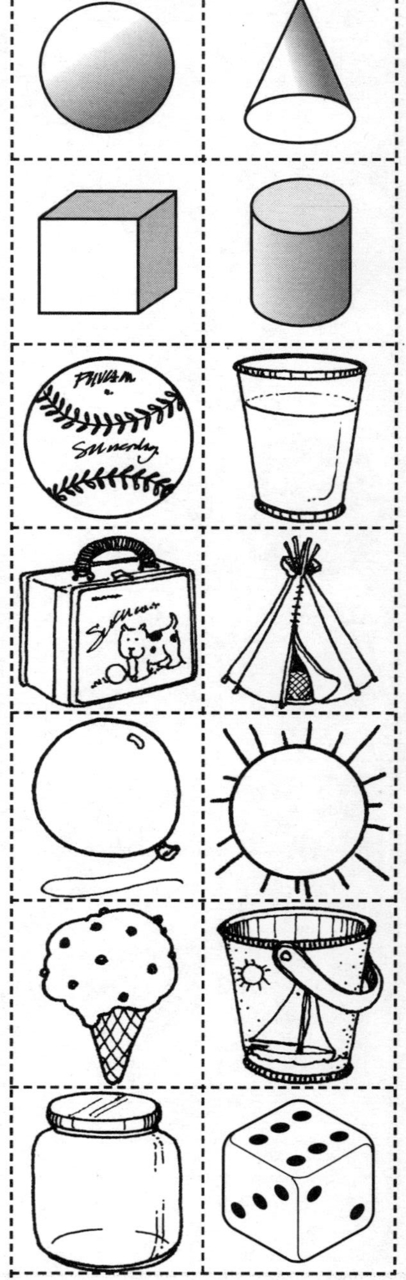

Name ______________________

IDENTIFYING SYMMETRICAL HALVES

Shape Symmetry

Symmetry is when both pieces of an item are the same size and the same shape. Look at each item and decide if it is symmetrical. Circle **yes** or **no**.

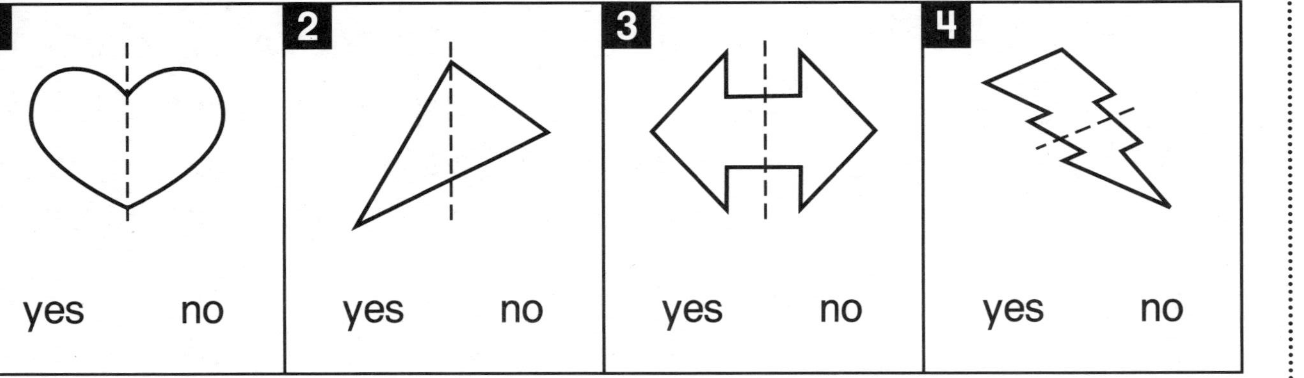

Draw a line to divide each shape into two symmetrical parts.

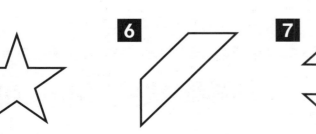

5 6 7 8

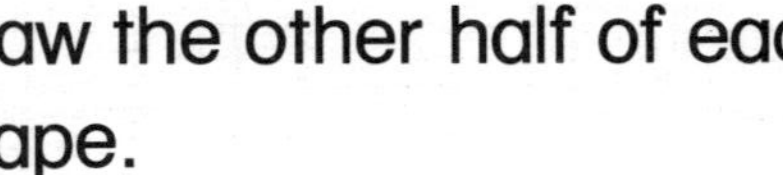

Draw the other half of each shape.

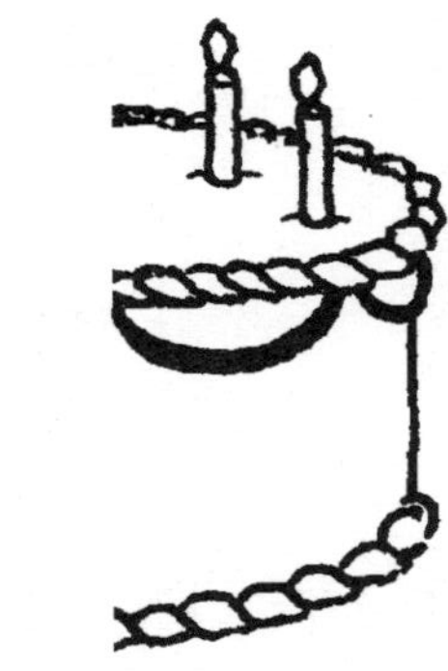

Math Mat 149 Name ____________

IDENTIFYING SIMPLE FRACTIONS

Dividing Shapes

Draw a line dividing each shape in two equal halves.

1 

2 

3 

4 

A fraction tells the number of parts in a whole object. The fraction $\frac{1}{3}$ says there are 3 parts and 1 part is used or needed.

Each shape has 3 equal parts.
Color $\frac{1}{3}$ of each shape.

5 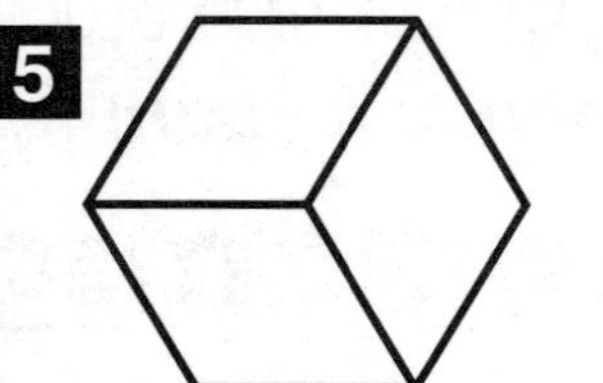

6 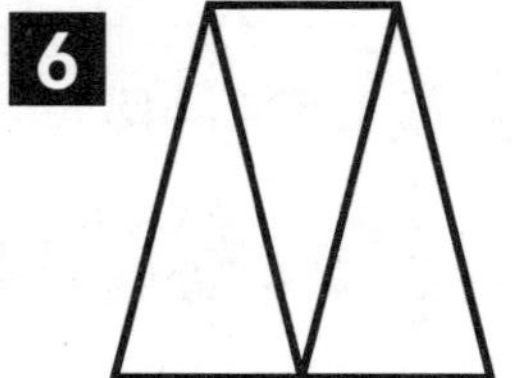

7 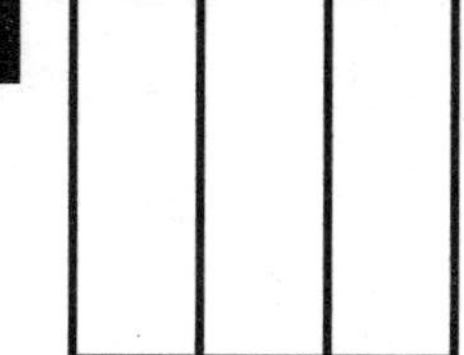

8 

What's the fraction?

9 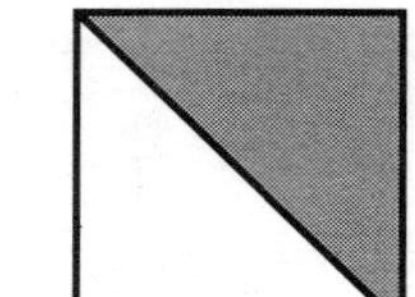

How many parts are shaded? ______

How many parts are there in all? ______

Circle the fraction.

$\frac{1}{3}$ $\frac{1}{2}$

10 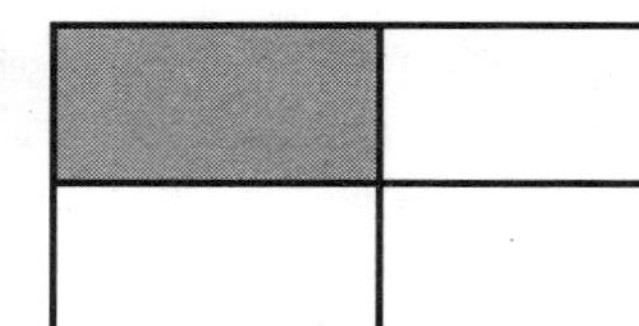

How many parts are shaded? ______

How many parts are there in all? ______

Circle the fraction.

$\frac{1}{4}$ $\frac{1}{3}$

Name ____________________

WRITING SIMPLE FRACTIONS

Fraction Fun

Write the fraction shaded for each shape.

1 

$\frac{\quad}{3}$

2 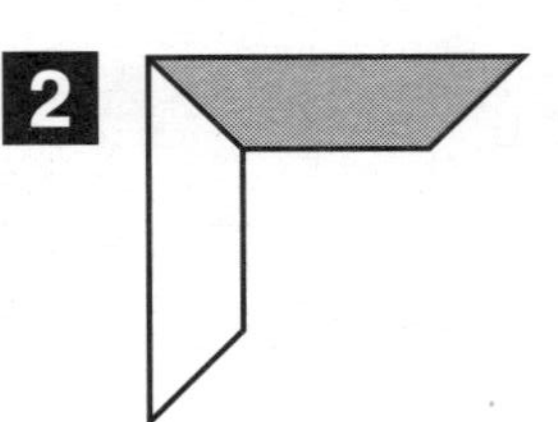

$\frac{\quad}{2}$

3 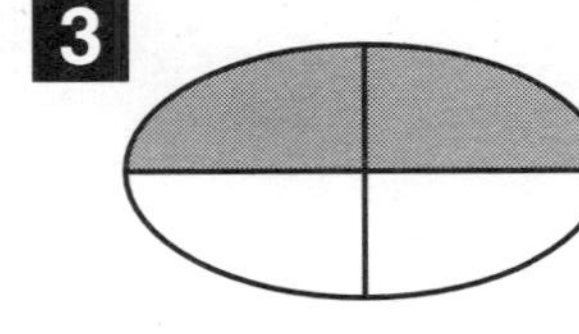

$\frac{\quad}{4}$

4 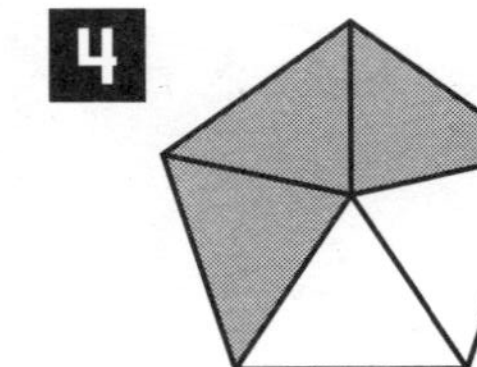

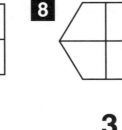

$\frac{\quad}{5}$

Color the shape to show the fraction.

5 

$\frac{1}{2}$

6 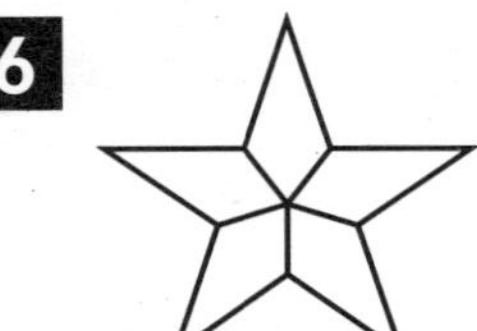

$\frac{1}{5}$

7 

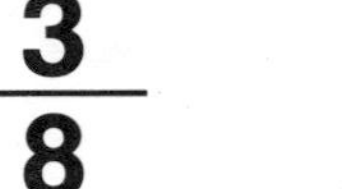

$\frac{3}{8}$

8 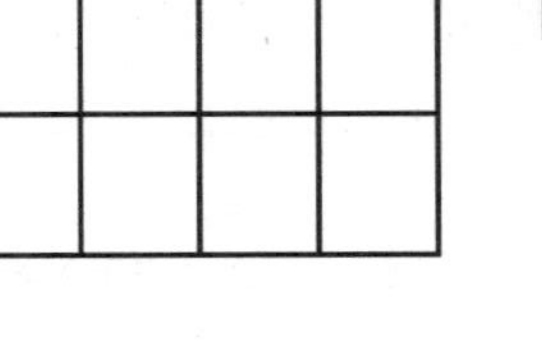

$\frac{3}{4}$

Fraction Tips

numerator: The top number of a fraction. It tells how many parts are shaded.

denominator: The bottom number of a fraction. It tells the total number of parts.

$\frac{3}{4}$ numerator / denominator

Draw a square around the shape that shows $\frac{3}{6}$.

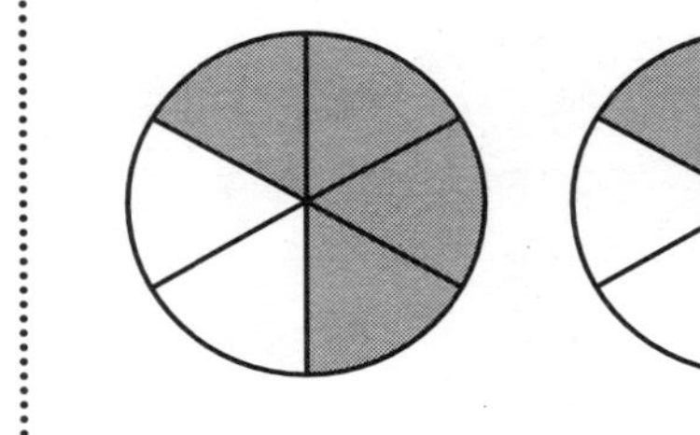

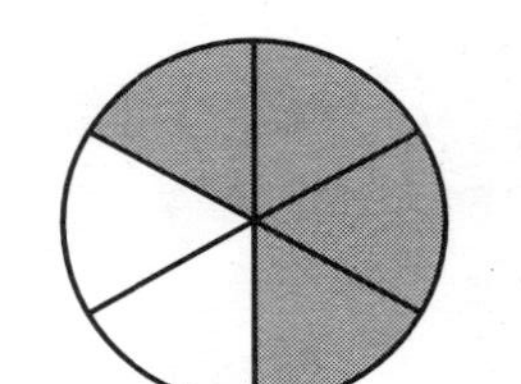

Math Mat 151 Name ______________ IDENTIFYING SETS

How Many Tens and Ones?

Circle sets of 10 fish. Record the number of tens and ones.

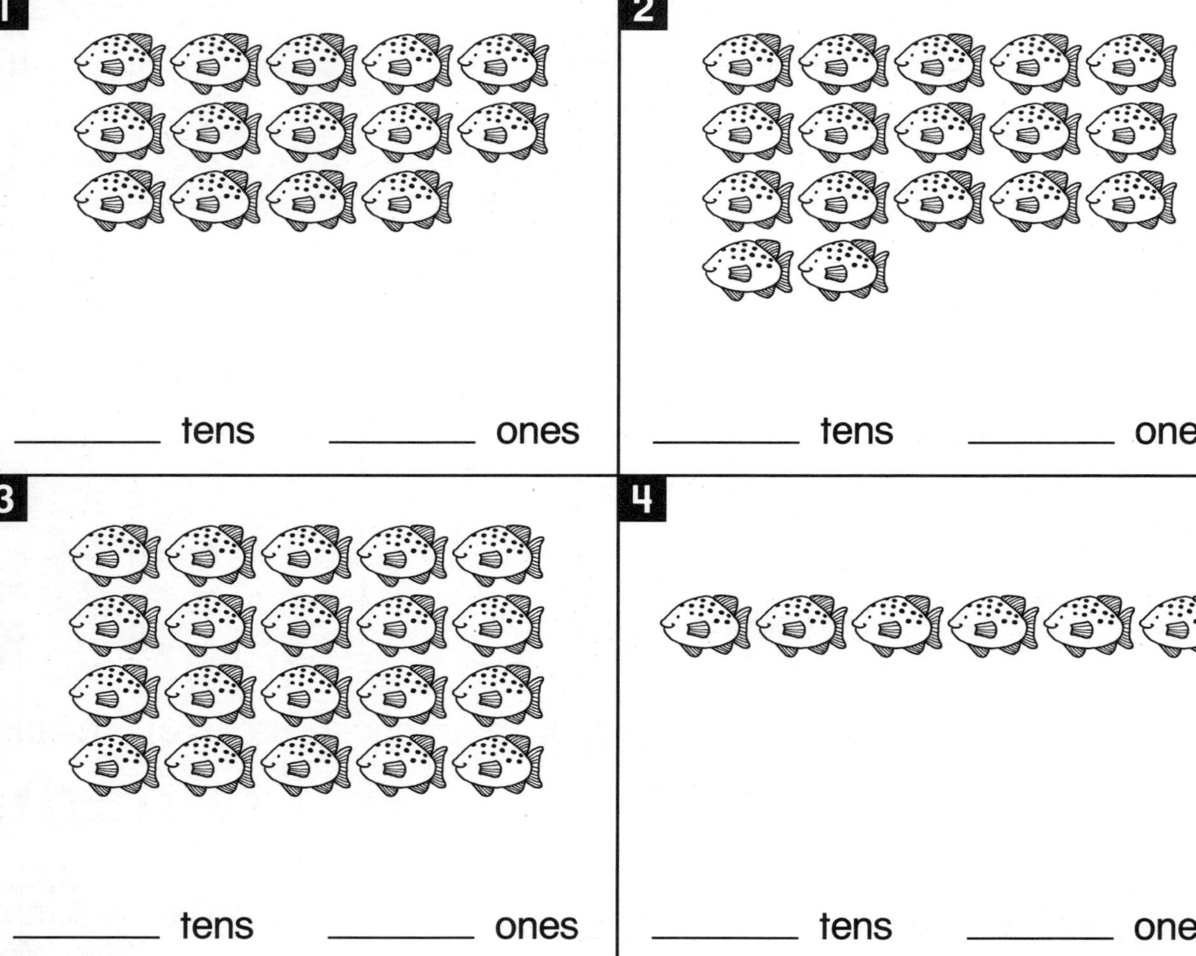

1 ______ tens ______ ones

2 ______ tens ______ ones

3 ______ tens ______ ones

4 ______ tens ______ ones

Circle the numbers. Then write the place value of each number (**tens** or **ones**) on the line.

5 Circle the 2s.

9(2) ones

21 ______

6 Circle the 5s.

56 ______

85 ______

7 Circle the 1s.

10 ______

31 ______

8 Circle the 8s.

84 ______

48 ______

Name ______________________

IDENTIFYING PLACE VALUE

Apples

Cut out the apples. Use the apples to show each number.

I apple = I one
I basket = I ten

1 36	**2** 25	**3** 3
4 84	**5** 48	**6** 57
7 92	**8** 69	**9** 70

Name ____________

IDENTIFYING NUMERICAL ORDER

Who Is My Neighbor?

Use the hundreds board to figure out each number's neighbors.

↑Up

←Left

1	2	3	4	5	6	7	8	9	10
11	12	13	14	15	16	17	18	19	20
21	22	23	24	25	26	27	28	29	30
31	32	33	34	35	36	37	38	39	40
41	42	43	44	45	46	47	48	49	50
51	52	53	54	55	56	57	58	59	60
61	62	63	64	65	66	67	68	69	70
71	72	73	74	75	76	77	78	79	80
81	82	83	84	85	86	87	88	89	90
91	92	93	94	95	96	97	98	99	100

Right→

↓Down

		Left	Right
	19	18	20
1	44	____	____
2	87	____	____
3	56	____	____
4	23	____	____
5	68	____	____
6	75	____	____

Find the Mystery Number

7 Start at 10.
Go down 3 spaces.
Go to the left 5 spaces.
What is the
mystery number? ________

8 Start at 56.
Go up 2 spaces.
Go to the right 2 spaces
What is the
mystery number? ________

Name ______________________ FOLLOWING DIRECTIONS

Find the Mystery Number!

Read the clues and color the numbers.

- Color the numbers that are used when counting by 5s.
- Color the numbers that have a 1 or a 2 as a digit.
- Color the numbers that are used when counting by 2s.
- Color all the numbers that **don't** have two digits that are the same.

1	2	3	4	5	6	7	8	9	10
11	12	13	14	15	16	17	18	19	20
21	22	23	24	25	26	27	28	29	30
31	32	33	34	35	36	37	38	39	40
41	42	43	44	45	46	47	48	49	50

The mystery number is ______________.

What's the Rule?

Look at each set of numbers and write the rule the pattern follows.

Example:

2, 12, 32, 22, 42, 62

They all have a 2 in the ones place.

1 11, 22, 33, 44, 55, 66

____

2 10, 20, 30, 40, 50

____

3 2, 4, 6, 8, 10, 12, 14

____

4 10, 11, 12, 13, 14, 15

____

Name ____________

SUBTRACTING WITH DOUBLE DIGITS

How Many Miles?

Find the difference (subtract) driving from one town to the next.

Miles to the Next City	
Hudson	21 miles
Irvington	34 miles
Bayport	46 miles
York	59 miles

1 Irvington to Hudson

34 miles to Irvington
− 21 miles to Hudson
13 miles

2 Bayport to Hudson

3 York to Hudson

4 Bayport to Irvington

5 York to Irvington

6 York to Bayport

7 What was the longest distance from one town to another town?

____

8 What was the shortest distance from one town to another town?

____

9 What is the name of your town?

____

Name ______________________

FINDING MISSING ADDENDS

The Garden Shop's Inventory

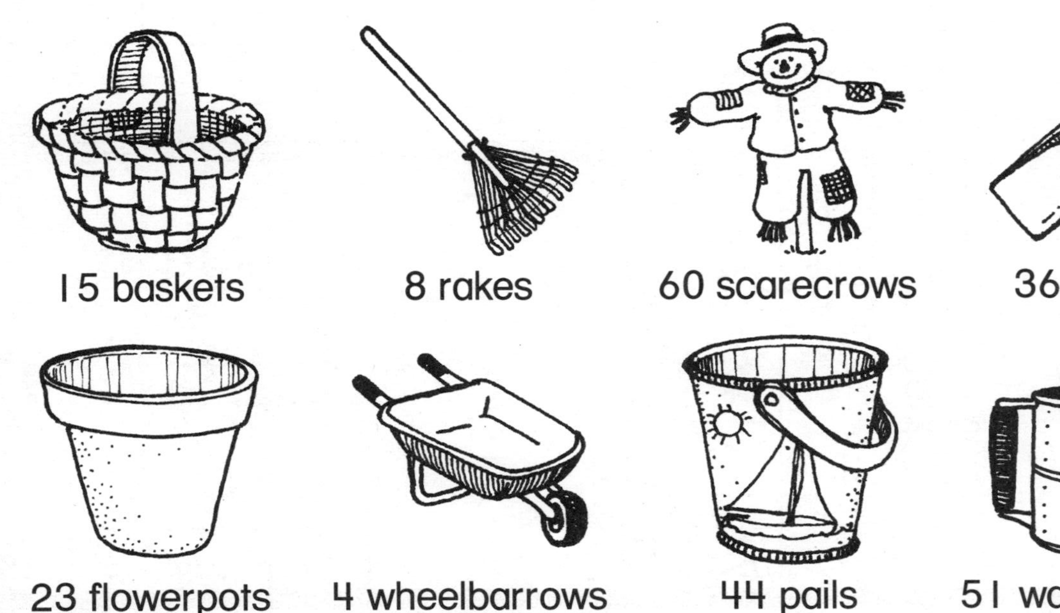

Use the information from the box above to solve each word problem.

1 Norma counted the rakes and the baskets. How many items did Norma count?

Norma counted ______ items.

2 John counted the shovels and the scarecrows. How many items did John count?

John counted ______ items.

Solve each problem.

3

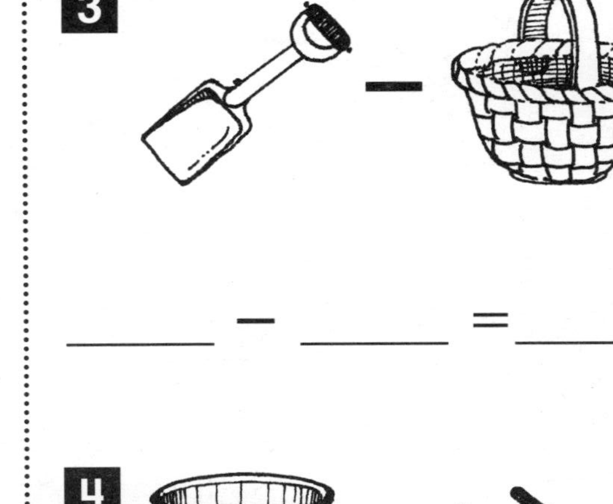

______ − ______ = ______

4

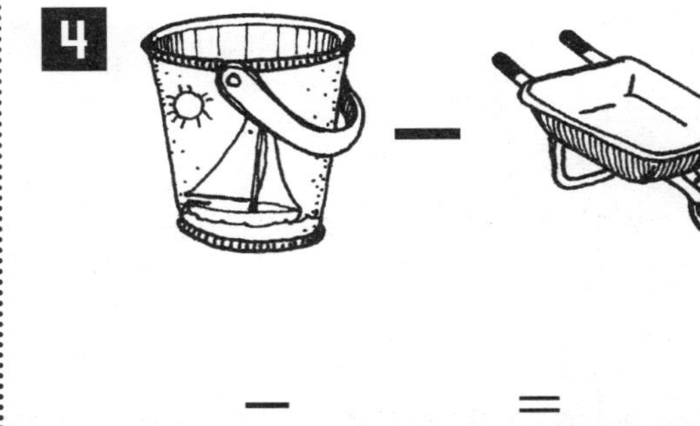

______ − ______ = ______

5

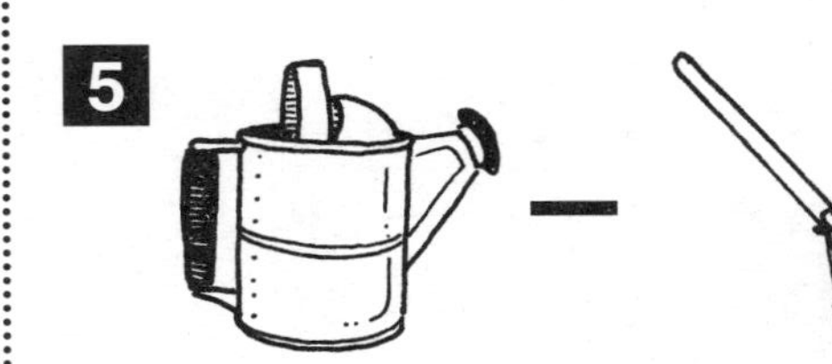

______ − ______ = ______

Math Mat 157 Name ____________________

Hundreds Puzzles

Write the missing numbers.

1

1	2	3
11		13
21	22	23

2

8	9	10
18	19	20
28	29	

3

53	54	
		65
73	74	

Cut out the pieces to the puzzle.
On a separate sheet of paper
put the puzzle together.

	84	74			
	85	75			
	86	76		56	46
97	87	77	67	57	47
98	88	78	68	58	48

61	62	63	64	65	66
71	72	73			
81	82	83			
91	92	93	94	95	96

10	20	30	40
9	19	29	39
8	18	28	38
7	17	27	37
6	16	26	
	15		

			24	25	
	32	33	34	35	36
41	42	43	44	45	
51	52	53	54	55	

5			
4	14		
3	13	23	
2	12	22	
1	11	21	31

49	50
59	60
69	70
79	80
89	90
99	100

Name ____________________

REPRESENTING PLACE VALUE

Grape Going!

Cut out the grapes and sort them into three groups of ones, tens, and hundreds. Use the grapes to show each number.

 		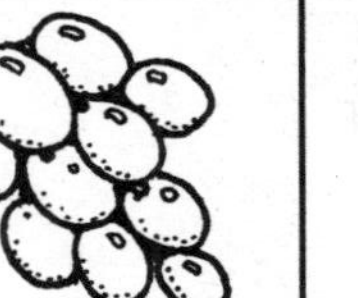
1 grape = 1 one	10 grapes = 1 ten	100 grapes = 1 hundred

1 326	3 401
2 247	4 734

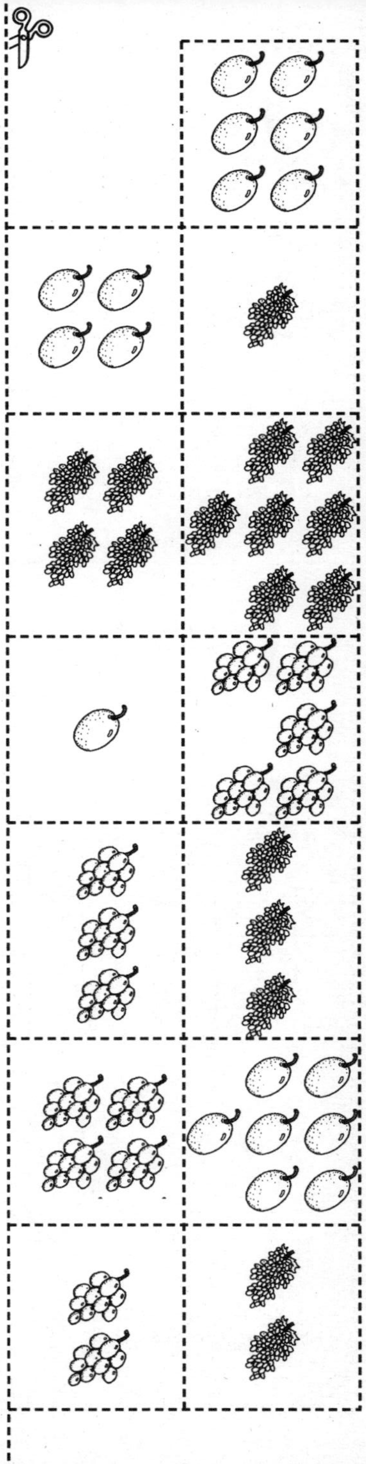

Name ______________________________

ASSIGNING PLACE VALUE

Making Numbers

Cut out the numbers, shuffle them, and place them in a stack facedown. Turn over the top three cards and use them to complete a problem. Glue them in place. Repeat three times.

Make the largest number.

Make the smallest number.

Make an odd number.

Make an even number.

Write the numbers above in order, smallest to largest.

__________, __________, __________, __________

1	2
3	4
5	6
7	8
9	1
2	3
4	5
6	7

Math Mat 160

Name ____________________

USING DEDUCTIVE REASONING

Number Hunt

Read and follow the clues to discover the mystery number.

1	2	3	4	5	6	7	8	9	10
11	12	13	14	15	16	17	18	19	20
21	22	23	24	25	26	27	28	29	30
31	32	33	34	35	36	37	38	39	40
41	42	43	44	45	46	47	48	49	50
51	52	53	54	55	56	57	58	59	60
61	62	63	64	65	66	67	68	69	70
71	72	73	74	75	76	77	78	79	80
81	82	83	84	85	86	87	88	89	90
91	92	93	94	95	96	97	98	99	100

Clues

- I am a 2-digit number.
- I do not have a 2, 3, or 4 as a digit.
- When counting by 2s, my name is said.
- I have a 6 in the ones place.
- When my 2 digits are added together, the answer is less than 10.

1 Write the mystery number

____

2 Write the number that is 10 more than my number.

____

3 Write the number that is 10 less than my number.

____

Math Mat 161 Name ______________ **EXPRESSING COMPARISON**

Using Symbols

Write the > (greater than) or < (less than) symbol in the circle.

1 438 ◯ 740

2 164 ◯ 511

3 275 ◯ 952

4 893 ◯ 329

Circle the largest digit (number).
Write its place (ones, tens, or hundreds) on the line.

5 438 ______________

6 607 ______________

7 511 ______________

8 164 ______________

9 740 ______________

10 680 ______________

11 Divide the footballs into 2 equal sets.

How many footballs are in each set?

____

12 Divide the basketballs into 3 equal sets.

How many basketballs are in each set?

____

Bonus: Each football is what fraction of the set?

$\frac{1}{5}$ $\frac{1}{4}$

Math Mat 162 Name ________

Making Numbers

Cut out the numbers. Place each set of numbers in the boxes to make the different number combinations.

1 Numbers: 1, 2, 3

Largest number: ________
Smallest number: ________
An odd number: ________
An even number: ________

2 Numbers: 4, 6, 7

Largest number: ________
Smallest number: ________
An odd number: ________
An even number: ________

3 Numbers: 2, 5, 8

Largest number: ________
Smallest number: ________
An odd number: ________
An even number: ________

4 Numbers: 1, 4, 9

Largest number: ________
Smallest number: ________
An odd number: ________
An even number: ________

5 Largest number using 2, 4, 6: ________

6 Smallest number using 3, 5, 9: ________

7 Odd number using 2, 6, 7: ________

8 Even number using 4, 3, 8: ________

1 2 3 4 5 6 7 8 9

Name ____________________

Magic Number

Read and follow the clues to discover the magic number.

1	2	3	4	5	6	7	8	9	10
11	12	13	14	15	16	17	18	19	20
21	22	23	24	25	26	27	28	29	30
31	32	33	34	35	36	37	38	39	40
41	42	43	44	45	46	47	48	49	50
51	52	53	54	55	56	57	58	59	60
61	62	63	64	65	66	67	68	69	70
71	72	73	74	75	76	77	78	79	80
81	82	83	84	85	86	87	88	89	90
91	92	93	94	95	96	97	98	99	100

Clues

- I am a 2-digit number.
- I do not have a 1 or a 3 as a digit.
- I have one odd number and one even number.
- When my 2 digits are added together, they equal 11.
- I have an odd number in the tens place.
- When the number in the ones place is subtracted from the number in the tens place, the answer is 7.

1 Write the magic number.

____

2 Write the number that is 20 more than my number.

____

Math Mat 164

Name ________________

ADDING THREE-DIGIT NUMBERS

Adding Large Numbers

Solve each problem. Remember to start in the ones column.

1
```
  325
+ 241
-----
```

2
```
  607
+ 180
-----
```

3
```
  534
+ 245
-----
```

4
```
  800
+ 117
-----
```

5
```
  750
+ 203
-----
```

6
```
  811
+ 160
-----
```

7
```
  466
+ 300
-----
```

8
```
  189
+ 410
-----
```

9
```
  277
+ 422
-----
```

Complete the pattern.

100, 200, ______, 400, ______, ______, 700, ______, ______, 1,000

Find and color each word.

ones	hundreds
tens	thousand
place	value
add	equal
subtract	sum

```
O H T O F T P V K E
N V A L U E L A Z Q
E N F V Q R A F V U
S T T I Y H C I D A
S P E T G D E A T L
W F N D O A C L H T
B L S F S H L G O P
H U N D R E D S U E
S Y E I E Z L Z S C
L A D D Y B X H A S
F Q P L M P Q W N U
S U B T R A C T D M
```

Name ____________________

What's the Secret Number?

Read and follow the clues to discover the secret number.

1	2	3	4	5	6	7	8	9	10
11	12	13	14	15	16	17	18	19	20
21	22	23	24	25	26	27	28	29	30
31	32	33	34	35	36	37	38	39	40
41	42	43	44	45	46	47	48	49	50
51	52	53	54	55	56	57	58	59	60
61	62	63	64	65	66	67	68	69	70
71	72	73	74	75	76	77	78	79	80
81	82	83	84	85	86	87	88	89	90
91	92	93	94	95	96	97	98	99	100

Clues

- Color all the numbers with two even digits.
- Color all the numbers with two digits that are the same.
- Color all the numbers with a digit greater than 6.
- Color all the numbers with two digits that add up to 6. (Example: 15: 1 + 5=6)
- Color all the numbers greater than 50.
- Color all the numbers less than 35.
- Color all the numbers with two odd digits.
- Color all the digits with an odd number in the ones place.
- Color all the numbers not used when counting by 5s.
- Color the smaller number.

What is the secret number?

____

Name ____________

SUBTRACTING THREE-DIGIT NUMBERS

Subtracting Large Numbers

Solve each problem. Remember to start in the ones column.

1
```
  876
- 305
-----
```

2
```
  422
- 222
-----
```

3
```
  658
- 528
-----
```

4
```
  259
- 148
-----
```

5
```
  754
- 233
-----
```

6
```
  437
- 216
-----
```

7
```
  599
- 397
-----
```

8
```
  300
- 200
-----
```

9
```
  981
- 800
-----
```

Draw a line matching each number to its number word.

3 tens	10
4 hundreds	60
1 ten	5,000
2 thousands	400
6 tens	80
5 thousands	700
7 hundreds	30
8 tens	2,000

Write your favorite three-digit number.

____

Math Mat 167 Name ____________

IDENTIFYING HOURS AND MINUTES

The Hands of a Clock

Cut out the hour hand and minute hand and fasten them to the face of the clock with a paper fastener. With a partner, take turns moving the hands and telling the time

The hour hand points to the hour. Write the hour shown on each clock.

1

____:00

2

____:00

3

____:00

4

____:00

Minute Hand

Hour Hand

Name ______________________

READING CLOCKFACES

Telling Time

Write the time shown on each clock on the line.

1	2	3	4
___:___ ___	___ ___:___ ___	___:___ ___	___:___ ___

5	6	7	8
___:___ ___	___ ___:___ ___	___:___ ___	___:___ ___

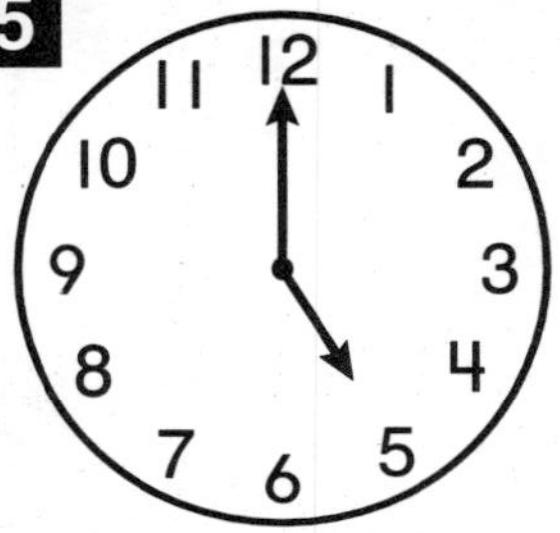

Write the times in order from earliest to latest, starting at 1:00.

______, ______, ______, ______, ______, ______, ______, ______

Draw the hands on each clock to show the time you do each activity.

I get up each morning at

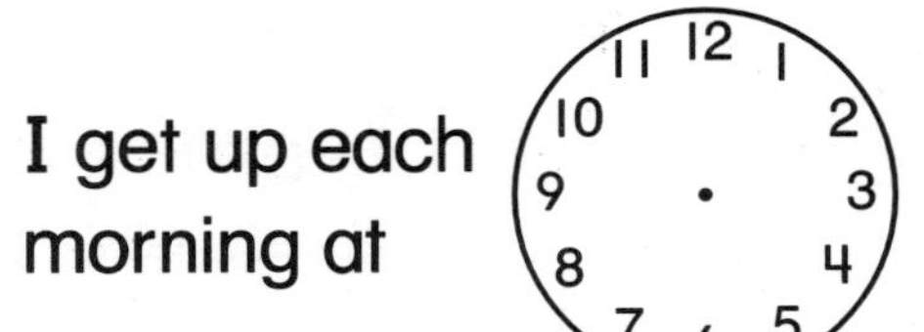

I eat breakfast at

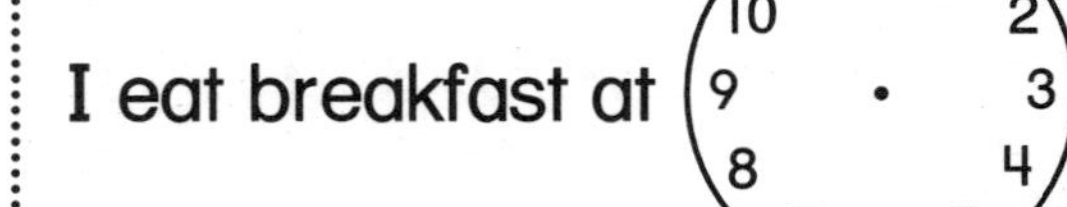

I eat dinner at

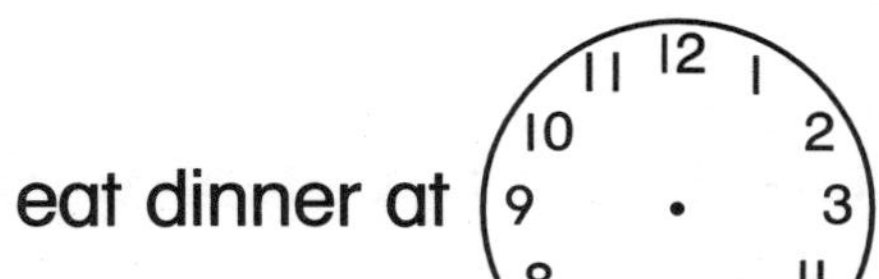

I go to bed at

Math Mat 169 Name ______________________

MATCHING TIMES TO CLOCKFACES

What Time Is It?

Cut out the different times at the bottom of the page.
Glue each time under the correct clock.

1	2	3	4

5	6	7	8

Find and color the words in the word search.

time	hour	minute
hands	face	day
	clock	

T	O	I	M	J	D	W	I	L	H
I	H	Z	H	T	A	O	F	T	A
M	V	K	N	X	Y	A	Z	O	N
E	B	N	F	V	Q	R	F	V	D
D	M	I	N	U	T	E	C	T	S
I	Y	H	I	D	T	V	S	P	T
G	D	A	B	X	C	L	O	C	K
U	W	F	D	O	A	C	L	T	R
F	A	C	E	O	H	O	U	R	B
L	F	S	H	L	G	P	N	Q	E

4:00	6:30
12:00	8:30
3:00	1:30
7:00	11:30

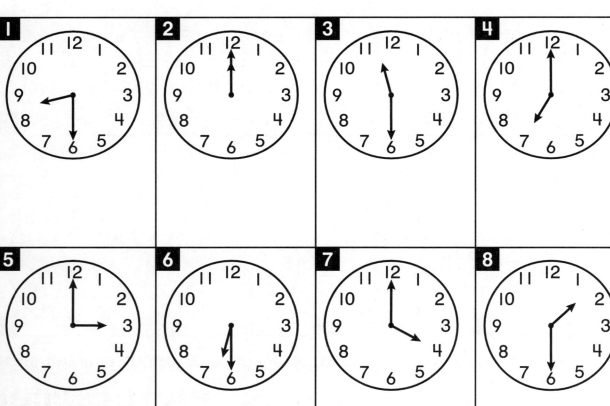

Math Mat 170

Name ____________________

READING CLOCKFACES

Reading Clocks

Count by 5s to find the number of minutes for each hour.

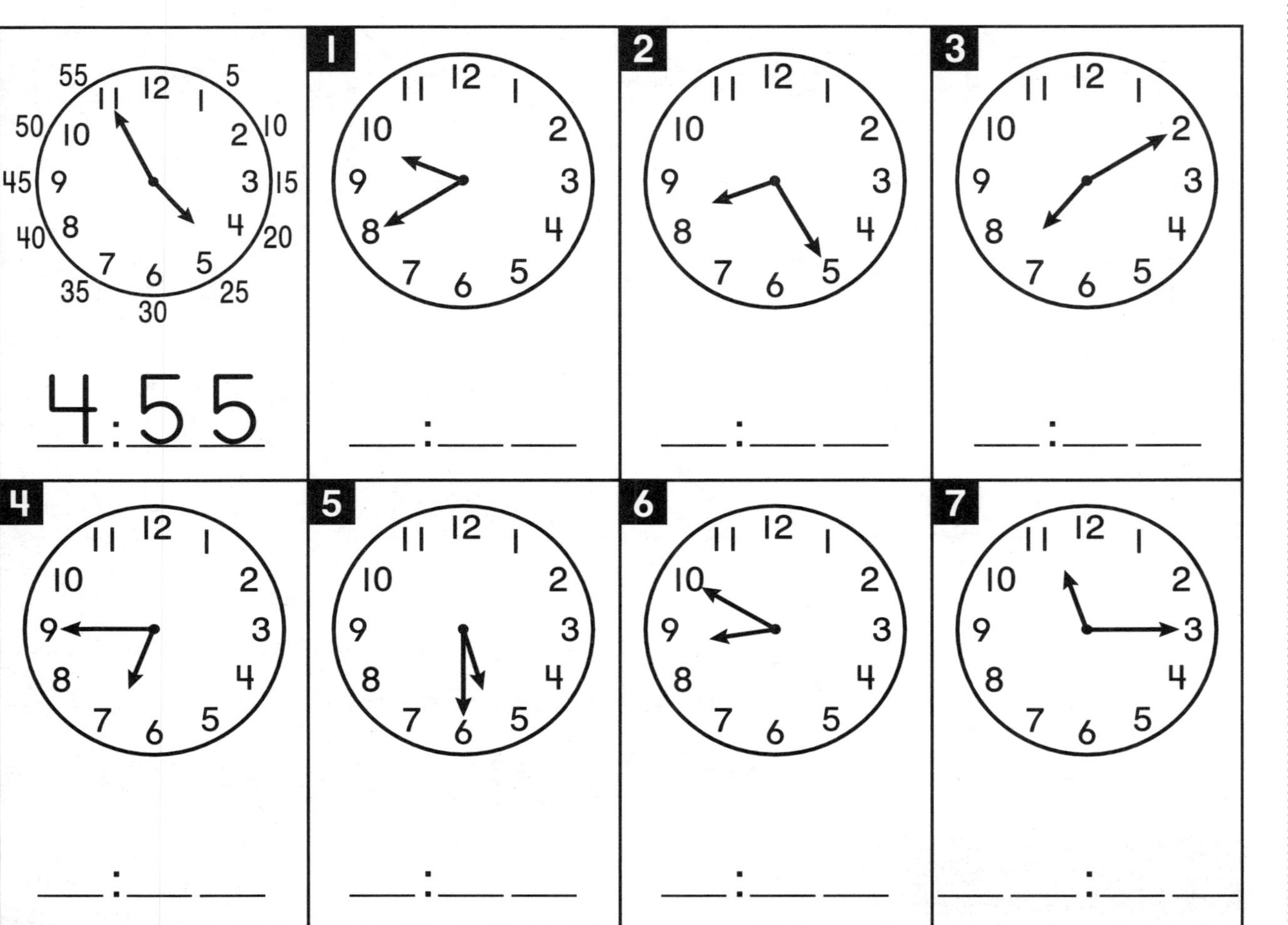

Write the number on a clock that shows the number of minutes.

8 :15 ___3___

9 :35 ______

10 :05 ______

11 :40 ______

12 :00 ______

13 :20 ______

14 :55 ______

Look at the classroom clock. Draw the hour and minute hands to show the time in 15 minutes.

Math Mat 171

Name ____________________

MATCHING TIME PHRASES AND CLOCK FACES

Half Past or Thirty Minutes

The time 12:30 can be read as twelve thirty or half past twelve. (One half hour is 30 minutes.) Cut out the time phrases and glue each one under the correct clock.

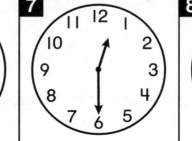

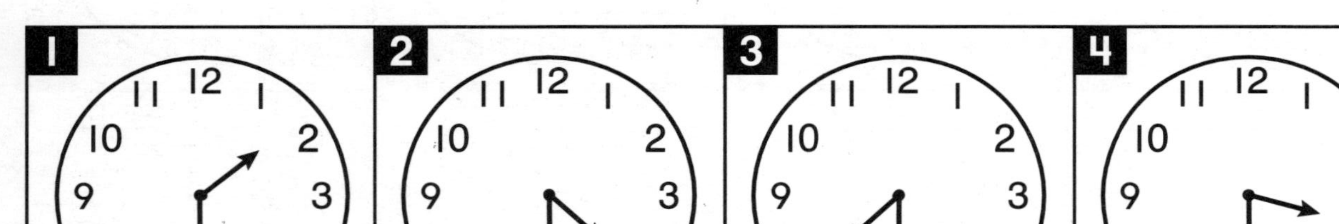

Draw the hour and minute hands to show the time.

6:30

half past 8

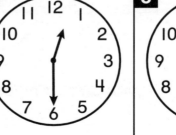

half past 7	12:30
half past 2	5:30
half past 9	4:30
half past 1	3:30

Name ____________________

IDENTIFYING TIME PHRASES

A Quarter of an Hour

There are 4 quarters in one hour. Each quarter is 15 minutes long.

- **7:15** can be read as **quarter past 7**.
- **7:45** can be read as **quarter 'til 8**.

Read each time and circle **quarter past** or **quarter 'til**.

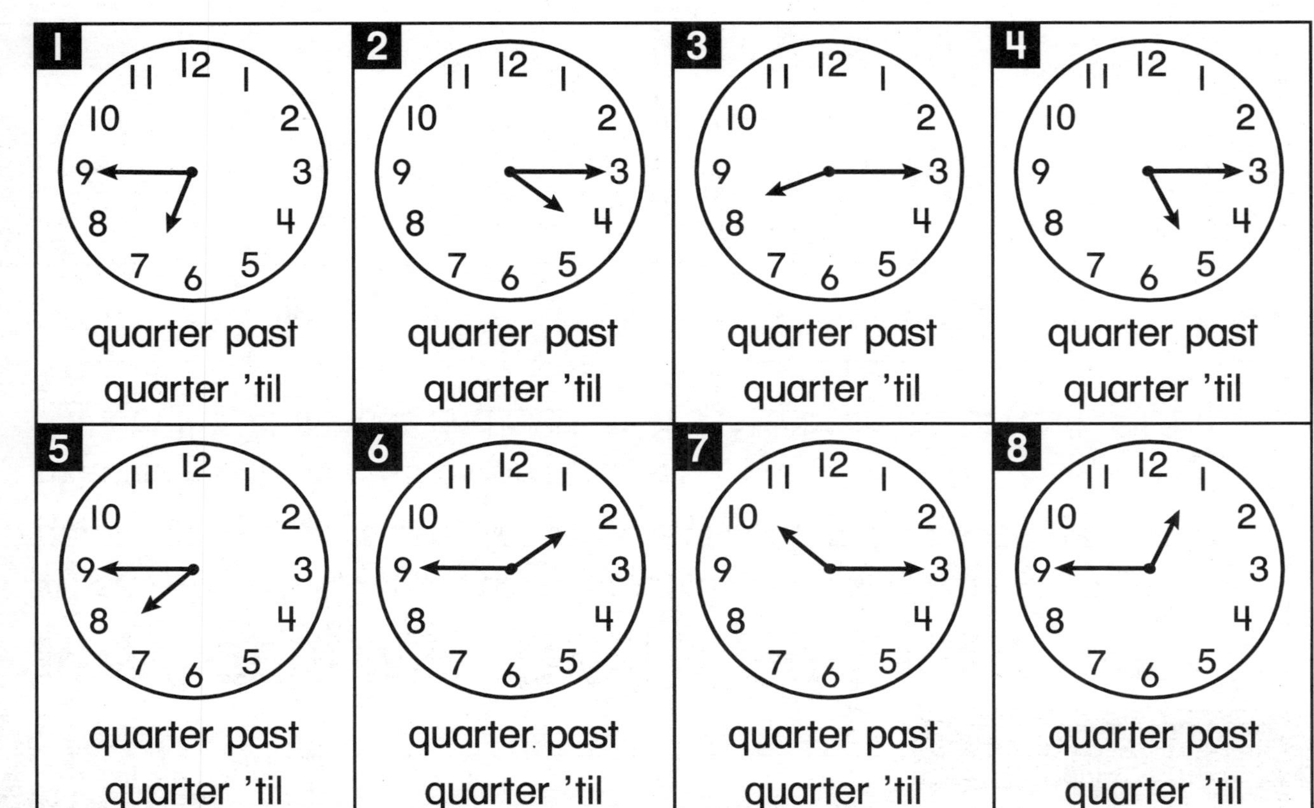

9 How many minutes are in one quarter of an hour?

____

10 How many quarters are in one hour?

____

11 Circle the longer length of time.

one quarter hour

half an hour

Bonus: How many quarters are in 2 hours?

____

Name ______________________

SORTING TIME SENTENCES

A.M. or P.M.

When telling time, A.M. is used for times that occur after midnight and before noon. P.M. is used for times that occur after noon and before midnight.

Cut out the sentences and glue each sentence in the correct column.

A.M.	P.M.

Izzy went to a birthday party at 2:00.

School begins at 8:00 each day.

Tomas eats a snack at 3:45.

Amelia eats breakfast at 8:00.

Sheila goes to bed at 7:30.

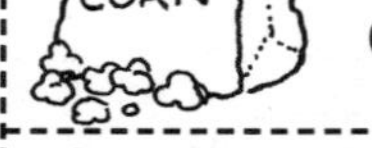

The movie began at 4:15.

The parade begins at 9:00.

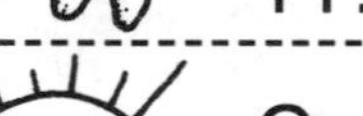
Grant has a dentist appointment at 11:00.

Carla wakes up at 6:15 each day.

Name ______________________

INTERPRETING CALENDAR DATA

The Weather Calendar

Answer the questions about the weather for the month.

Sunday	Monday	Tuesday	Wednesday	Thursday	Friday	Saturday
		1	2	3	4	5
6	7	8	9	10	11	12
13	14	15	16	17	18	19
20	21	22	23	24	25	26
27	28	29	30	31		

Calendar Questions

1. How many days are in the month? ________
2. How many days are in 1 week? ________
3. On what day of the week does the month begin?

   ____
4. On what day of the week does the month end?

   ____
5. On what date did it snow?

   ____
6. Which week had the most rain?

   ____
7. Which day was windy?

   ____

Math Mat 175

Name ______________________

INTERPRETING CALENDAR DATA

Happy New Year!

Cut out the pictures and place them on the correct day. Answer the questions.

January

Sunday	Monday	Tuesday	Wednesday	Thursday	Friday	Saturday
				1	2	3
4	5	6	7	8	9	10
11	12	13	14	15	16	17
18	19	20	21	22	23	24
25	25	27	28	29	30	31

- On January 15, Lee got new mittens.
- On January 31, Lee made a snowman.
- On January 8, Lee found earmuffs.
- On January 23, Lee went skating.
- On January 9, it started to snow.
- On January 21, Lee built an igloo.
- On January 12, Lee went sledding.
- The New Year began on January 1.

1 Circle the busier week.

January 11–17   January 25–31

2 On what day of the week did January begin?

____

3 On what day of the week did Lee go sledding?

____

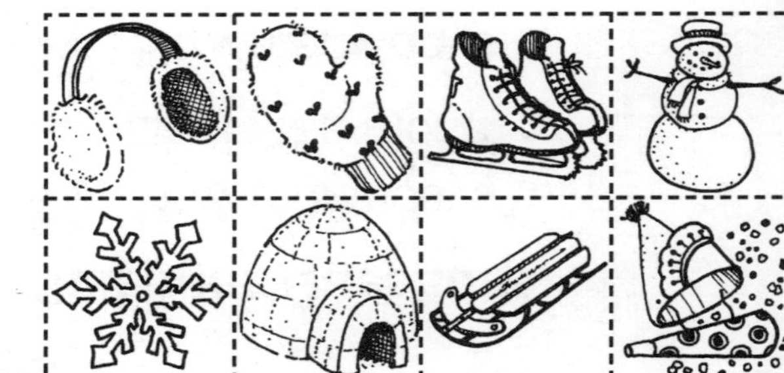

Name ____________________ USING CALENDARS

Roberto's Busy Month

Fill in the dates for the current month. Cut out the pictures and glue them in the correct spaces.

month ____________________ year ____________

Sunday	Monday	Tuesday	Wednesday	Thursday	Friday	Saturday

- On the 1st, Roberto lost a tooth.
- On the 3rd, Roberto went to a birthday party.
- On the 10th, Roberto went on a trip.
- On the 15th, Roberto had art class.
- On the 20th, Roberto flew a kite.
- On the 22nd, Roberto packed his own lunch.

1 On what date did Roberto go on a trip?

____

2 On what day of the week did he fly a kite?

____

Name ______________________ USING CALENDARS

Latisha's Plans

Fill in the calendar for the current month. Cut out the pictures and place them in the correct space on the calendar.

month ______________________ year __________

Sunday	Monday	Tuesday	Wednesday	Thursday	Friday	Saturday

Write the date for each activity on the lines below.

- Latisha went to the park on the third Monday. __________
- Latisha baked a cake on the second Saturday. __________
- Latisha played football on the first Wednesday. __________
- Latisha watched a baseball game on the fourth Friday. __________
- Latisha picked apples on the second Tuesday. __________
- Latisha went sailing on the last Saturday. __________

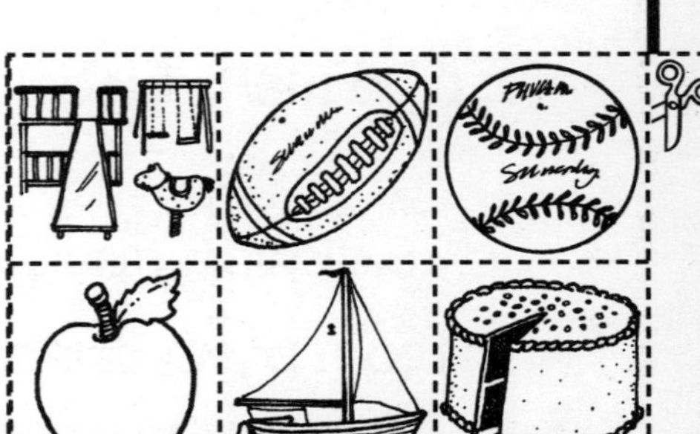

Name ____________________ SEQUENCING EVENTS

A Caterpillar's Life

Cut out the pictures and glue them in order on the time line.

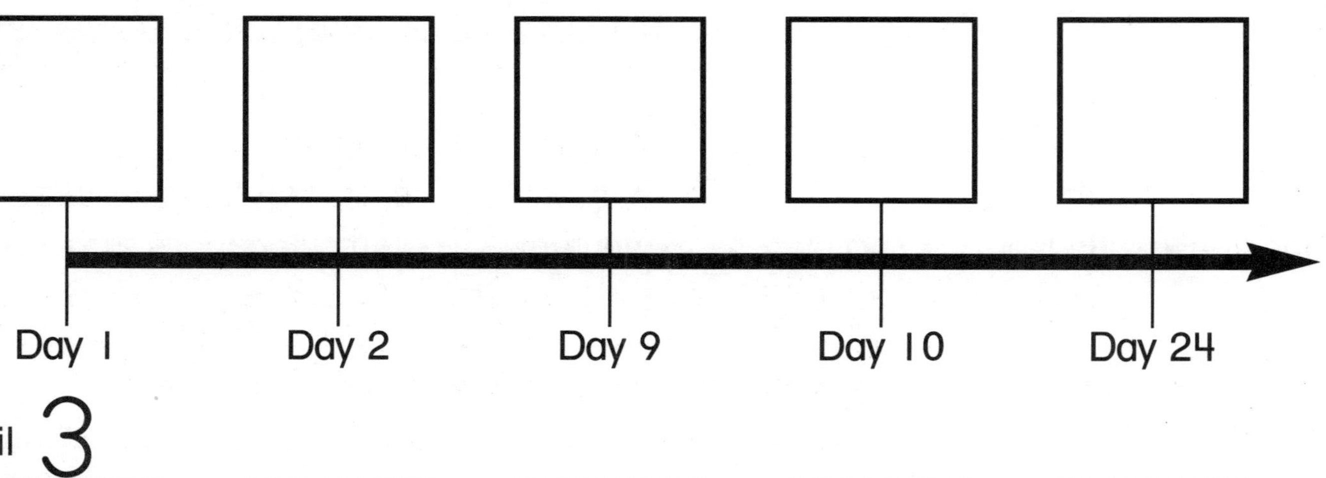

The egg hatched on April 3. Use the calendar to write the dates for the other events on the lines above.

April

Sunday	Monday	Tuesday	Wednesday	Thursday	Friday	Saturday
	1	2	3	4	5	6
7	8	9	10	11	12	13
14	15	16	17	18	19	20
21	22	23	24	25	26	27
28	29	30				

Describe one of the days in the caterpillar's life. Use the back of this paper to write what happened on that day.

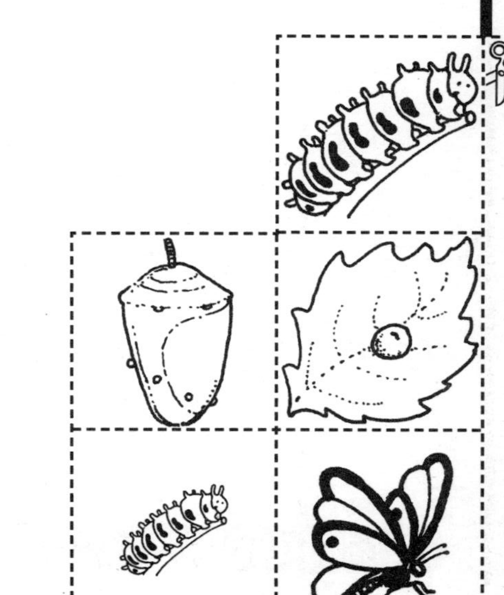

Name ______________________

Holidays

Cut out the holidays and glue them in the correct order.

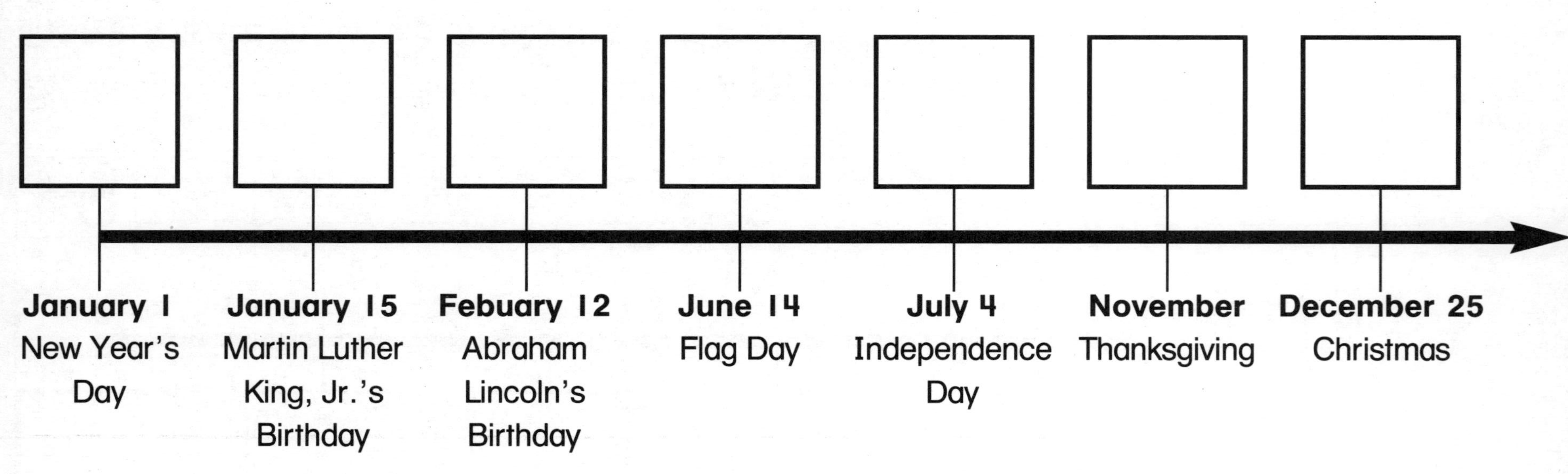

1 Which two holidays occur during the summer? ______________ and ______________

2 Which holiday is the birthday of the United States? ______________________

Math Mat 180 Name ____________________

Birthdays

Ask eight classmates to record their names and birthdays in the boxes below.

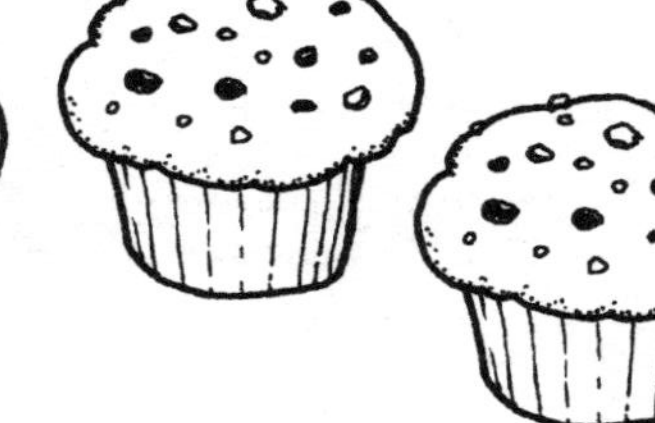

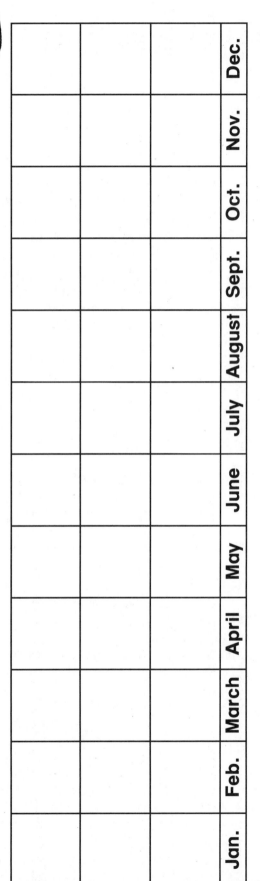

Jan.	Feb.	March	April	May	June	July	August	Sept.	Oct.	Nov.	Dec.

1 Who had the first birthday? ____________________

2 Who had the last birthday? ____________________

3 Which month had the most birthdays? ____________________

4 Which month had the fewest birthdays? ____________________

5 Do any classmates share the same birthday? ____________________

Answer Key

Math Mat 1: Adding 1 to 5

1. 5
2. 4
3. 5
4. 3
5. 4
6. 5
7. see right
8. Configurations will vary; 3
9. 1

3 2 4 1
5 0 1 3
0 5 2 4

Math Mat 2: Ways to Make 5

2. 3 + 2 = 5
3. 2 + 3 = 5
4. 4 + 1 = 5
5. 5 + 0 = 5
6. 2
7. 5
8. 4

Math Mat 3: Counting Cats

1. 4 + 1 = 5; Four cats are in the grass and one is in the tree.
2. 3
3. 16
4. 32

Math Mat 4: Gathering Acorns

6 + 4 = 10; ten

Math Mat 5: Dog Bone Directions

Students need to glue a bone next to the food bowl, in the wheelbarrow, in the grass below the tree, under the wheelbarrow's tire, and in front of the fence.

1. 5
2. 8
3. 8
4. 8
5. 8

Math Mat 6: Brown Bear's Berries: Song

1. 1 + 2 + 3 = 6
2. 4
3. 10 – 6 = 4

Math Mat 7: Stars on Flags

2 + 2 + 1 = 5
3 + 1 + 1 = 5
4 + 1 + 0 = 5
5 + 0 + 0 = 5

Math Mat 8: Bird Nests

Students need to draw two nests, then glue two baby birds in one nest and three in the other.

1. 2 + 3 = 5; Three babies can fit in the first nest and two more baby birds fit in the second nest.
2. Possible answers: feathers, two legs, beak

Math Mat 9: Many Mice

Students need to draw a cupboard and hole in the wall, then glue three mice in the cupboard and four mice in the wall.

3 + 4 = 7; Three mice are in the cupboard and four are in the wall.

Math Mat 10: Frogs in a Bucket

Students need to glue six frogs outside the bucket and three inside.

1. 9 – 6 = 3; Sam had nine frogs and six escaped. Three frogs are left.
2. 15¢

Math Mat 11: Apple Picking

Problems will vary; 11

Math Mat 12: Butterfly Wing Addition

Answers will vary.

Math Mat 13: Sort the Fish!

Column 10: 2 + 8; 13 – 3
Column 11: 6 + 5; 15 – 4; 13 – 2
Column 12: 3 + 9; 12 – 0; 0 + 12

Math Mat 14: Cat and Dog Pogs

Answers will vary.

Math Mat 15: Domino Sort and Tally

Students need to record tally marks ten times. Answers will vary.

1. 4
2. 9
3. 14

Math Mat 16: Birthday Candles

Students need to glue two rows of candles with three candles in each row.

3 + 3 = 6; six

Math Mat 17: Party Balloons

Students need to glue five balloons in the red box, three in the orange, four in the yellow, and four in the green; four

Math Mat 18: Playing Card Addition

Answers will vary.

Math Mat 19: Four in a Row

3 – 2 = 1	3 – 3 = 0	2 – 1 = 1
4 – 4 = 0	4 – 3 = 1	5 – 4 = 1
2 – 2 = 0	2 – 0 = 2	3 – 1 = 2
5 – 2 = 3	4 – 2 = 2	5 – 3 = 2
5 – 5 = 0	1 – 1 = 0	3 – 0 = 3
1 – 0 = 1	4 – 1 = 3	5 – 2 = 3

Math Mat 20: Scarecrow Subtraction

1. 2
2. 2
3. 5
4. 1
5. 3

Math Mat 21: Finding the Difference

1. 4
2. 0
3. 0
4. 8
5. 2
6. 6
7. 8 – 6 = 2
8. 4 – 2 = 2
9. 0 – 0 = 0
10. 2 – 0 = 2
11. 8 – 4 = 4
12. 6 – 0 = 6

Math Mat 22: Count and Subtract

1. 9 – 3 = 6
2. 7 – 3 = 4
3. 11 – 3 = 8
4. 12 – 3 = 9
5. 10 – 3 = 7
6. 8 – 3 = 5
7. Across: 9 – 8 = 1; 5 – 4 = 1
Down: 9 – 5 = 4; 8 – 4 = 4
8. Across: 7 – 5 = 2; 4 – 2 = 2
Down: 7 – 4 = 3; 5 – 2 = 3

Math Mat 23: Dominoes Subtraction

6 – 5 = 1	5 – 3 = 2	4 – 1 = 3
6 – 2 = 4	5 – 2 = 3	3 – 2 = 1

Math Mat 24: How Many Are Left?

1. 8 – 4 = 4
2. 9 – 7 = 2
3. 10 – 7 = 3
4. 10 – 1 = 9
5. 2
6. 1
7. 5

Math Mat 25: At the Fruit Stand

1. 5
2. 3
3. 3
4. 6

Crossword Puzzle

Across	**Down**
1. four	**1.** five
3. eight	**2.** three
5. seven	**4.** one
7. ten	**5.** six
8. zero	**6.** nine
	7. two

Math Mat 26: Rupert's Cheese

Students need to cross out three pieces of cheese. Rupert has six left.

1. six
2. 7
3. 5
4. 5

Math Mat 27: On the Ranch

1. 6
2. 0
3. 3
4. 2
5. 5 hens
6. 10 cows
7. 2 pigs

Math Mat 28: Apples in a Row

1. 14
2. 11
3. 9
4. 10
5. 8
6. 9
7. 12
8. 12
9. 18
10. 9

Addition Square

Across: 6 + 1 + 3 = 10; 3 + 5 + 2 = 10; 1 + 4 + 5 = 10

Down: 6 + 3 + 1 = 10; 1 + 5 + 4 = 10; 3 + 2 + 5 = 10

Math Mat 29: 1, 2, 3, Go!

1. 3 + 6 = 9 + 2 = 11
2. 2 + 4 = 6 + 8 = 14
3. 1 + 0 = 1 + 9 = 10
4. 2 + 7 = 9 + 8 = 17
5. 5 + 6 = 11 + 0 = 11
6. 4 + 4 = 8 + 4 = 12
7. 444
8. 178
9. 856

Math Mat 30: Number Sentences

Matching

13: 9 + 4, 4 + 9
14: 6 + 8, 8 + 6
15: 9 + 6, 6 + 9
16: 9 + 7, 7 + 9
17: 8 + 9, 9 + 8
18: 8 + 10, 10 + 8

Circle all the ways to make 15.
see right

9 8 7 6 5 7 8
8 7 6 5 9 6 9
7 6 5 9 8 7 5
6 5 9 8 7 9 6
8 7 5 6 9 7 8
9 6 9 6 5 8 7
6 7 8 9 5 7 6

Math Sentences

9 + 6
6 + 9
8 + 7
7 + 8

Math Mat 31: Spin the Spinners!

Answers will vary.

1. >
2. <
3. <
4. =

Math Mat 32: Apple Number Line

1. 15
2. 18
3. 11
4. 20
5. 19
6. 14
7. 15
8. 17
9. 10
10. –
11. +
12. –
13. –
14. –
15. +

Math Mat 33: Find the Missing Number

1. 3 + 3 = 6
2. 10 – 7 = 3
3. 9 – 4 = 5
4. 8 – 6 = 2
5. 7 – 6 = 1
6. 6 + 0 = 6
7. 5 – 4 = 1
8. 6 + 2 = 8
9. zero
10. nine
11. eight
12. three
13. ten

Math Mat 34: Ready, Set, Start!

1. 13 – 8 = 5
2. 19 – 8 = 11
3. 14 – 2 = 12
4. 15 – 6 = 9
5. 11 – 8 = 3
6. 14 – 8 = 6
7. 18 – 9 = 9
8. 20 – 10 = 10

Math Riddle

5 apples

Math Mat 35: Arabic and Roman Numerals

2. 17 – 1 = 16
3. 15 – 6 = 9
4. 10 – 5 = 5
5. 19 – 7 = 12
6. 14 – 2 = 12
7. XXV
8. XXX

Math Mat 36: Subtraction Crossword Puzzle

Across	Down
1. eighteen	**2.** ten
3. twenty	**3.** twelve
5. two	**4.** eleven
7. seven	**5.** three
8. four	**6.** one
9. zero	**8.** five
10. nine	

Math Mat 37: Apples and Cores

1. 3	**4.** 1
2. 4	**5.** 5
3. 2	**6.** 5

Math Mat 38: Stinky Skunks!

1. 4
2. 5
3. 9

Complete each pattern.
2, 4, 6, 8, 10; 5, 7, 9, 11, 13; 28, 30, 32, 34

What's the rule?
Add 2.

Math Mat 39: Animal Sorting

1. They are all cats.
2. They are all dogs.
3. They are all birds.
4. They may be sorted by color, tail length, body position, and so on. Answers will vary.

Math Mat 40: Chocolate Desserts

Students need to glue two pictures of chocolate cake in the Chocolate Cake oval, three bowls of ice cream in the Chocolate Ice Cream oval, and one picture of chocolate cake with ice cream in the Both oval.

Six people voted.

Math Mat 41: Ladybugs and Butterflies

Students need to glue two ladybugs in the square, one ladybug and two butterflies in the overlapping area, and three ladybugs and one butterfly in the circle.

1. 9
2. ladybug

Math Mat 42: Find Me!

Students need to make Xs on every animal, except for the frog.

1. frog; Possible answers: I catch flies with my tongue, I have a long tongue, I can croak.
2. Possible answers: They all can fly, have wings.
3. Possible answers: They all live in trees, have tails.
4. Possible answers: They all are black and white, cannot fly.

Math Mat 43: Woodland Animal Clues

Students need to make Xs on every animal picture, except for the owl.

1. owl
2. owl
3. opossum
4. skunk
5. snake

Math Mat 44: My Favorite Hat

Students need to make Xs on every hat, except for the sombrero.

sombrero

Math Mat 45: Albert Goes to School

Students need to make Xs on every vehicle, except for the bus.

bus

Math Mat 46: Sports Tally

Angela's row should have Xs for football and Frisbee, with an O in the basketball column.

Kate's row should have Xs for both Frisbee and basketball, with an O in the football column.

Mark's row should have Xs for football and basketball, with an O in the Frisbee column.

Which sport does each play?
Angela: basketball
Kate: football
Mark: Frisbee

Math Mat 47: Favorite Fruits

Leo's row should have Xs for grapes, oranges, and strawberries. An O should be in the pears column.

Sonja's row should have Xs for grapes, oranges, and pears. An O should be in the strawberries column.

Henry's row should have Xs for grapes, pears, and strawberries. An O should be in the oranges column.

Rebecca's row should have Xs for grapes, pears, and strawberries. An O should be in the grapes column.

Matching

Leo: pear
Sonja: strawberry
Henry: orange
Rebecca: grapes

Math Mat 48: At the Toy Store

Daniel's row should have Xs for bears, cats, and turtles. An O should be in the dogs column.

Lisa's row should have Xs for bears, dogs, and turtles. An O should be in the cats column.

Maria's row should have Xs for bears, cats, and dogs. An O should be in the turtles column.

Bill's row should have Xs for cats, dogs, and turtles. An O should be in the bears column.

What did each person buy?

Daniel: dog
Lisa: cat
Maria: turtle
Bill: bear

Math Mat 49: Who Lives Where?

Sam: 4
Sarah: 5
Alanna: 6
Chris: 3
Steve: 1
Kevin: 2

Word Search

see right

F	O	T	H	E	A	S	J	P	H
N	K	A	S	C	F	I	F	T	H
T	J	S	E	C	O	N	D	U	O
H	J	Y	Q	E	J	N	T	Y	P
A	I	H	Q	D	T	H	I	R	D
W	W	P	S	D	S	H	Q	F	B
F	I	R	S	T	L	O	F	C	Z
E	M	J	F	O	U	R	T	H	P
V	D	H	U	S	I	X	T	H	T

Math Mat 50: Animal Order

Logic Clues

1. cat, lamb, chick, dog
   The lamb is second.
2. lamb, chick, dog, cat
   The chick is second.
3. cat, chick, lamb, dog
   The dog is fourth.
4. cat, lamb, chick, dog
   The cat is first.

Math Mat 51: Mix and Match Caps

1. A, B, C
2. A, C, B
3. B, A, C
4. B, C, A
5. C, A, B
6. C, B, A
7. 12

Math Mat 52: A Fall Day

1. 3; 5; 2
2. leaves
3. 10
4. 0, 1, 2, 3, 4, 5, 6, 7
5. 6, 7, 8, 9, 10, 11
6. 11, 12, 13, 14, 15, 16
7. 16, 17, 18, 19, 20
8. 9, 10, 11, 12, 13, 14

Math Mat 53: Favorite Ways to Eat an Apple

1. whole
2. slices
3. 12

Show the number of seeds.

five tally marks, two tally marks, three tally marks

Graph

Answers will vary.

Math Mat 54: A Roll of the Die!

Answers will vary.

Math Mat 55: Jason's Classmates

Students will need to color six squares in the D row, three squares in the H row, and five squares in the Z row.

1. D
2. H
3. 15 (Be sure to include Jason.)
4. Answers will vary.

Math Mat 56: Cowboys and Cowgirls

1. horses
2. boots
3. horseshoes
4. boots, horseshoes

Math Mat 57: Maria's Gardening Equipment

Students need to draw three Xs in the rake row, four Xs in the shovel row, five Xs in the watering can row, and six Xs in the wheelbarrow row.

1. 3; 4; 5; 6
2. wheelbarrows
3. watering cans

Math Mat 58: Favorite Hearts

Answers will vary.

Math Mat 59: Letters and Names

Answers will vary.

Math Mat 60:Voting for Presidents

Answers will vary.

Math Mat 61: Penny Toss

Answers will vary.

Math Mat 62: A Trip to the Orchard

1. 10; 2; 4; 8
2. Arlene and Ray

Math Mat 63: Flower Picking

1. 25; 15; 20; 5
2. Tuesday
3. Monday and Wednesday
4. Thursday

Math Mat 64: Fair and Square

Answers will vary.

Math Mat 65: Circles and Squares

Answers will vary.

Math Mat 66: Bear Buddies

1. Students need to finish numbering the bears from 1st to 10th.
2. Students need to color the second bear brown.
3. Students need to draw a circle around the third bear.
4. Students need to draw a line under the last, tenth, bear.
5. Students need to draw a diamond around the first bear.
6. Students need to draw a square around the fifth bear.
7. Students need to color the third, fifth, seventh, and ninth bears.

Math Mat 67: Animal Addresses

1. A3: cat; B1: bird; C4: dog; D2: fish
2. cat to round bed; bird to cage; fish to bowl; dog to doghouse

Math Mat 68: Creepy Crawlies

1. bee
2. snail

Math Mat 69: The Playground

1. Students need to glue grass under the school.
2. Students need to glue the sun over the school.
3. Students need to glue the tree to the left of the school.
4. Students need to glue the boy to the right of the school.
5. Students need to glue the girl to the left of the tree.
6. Students need to glue the swing set to the right of the boy.

Math Mat 70: Tiny Town

1. Rachel
2. Henry's
3. Henry's house
4. picnic area

Math Mat 71: A Trip to the Zoo

row one: monkey, penguin, zebra, duck pond
row two: panda, playground, hippo, polar bear
row three: will vary, will vary, ostrich, giraffe

Math Mat 72: Our Classroom

Answers will vary.

Math Mat 73: Design a Bedroom
Answers will vary.

Math Mat 74: Tasty Treat
an apple on a plate
Students need to connect:
- the word *six* to bottom apple and numeral 6.
- the word *eight* to the top apple and the numeral 8.
- the word *nine* to the second apple and the numeral 9.
- the word *ten* to the third apple and the numeral 10.

Math Mat 75: Furry Friend
a teddy bear

Math Mat 76: Me and My Big Trunk!
an elephant

Math Mat 77: Pencil Lengths
1. 6 apples
2. 2 apples
3. 4 apples
4. 3 apples
5. 5 apples

Math Mat 78: Ribbon Lengths
1. 7 inches
2. 5 inches
3. 6 inches
4. 2 inches
5. 1 inch

Math Mat 79: Shape Sizes
1. 4 square inches
2. 5 square inches
3. 6 square inches
4. 3 square inches

Color the squares.
Configurations will vary.

Math Mat 80: Estimating Weights
Less Than 1 Pound
pencil, ladybug, acorn, mouse, leaf, bumblebee, ant, balloon

More Than 1 Pound
airplane, desk, zebra, hippopotamus, car, bed

Math Mat 81: What's the Temperature
1. 20°F
2. 70°F
3. 50°F
4. 0°F
5. 100°F
6. 60°F

Weather Reports
Answers will vary.

Math Mat 82: More or Less Water
1. jar
2. watering can
3. teacup
4. measuring cup
5. pail
6. measuring cup

Math Mat 83: About a Cup
Less Than 1 Cup
thimble, spoon

About 1 Cup
teacup, jar, glass, measuring cup

More Than 1 Cup
watering can, fishbowl, gallon of milk, pond, pail, wheelbarrow

Math Mat 84: Ways to Measure Volume
1. 3 measuring cups
2. carton
3. measuring cup
4. 2 cartons

Number the containers.
3, 1, 2

Math Mat 85: More Ways to Measure Volume
1. 4 quarts
2. pint
3. 4 cups
4. quart

Word Search
see right

Math Mat 86: Animal Pens

1. 3 + 4 + 2 = 9
2. 3 + 3 + 2 + 2 = 10
3. 2 + 2 + 2 + 2 = 8

Math Mat 87: Measuring Me

Answers will vary.

Math Mat 88: Our Classroom

Measure the items.
Answers will vary.
Circle the answer.
Students need to circle the longest pencil, shortest crayon, and matching glue containers.

Math Mat 89: Campground Map

Campsite to Fishing pond: 3 in. = 6 mi.
Campsite to Canoes: 2 in. = 4 mi.
Canoes to Cabin: 3 in. = 6 mi.
Fishing Pond to Cabin: 2 in. = 4 mi.
Figure the Miles
1. 4 mi.
2. 6 mi.
3. 4 mi.
4. 6 mi.
Table
1, 2; 2, 4; 3, 6; 4, 8; 5, 10; 6, 12
Double each number.

Math Mat 90: Camping Out

1. 10 cm long
2. 7 cm long
3. 3 cm tall
4. 5 cm long
5. 6 cm tall

Math Mat 91: Find the Area

1. 10 square centimeters
2. 8 square centimeters
3. 12 square centimeters
4. 6 square centimeters
5. 9 square centimeters
6. 3 square centimeters
7. 5 square centimeters
Color the squares.
Configurations will vary.

Math Mat 92: About Meters

Answers will vary.
List three items.
Answers will vary.
Subtraction square
Across: 9 –5 = 4; 6 – 4 = 2; 3 – 1 = 2
Down: 9 –6 = 3; 5 – 4 = 1; 4 – 2 = 2

Math Mat 93: Kilometers

1. 7 km = 4.2 mi.
2. 12 km = 7.2 mi.
3. 14 km = 8.4 mi.
4. 22 km = 13.2 mi.
5. 25 km = 15 mi.
6. 15 km
7. 13 km
8. 8 km

Math Mat 94: Grams and Kilograms

1. kilograms
2. grams
3. kilograms
4. grams
5. kilograms
6. grams
7. 2.2 kg
8. 17.6 kg

Math Mat 95: Liters

Color the items.
Students need to circle the pitcher, thermos, and pot.
Complete the sentence.
1. ruler
2. thermometer
3. cup
4. clock

Math Mat 96: °Celsius

0°C/Cold Weather
mitten, snowman, snowflake, igloo, earmuffs, penguin, hibernating bear
40°C/Hot Weather
butterfly, ice cream cone, fireworks, sailboat, kite

Math Mat 97: Coin Values

Table

Students need to glue a penny, nickel, dime, and quarter beneath its name and value.

Values

1. quarter
2. penny
3. 4¢
4. 8¢

Math Mat 98: Making Cents

1. 9¢
2. 7¢
3. 8¢
4. two pennies
5. three pennies
6. 1¢
7. 5¢

Math Mat 99: Change for a Nickel

1. 5 pennies and 0 nickels
2. 0 pennies and 1 nickel
3. 12¢
4. 16¢

Math Mat 100: Change for a Dime

1.–5. 2 nickels; 1 nickel, 4 pennies, 1 penny; 1 nickel, 3 pennies, 2 pennies; 4 pennies, 4 pennies, 2 pennies; 3 pennies, 3 pennies, 2 pennies, 1 penny, 1 penny
6. 10¢

Math Mat 101: The School Store

1. 7¢
2. 4¢
3. 1¢
4. 4¢

Math Mat 102: Counting With Nickels

Count by 5s.

5, 10, 15, 20, 25, 30, 35, 40, 45, 50, 55, 60, 65, 70, 75, 80, 85, 90, 95

Number the nickels.

1. 7
2. 2
3. 10
4. 1

Math Mat 103: Counting With Dimes

1. and 2. 5 pennies, 1 nickel; 2 nickels; 1 dime; 10 pennies
3. 10, 20, 30, 40, 50, 60, 70, 80, 90, 100
4. 10, 20, 30, 40, 50, 60, 70, 80, 90, 100

Math Mat 104: Counting With Quarters

1. 1 quarter
2. 3 quarters
3. 4 quarters
4. 2 quarters
5. six quarters
6. $4.00

Math Mat 105: Counting Loose Change

1. 3 pennies
2. 1 nickel
3. 1 nickel, 2 pennies
4. 1 nickel, 4 pennies
5. 1 dime
6. 1 dime, 1 penny
7. 1 dime, 2 pennies
8. 3 nickels

Math Mat 106: Sweet Shop

Answers will vary.

Math Mat 107: Pennies and Dimes

1. 3 dimes, 2 pennies; 3 tens, 2 ones
2. 2 dimes, 5 pennies; 2 tens, 5 ones
3. 5 dimes, 4 pennies; 5 tens, 4 ones
4. 4 dimes, 3 pennies; 4 tens, 3 ones
5. Answers will vary.
6. Answers will vary.
7. Answers will vary.
8. Answers will vary.

Math Mat 108: Frisbee Dog

Write the math problem.

10 – 7 = 3; Bart brought back only seven of Miguel's ten Frisbees. Three weren't brought back.

Word Problem

100 Frisbees

Math Mat 109: Dollars and Cents

1. 1 dollar, 2 quarters
2. 2 dollars, 2 dimes
3. 2 dollars, 3 pennies
4. 1 dollar, 1 nickel
5. $2.20
6. $1.05

Math Mat 110: Bait and Tackle Shop

1. $4.75
2. $5.75
3. 5, 2, 6, 3, 1, 4
4. Students need to circle the net.
5. Students need to circle the fishing pole.
6. Students need to circle the net.

Math Mat 111: Matching Money

1. 1 five-dollar bill
2. 1 five-dollar bill, 2 dollar bills
3. 1 twenty-dollar bill
4. 1 five-dollar bill, 3 dollar bills
5. 1 ten-dollar bill
6. 1 ten-dollar bill, 3 dollar bills

Math Mat 112: Money Review

Write the value.

10 cents, 1 cent, 5 cents, 25 cents

Use the coins to make the amount.

1. Possible answer: 2 quarters, 1 dime
2. Possible answer: dollar bill, 1 quarter, 1 dime, 1 nickel
3. Possible answer: 2 quarters, 1 nickel, 3 pennies

Math Mat 113: Plenty of Penguins

1. $2 \times 2 = 4$
2. $3 \times 1 = 3$
3. $1 \times 3 = 3$
4. $4 \times 1 = 4$

Math Mat 114: Fabulous Fish

1. 1 fish
2. 2 fish
3. 8 fish
4. 9 fish
5. 7 fish
6. 10 fish
7. 3 fish
8. 5 fish
9. 6 fish
10. 4 fish

Math Mat 115: Busy Bees

1. 2
2. 4
3. 6
4. 8
5. 10
6. 12
7. 14
8. 16
9. 18
10. 20

Math Mat 116: Fresh Fruit

Complete the chart.

3, 6, 9, 12, 15, 18, 21, 24, 27, 30

Solve the problems.

1. 9
2. 3
3. 15
4. 6
5. 27
6. 18
7. 21
8. 12
9. 30
10. 24

Write the problems.

11. $2 \times 2 = 4$ pears
12. $1 \times 3 = 3$ bananas
13. $4 \times 1 = 4$ strawberries

Math Mat 117: Multiplication Chart

Complete the chart.

row 0: 0, 0, 0, 0, 0, 0
row 1: 0, 1, 2, 3, 4, 5
row 2: 0, 2, 4, 6, 8, 10
row 3: 0, 3, 6, 9, 12, 15
row 4: 0, 4, 8, 12, 16, 20
row 5: 0, 5, 10, 15, 20, 25

Solve the problem.

1. 6
2. 4

Math Mat 118: Apple Division

1. 1; $2 \div 2 = 1$
2. 3; $12 \div 4 = 3$
3. 2; $6 \div 3 = 2$
4. 5; $5 \div 1 = 5$

Math Mat 119: In the Woods

1. $4 \div 2 = 2$; 2 acorns
2. $9 \div 3 = 3$; 3 pinecones
3. $3 \div 3 = 1$; 1 leaf
4. $10 \div 2 = 5$; 5 flowers
5. $6 \div 3 = 2$
6. $8 \div 4 = 2$

Math Mat 120: Pizza Parlor

Matching

1. ½
2. ¼
3. ⅕
4. ⅓

Questions

Answers will vary.
Answers will vary.

Math Mat 121: Division Review

1. 1
2. 5
3. 1
4. 2
5. 3
6. 7
7. 1
8. 0
9. 1
10. 1 ÷ 1 = 1
11. 5 ÷ 0 = 0
12. 8 ÷ 8 = 1
13. 2 ÷ 1 = 2
14. 3 ÷ 3 = 1
15. 4 ÷ 1 = 4
16. 2 ÷ 1 = 2
17. 9 ÷ 1 = 9
18. 6 ÷ 1 = 6

Brain Teaser

100 ÷ 1 = 100
100 ÷ 0 = 0

Math Mat 122: Pencil Pairs

Circle the pairs.

1. 3 pairs, odd
2. 5 pairs, even
3. 1 pair, odd
4. 4 pairs, odd
5. 4 pairs, even
6. 2 pairs, even

Write the numbers.

1, 2, 3, 4, 5, 6, 7, 8, 9, 10

Circle the odd numbers with red.

1, 3, 5, 7, 9

Circle the even numbers with blue.

2, 4, 6, 8, 10

Math Mat 123: Odd or Even?

Table

Answers will vary.

Circle the even numbers.

2, 4, 6, 8, 10

Draw a square around odd numbers.

1, 3, 5, 7, 9

Write odd or even.

74: even
61: odd
28: even
17: odd
123: odd
249: odd

Math Mat 124: Lost Mittens

1. 3 children; 2 + 2 + 2 = 6; 3 mittens
2. Ted's row should have Xs in the blue and red columns, with an O in the green column.

Lia's row should have Xs in the green and red columns, with an O in the blue column.

Nick's row should have Xs in the blue and green columns, with an O in the red column. Nick wears red mittens.

Math Mat 125: What's the Pattern?

2, 4, 6, 8, 10, 12, 14, 16, 18, 20, 22, 24, 26, 28, 30, 32

Students will need to write 34 and 36.

I counted by 2s.

Math Mat 126: What's the Pattern?

5, 10, 15, 20, 25, 30, 35, 40, 45, 50, 55, 60, 65, 70, 75, 80

Students will need to write the numbers 85, 90, 95, and 100.

I counted by 5s.

Math Mat 127: What's the Pattern?

1. Students will need to glue the numbers 20, 30, 40, 50, 60, 70, 80, 90, and 100 in place.
I counted by 10s.

Write the missing numbers.

2. 10, 20, 30, 40, 50, 60, 70, 80, 90, 100
3. 10, 20, 30, 40, 50, 60, 70, 80, 90, 100
4. any number from 11 through 24
5. any number from 51 through 99

Math Mat 128: Planes and Trains

1. two
2. one
3. two
4. one
5. one
6. one
7. two
8. two

Word Search

Math Mat 129: Counting Apples

1. Students will need to draw three apples.
2. Students will need to draw four apples.
3. Students will need to draw four apples.
4. Students will need to draw three apples.
5. Students will need to draw four apples.
6. Students will need to draw three apples.

Circle the apple that does not belong.
Students need to circle the apple core.

Math Mat 130: Snack Food

1. 5 pennies
2. 6 pennies
3. 5 pennies
4. 6 pennies

Math Mat 131: How Many Shoes?

1. seven
2. eight
3. seven
4. eight
5. seven
6. eight

Maze
see right

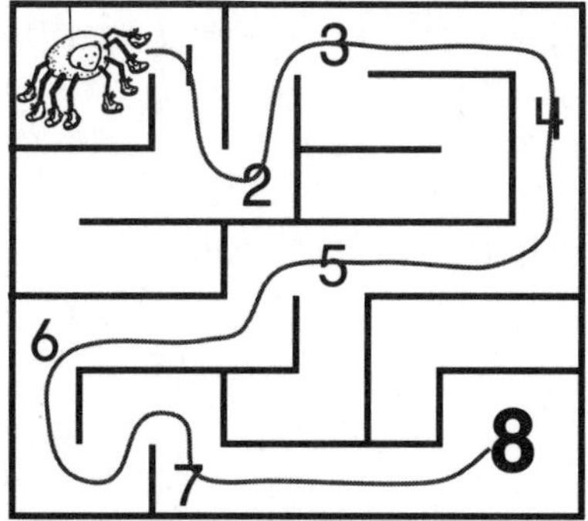

Math Mat 132: School Supplies

1. ten
2. nine
3. ten
4. ten
5. nine
6. nine

Math Mat 133: Counting Books

Write the number.

1. nine
2. six
3. eight
4. seven
5. three
6. ten

Word Problem
2 + 3 = 5

Math Mat 134: Mice Count

1. 11
2. 12
3. 11
4. 12
5. 11
6. 12

Word Search

T W E L V E V K N
E L E V E N A Z O
N F V T W E L V E
R T W E L V E F V
E L E V E N H I D
V T W E L V E S P
O B D E L E V E N

Math Mat 135: Seeing Stars

1. 4 + 9 = 13
2. 7 + 7 = 14
3. 5 + 8 = 13
4. 3 + 10 = 13
5. 9 + 5 = 14
6. 2 + 12 = 14

Mystery number: 9

Math Mat 136: Pennies

1. 15¢
2. 16¢
3. 15¢
4. 15¢
5. 15¢
6. 16¢

Word Problem
15 pennies

Math Mat 137: Pet Math

1. 17
2. 18
3. 18
4. 17

How many pets?
add

Math Mat 138: Missing Numbers

1. 1, 2, 3, 4, 5, 6, 7, 8, 9, 10, 11
2. 11, 12, 13, 14, 15, 16, 17, 18, 19
3. 10, 11, 12, 13, 14, 15, 16, 17
4. 5; 13; 9
5. 8; 12; 16
6. 4; 9; 17

Word Search
see right

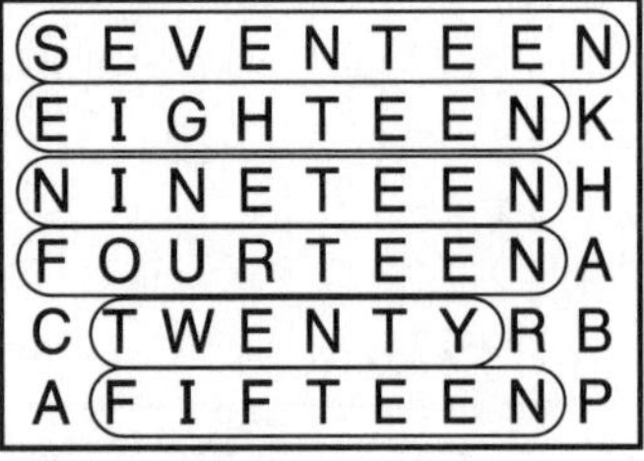

Math Mat 139: Teddy-ominoes

Answers will vary.

Math Mat 140: Partners Bingo

Answers will vary.

Math Mat 141: Naming Shapes

1. Students need to match:
   - the word *triangle* to the triangle shape.
   - the word *circle* to the circle shape.
   - the word *square* to the square shape.
   - the word *rectangle* to the rectangle shape.
2. Students need to draw an X on the square.
3. Answers will vary.
4. circle
5. square
6. oval

Math Mat 142: What Comes Next?

1. star, circle
2. heart, arrow
3. arrow, star
4. Answers will vary.

Math Mat 143: Button Patterns

1. A, B
2. A, B
3. B, C
4. AB
5. ABC
6. ABC

Math Mat 144: Seeing Patterns

1. 123123123
2. 112311231
3. 121312131
4. star, circle, star, circle, star, circle
5. star, star, circle, circle, star, star, circle, circle

Math Mat 145: Shapes, Sides, and Corners

1. square; 4; 4
2. triangle; 3; 3
3. diamond or rhombus; 4; 4
4. pentagon; 5; 5
5. Students need to draw a line between opposite parallel sides, dividing the square into two rectangles.
6. Students need to draw a line between opposite angles, dividing the square into two triangles.
7. Students need to draw a line between opposite angles, dividing the diamond into two triangles.

Math Mat 146: Seeing Shapes

11 shapes with only straight lines

Math Mat 147: Sorting Shapes

Sphere: baseball, balloon, sun, sphere
Cone: teepee, ice-cream cone, cone
Cube: lunch box, die, cube
Cylinder: jar, glass, pail, cylinder

Math Mat 148: Shape Symmetry

1. yes
2. no
3. yes
4. no

5. 6. 7. 8.

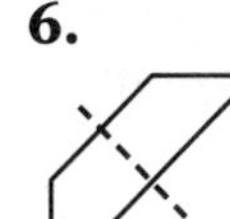

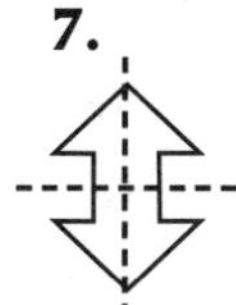

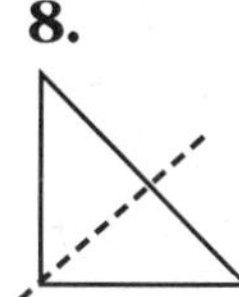

Math Mat 149: Dividing Shapes

1. 2. 3. 4.

5.–8. Students will need to shade one section of the shape. Shading will vary.

9. 1; 2; ½
10. 1; 4; ¼

Math Mat 150: Fraction Fun

1. ⅓
2. ½
3. 2⁄4
4. ⅗
5. Students need to shade one-half of the arrow. Shading will vary.
6. Students need to shade one-fifth of the star. Shading will vary.
7. Students need to shade three-eighths of the rectangle. Shading will vary.
8. Students need to shade three-fourths of the hexagon. Shading will vary.

Draw a square.

Students need to draw a square around the circle on the right, which shows 3 of 6 sections shaded.

Math Mat 151: How Many Tens and Ones?

1. 1 ten, 4 ones
2. 1 ten, 7 ones
3. 2 tens, 0 ones
4. 0 tens, 6 ones
5. 2 ones; 2 tens
6. 5 tens; 5 ones
7. 1 tens; 1 ones
8. 8 tens; 8 ones

Math Mat 152: Apples

1. 3 baskets, 6 apples
2. 2 baskets, 5 apples
3. 3 apples
4. 8 baskets, 4 apples
5. 4 baskets, 8 apples
6. 5 baskets, 7 apples
7. 9 baskets, 2 apples
8. 6 baskets, 9 apples
9. 7 baskets

Math Mat 153: Who Is My Neighbor?

1. 43, 45
2. 86, 88
3. 55, 57
4. 22, 24
5. 67, 69
6. 74, 76
7. 35
8. 38

Math Mat 154: Find the Mystery Number!

Students need to color all the numbers, except for 33.

33

What's the Rule?

1. Count by 11s
2. Count by 10s
3. Count by 2s
4. They all have a 1 in the tens place and you count by 1s.

Math Mat 155: How Many Miles?

2. 46 – 21 = 25
3. 59 – 21 = 38
4. 46 – 34 = 12
5. 59 – 34 = 25
6. 59 – 46 = 13
7. 59 – 21 = 38 miles
8. 46 – 34 = 12 miles
9. Answers will vary.

Math Mat 156: The Garden Shop's Inventory

1. 8 + 15 = 23
2. 36 + 60 = 96
3. 36 – 15 = 21
4. 44 – 4 = 40
5. 51 – 8 = 43

Math Mat 157: Hundreds Puzzle

1. 12
2. 30
3. 55; 63; 64; 75

1	2	3	4	5	6	7	8	9	10
11	12	13	14	15	16	17	18	19	20
21	22	23	24	25	26	27	28	29	30
31	32	33	34	35	36	37	38	39	40
41	42	43	44	45	46	47	48	49	50
51	52	53	54	55	56	57	58	59	60
61	62	63	64	65	66	67	68	69	70
71	72	73	74	75	76	77	78	79	80
81	82	83	84	85	86	87	88	89	90
91	92	93	94	95	96	97	98	99	100

Math Mat 158: Grape Going!

1. three groups of one hundred, two groups of ten, six grapes
2. two groups of one hundred, four groups of ten, seven grapes
3. four groups of one hundred, one grape
4. seven groups of one hundred, three groups of ten, four grapes

Math Mat 159: Making Numbers

Largest number possible: 987
Smallest number possible: 112
Odd number: Answers must end in 1, 3, 5, 7, or 9.
Even number: Answers must end in 2, 4, 6, or 8.
Smallest to largest: Answers will vary.

Math Mat 160: Number Hunt

1. 16
2. 26
3. 6

Math Mat 161: Using Symbols

1. <
2. <
3. <
4. >
5. circle 8; ones
6. circle 7; ones
7. circle 5; hundreds
8. circle 6; tens
9. circle 7; hundreds
10. circle 8; tens
11. 5 in each set
12. 4 in each set
Bonus: ⅕

Math Mat 162: Making Numbers

1. 321; 123; 123, 213, 231, or 321; 132 or 312
2. 764; 467; 467 or 647; 476, 674, 746, or 764
3. 852; 258; 285 or 825; 258, 528, 582, or 852
4. 941; 149; 149, 419, 491, or 941; 194 or 914
5. 642
6. 359
7. 267 or 627
8. 348, 384, 438, or 834

Math Mat 163: Magic Number

1. 92
2. 112

Math Mat 164: Adding Large Numbers

1. 566 **4.** 917 **7.** 766
2. 787 **5.** 953 **8.** 599
3. 779 **6.** 971 **9.** 699

Complete the pattern.
100, 200, 300, 400, 500, 600, 700, 800, 900, 1,000

Word Search

```
O H T O F T P V K E
N V A L U E L A Z Q
E N F V Q R A F V U
S T T I Y H C I D A
S P E T G D E A T L
W F N D O A C L H T
B L S F S H L G O P
H U N D R E D S U E
S Y E I E Z L Z S C
L A D D Y B X H A S
F Q P L M P Q W N U
S U B T R A C T D M
```

Math Mat 165: What's the Secret Number?

50

Math Mat 166: Subtracting Large Numbers

1. 571 **4.** 111 **7.** 202
2. 200 **5.** 521 **8.** 100
3. 130 **6.** 221 **9.** 181

Matching
3 tens: 30
4 hundreds: 400
1 ten: 10
2 thousands: 2,000
6 tens: 60
5 thousands: 5,000
7 hundreds: 700
8 tens: 80

Math Mat 167: The Hands of a Clock

1. 3:00
2. 7:00
3. 10:00
4. 5:00

Math Mat 168: Telling Time

1. 3:00 **5.** 5:00
2. 10:00 **6.** 11:00
3. 2:00 **7.** 1:00
4. 7:00 **8.** 4:00

Write the time in order.
1:00, 2:00, 3:00, 4:00, 5:00, 7:00, 10:00, 11:00

Draw the hands.
Answers will vary.

Math Mat 169: What Time Is It?

1. 8:30 **5.** 3:00
2. 12:00 **6.** 6:30
3. 11:30 **7.** 4:00
4. 7:00 **8.** 1:30

Word Search

T	O	I	M	J	D	W	I	L	H
I	H	Z	H	T	A	O	F	T	A
M	V	K	N	X	Y	A	Z	O	N
E	B	N	F	V	Q	R	F	V	D
D	M	I	N	U	T	E	C	T	S
I	Y	H	I	D	T	V	S	P	T
G	D	A	B	X	C	L	O	C	K
U	W	F	D	O	A	C	L	T	R
F	A	C	E	O	H	O	U	R	B
L	F	S	H	L	G	P	N	Q	E

Math Mat 170: Reading Clocks

1. 9:40 **8.** 3
2. 8:25 **9.** 7
3. 7:10 **10.** 1
4. 6:45 **11.** 8
5. 5:30 **12.** 12
6. 8:50 **13.** 4
7. 11:15 **14.** 11

Classroom clock
Answers will vary.

Math Mat 171: Half Past or Thirty Minutes

1. half past 1
2. 4:30
3. half past 7
4. 3:30
5. half past 9
6. half past 2
7. 12:30
8. 5:30

Draw the hands.
Students need to draw the hour hand between 6 and 7 and the minute hand on the 6.

Students need to draw the hour hand between 8 and 9 and the minute hand on the 6.

Math Mat 172: A Quarter of an Hour

1. quarter 'til
2. quarter past
3. quarter past
4. quarter past
5. quarter 'til
6. quarter 'til
7. quarter past
8. quarter 'til
9. 15 minutes
10. 4 quarters
11. half an hour
Bonus: 8 quarters

Math Mat 173: A.M. or P. M.

A.M.

School begins at 8:00 each day.
Amelia eats breakfast at 8:00.
The parade begins at 9:00.
Grant has a dentist appointment at 11:00.
Carla wakes up at 6:15 each day.

P.M.

Izzy went to a birthday party at 2:00.
Tomas eats a snack at 3:45.
Sheila goes to bed at 7:30.
The movie began at 4:15.

Math Mat 174: The Weather Calendar

1. 31
2. 7
3. Tuesday
4. Thursday
5. Saturday the 12th
6. The week of the 13th
7. Friday the 25th

Math Mat 175: Happy New Year!

Students need to glue the items as follows:

- the mittens on January 15
- the snowman on January 31
- the earmuffs on January 8
- the skates on January 23
- the snowflake on January 9
- the igloo on January 21
- the sled on January 12
- the party hat on January 1

1. January 11–17
2. Thursday
3. Monday

Math Mat 176: Roberto's Busy Month

Students need to fill in the dates for the current month. Students need to glue the items as follows:

- the tooth on the 1st
- the birthday cake on the 3rd
- the car on the 10th
- the paint box on the 15th
- the kite on the 20th
- the lunchbox on the 22nd

1. His trip was on the 10th day of the current month.
2. He flew his kite on (day of the week) the 20th of the current month.

Math Mat 177: Latisha's Plans

Answers will vary.

Math Mat 178: A Caterpillar's Life

Glue pictures in order.

Day 1: egg on a leaf
Day 2: small caterpillar
Day 9: fat caterpillar
Day 10: chrysalis
Day 24: butterfly

Write the dates.

3, 4, 11, 12, 26

Math Mat 179: Holidays

Students need to glue the items as follows:

- the party hat on January 1
- the portrait of Martin Luther King, Jr. on January 15
- the portrait of Abe Lincoln on January 12
- the flag on June 14
- the fireworks on July 4
- the turkey on November
- the holiday tree on December 25

1. Flag Day; Independence Day
2. Independence Day

Math Mat 180: Birthdays

Answers will vary.

Notes

Notes